TRANSACTIONS

of the

American Philosophical Society

Held at Philadelphia for Promoting Useful Knowledge

VOLUME 81 Part 3

Settlement and Land Use in Micheldever Hundred, Hampshire, 700–1100

Eric Klingelhöfer

American Philosophical Society
Independence Square • Philadelphia

Library of Congress Catalog Card No.: 91-55253
International Standard Book No.: 0-87169-813-7
US ISSN: 0065-9746

TABLE OF CONTENTS

ILLUSTRATIONS

ABBREVIATIONS

AJ	*Archaeological Journal*
AASE	*The Archaeology of Anglo-Saxon England*, D. M. Wilson (1976)
AHEW	*The Agrarian History of England and Wales*, Ed. H. P. R. Finberg, Vol. I, part 2 (1972), Vol. I, part 1 (1978)
ASE	*Anglo-Saxon England*, F. Stenton, 3rd ed. (1971)
DB	*Domesday Book*, A. Farley (1783)
DB Hants.	*Domesday Book. Hampshire*, J. Munby (1982)
DBB	*Domesday Book and Beyond*, F. Maitland (1897)
EHD	*English Historical Documents c. 500–1042*, D. Whitlock (1955)
Gesetze	*Die Gesetze der Angelsachsen*, F. Liebermann (Halle, 1898–1916)
HE	*Historia Ecclesia*, Bede
HRO	Hampshire Record Office
Liber de Hyda	*Liber Monasterii de Hyda*, E. Edwards (1866)
Medieval Settlement	*Medieval Settlement: Continuity and Change*, P. Sawyer (1976)
"Micheldever"	"Manor, Vill, and Hundred: Rural Development in the Region of Micheldever, Hampshire, 700–1100," E. Klingelhöfer, Ph.D. dissertation, The Johns Hopkins University (1985)
ODEPN	*The Concise Oxford Dictionary of English Place-Names*, E. Ekwall, 4th ed. (1960)
VCH	*The Victoria County History of England. A History of Hampshire.* Vols. I, II, A. Doubleday (1900–1903); Vols. III, IV, W. Page (1908, 1911)

PREFACE

The historical and archaeological riches of Winchester, the Anglo-Saxon capital, were familiar to me through my participation in Martin Biddle's excavations, when in 1973 I joined Peter Fasham's archaeological team, MARC3, that was surveying the countryside north of Winchester in advance of the M3 motorway construction. During that project, I came to recognize the research potential of the Micheldever estate, with its concentration of Anglo-Saxon charters and its depth of archaeological investigation. Some years later, I was able to return to Micheldever when the evolution of its landscape and institutions became the subject of my 1985 doctoral thesis for The Johns Hopkins University. Much of that study was concerned with territorial divisions; in it was proposed the existence of an early Saxon "archaic hundred," the economic, spiritual, and political functions of which devolved into the typical medieval institutions of manor, parish, and hundred. Through the examination of patterns of settlement and land use from the Roman period to that of the Normans, this work traces the agricultural changes that brought about the nucleated village with its surrounding lands. The growth of the vill is here seen as instrumental to the development of the rural institutions of medieval England.

In England, I have received much assistance over the years from the staffs of the Hampshire County Archives, The Winchester Research Unit, its City Archaeologist, and The British Library. I have been shown continued help and hospitality by Kenneth Qualman, Katherine Barclay, and Caroline Raison Schadla-Hall. David Hinton and Derek Keene kindly examined the dissertation and offered many useful corrections and recommendations.

In America, my doctoral advisers at The Johns Hopkins University, John Baldwin and Michael McCormick, were willing to consider my claim for an archaeological approach to agrarian history. Mercer University faculty development grants supported supplemental research in 1985 and time for writing in 1986. My colleague Carlos Flick was kind enough to review the manuscript in final draft, but any errors and omissions are mine alone.[1]

---

[1] Several pertinant works appeared after the text was completed: G. Astil and A. Grant, eds., *The Countryside of Medieval England* (New York, 1988); H. E. Hallam, ed., *The Agrarian History of England and Wales*, Vol. 2, 1042–1350 (Cambridge, 1989); M. Astin, D. Austin, and C. Dyer, eds., *The Rural Settlements of Medieval England. Studies dedicated to Maurice Beresford and John Hurst* (Oxford, 1989); L. Genicot, *Rural Communities in the Medieval West* (Baltimore, 1990); and M. Beresford and J. Hurst, *Wharram Percy: Deserted Medieval Village* (London, 1990; New Haven, 1991).

I. INTRODUCTION

The early Middle Ages was a time when few men gave thought to events beyond their native valleys. Yet it was then that rural England underwent a fundamental change, as primitive tribal communities were transformed into economically functional manors. The details of this development must necessarily be sought at the local level, not only in the institutions possessed by a locality's inhabitants, but also in their activities: the type and pattern of settlement, the physical components of agriculture and husbandry (e.g., fields, sheepfolds, fishponds), and the exploitation of the non-agrarian resources (e.g., timber, clay, ore, wild animals, water power). Here is reviewed the background to the questions and approaches used in research on early medieval Micheldever Hundred in north-central Hampshire.

The history of the Middle Ages is based upon a variety of sources. They are largely legal and judicial, regulating personal and property rights, or administrative, directing governmental transactions, but there are also the correspondence and literature (including chronicles) of religious and social organizations. From the earliest medieval period, with rare exception, there are no written sources, no recorded memory. For early medieval men, an event once forgotten and removed from oral tradition, was as if it had never occurred, for ". . . the fragile memory of men loses by death what letters retain."[1] But even then, substitutes for such consciously preserved actions and conditions may be found in the unconscious record that past activity has deposited in the surviving landscape, language, and society.

Reliable information is only now being made available, through the combined efforts of toponymic specialists, medieval archaeologists, and historical geographers. The conclusions formed by these researchers are that past generations of scholars, misled by incomplete and faulty data, have made invalid assumptions about the nature of rural development in early England, although many earlier scholars were aware of the limitations of the sources at their disposal. Nearly fifty years ago, Helen Cam recognized the value of the "continental technique" of comparative

---

[1] The process by which different aspects of social interaction become recorded in medieval England was presented in M. T. Clanchy, *From Memory to Written Record, England, 1066–1307* (Cambridge, Mass., 1979). But see also F. M. Stenton, "The Foundation of Early English History," *Trans. Royal Hist. Soc.*, 4th ser., 9 (1929), pp. 195–73. The quotation is from Stenton's translation of a charter of Ethelred II dated 995 (K1289), in Stenton, *The Latin Charters of the Anglo-Saxon Period* (Oxford, 1955), p. 77.

topography, and pointed to other fields rich in information for the historian:

The harvest, again, that is beginning to be reaped from the work of the English Place-Name Society is evidence of the soundness of the piecemeal method in evoking the contribution of philology and topography to history, and the same can be said of the achievements of the Romano-British and Anglo-Saxon archaeologist. But such a procedure is above all necessary for the student of institutions, where some facile generalization on legal, social, or administrative matters, passed on from pen to pen, may, without such checking by the facts, destroy both the life and the truth of pictures of the past.[2]

The lasting controversies over early English history testify to the complexity and questionable accuracy of the early historical material. In rural history, a true consensus has perhaps never been reached, although "established views" have appeared from time to time. A lack of fixed identities for the elements of the countryside makes the scanty documentary references even more difficult to use. Any recorded settlement could range in size from the isolated farmstead of a single family to a nucleated village of perhaps several hundred persons. Likewise, each settlement and its fields could be one unit of a larger manorial estate, but at the same time a manor might encompass only one corner of a village.[3] By the time written records appear in any quantity, there are no firmly fixed relationships among tithing, village, parish, manor, and even hundred; nearly any one of these divisions may be territorially identical to one, or more, of the others. The explanation of rural development must be sought not only among the limited documentary material, but in all other available sources, that is, in those which bear the unconscious record of the past.

THE SYNTHETIC APPROACH

Advances in palaeography and diplomatics have given historians better control over primary documentary sources. The major historiographical development of the later twentieth century, however, has been the increased specialization of research, with an accompanying rapid accumulation (though not necessarily dissemination) of data by these specialists. The multiplicity of the disciplines and their particularistic meth-

---

[2] Helen Cam, *Liberties and Communities in Medieval England, Collected Studies on Local Administration and Topography* (Cambridge, 1974), pp. x, xi.

[3] See B. H. Slicher van Bath, *The Agrarian History of Western Europe, A.D. 500–1850* (New York, 1963), pp. 41–59. In this section he delineated four types of estate, four kinds of manor, four field systems, and five methods of cultivation for the early medieval period. If all were jointly applicable, 320 analyzable factors would exist for this aspect of rural development alone.

odology and terminology have made it increasingly difficult to bring together the diverse elements necessary for a general synthesis.

Students of rural history are aware of the multiple facets of the subject; tenurial relations, agriculture, social organization, archaeology, physical geography, and toponymic studies are but the major divisions. An alternate approach, local history, while associated with the often uneven efforts of amateur historical societies, has nonetheless a long tradition of superior scholarship as seen in the valuable volumes of the *Victoria County History of England* with contributions by Maitland, Round, and Stenton. Helen Cam's view has been presented above. In more recent years, H.P.R. Finberg extensively applied local history to general problems. Dorothy Whitelock also found this focus of inquiry most valuable.[4]

The most effective way to address the issue of rural development is by using the multiple approaches of rural history within the parameters of a local history. This method has the potential to recreate the particulars of early medieval rural development, area by area, until a greater regional, or even national, pattern is established. The study of early land tenure and local administration produces information on how the land was divided into tenurial holdings and how these were grouped into administrative units. Similarly, settlement studies, and the contributory disciplines of historical geography, archaeology, and toponymics produce data on the physical location and character of the rural population.

Until recently, the contribution of historical geography to English rural history was largely to be found in the works of two scholars. W.G. Hoskins's landmark *The Making of the English Landscape* (1955) and H.C. Darby's several studies of *The Domesday Geography of England* (from 1936 on) are familiar to students of rural history.[5] The validity of some of their findings, however, has been called into question by younger geographers and by historians working with the primary documents.[6] Since the 1960s, historical geography has undergone a dramatic change. Emphasis is now placed on theoretical approaches and model building, following the trend set by Peter Haggett's *Locational Models in Human Geography*, in which he proposed that analysis of the spatial relationship between settlements reveals the reasons for the distribution pattern.[7]

---

[4] *E. H. D.*, vol. I. On p. 353 Dr. Whitlock refers to topographic boundary studies based only on maps as having "not the value of detailed perambulations on the spot, such as lie behind Mr. Finberg's work."

[5] W. G. Hoskins, *The Making of the English Landscape* (London, 1955); H. C. Darby, *The Historical Geography of England before 1800: Fourteen Studies* (Cambridge, 1936); and the subsequent *Domesday Geography* series from Cambridge. Recent works by Darby are *A New Historical Geography of England* (Cambridge, 1977), and *Domesday England* (Cambridge, 1974).

[6] E.g., Peter Sawyer, "Anglo-Saxon Settlement: The Domesday Evidence," pp. 108–19, in Trevor Rowley, ed., *Anglo-Saxon Settlement and Landscape. Papers Presented to a Symposium, Oxford, 1973* (Oxford, 1974).

[7] Peter Haggett, *Locational Analysis in Human Geography* (London, 1965); Peter Haggett and Richard J. Chorley, *Network Analysis in Geography* (London, 1969); expanded in R. J. Chorley and P. Haggett, eds., *Models in Geography* (London, 1967).

The techniques of the "new geography" have become interdisciplinary and an accepted component of much prehistoric research, and they have been tested on Roman and Anglo-Saxon settlements.[8] The results have not been altogether successful, nor has this methodology been without critics. Anthropologically oriented researchers may consider it a valid extension of premises which they hold concerning human nature, motivation (e.g., shortest distance theory), and the conditions of rural settlement, but a specialist in historic landscapes, C.C. Taylor, has concluded that "the study of settlement patterns in pre-Saxon Britain, at least in the sense that historical geographers understand it, seems . . . impossible either now or in the foreseeable future."[9] It is of course possible that the findings of a simple spatial analysis are valid, but the complex chronology of local history in any area of Britain (and Europe) suggests that conclusions drawn from such findings have to be highly qualified.

The geographer Brian Roberts presented a study, *Rural Settlement in Britain* (1977), in which he referred to the theoretical interests and computations of others, but preferred to use a wider range of data with which to analyze the patterns of rural settlement.[10] In doing so, he took a multi-disciplinary approach, drawing material from all appropriate sources. Roberts's work was limited in depth and detail because of its wide time span, but it presented a good overview of the changes which took place in the British countryside over millennia, as well as a review of the literature contributing to rural studies.

At the same time as a new methodology was forming in historical geography, great changes were taking place in the study of toponymics, or place names, as British scholars refer to them. To supplement the scarce historical sources, a careful evaluation of toponymic forms and their evolution provides much valuable data. The etymological work of Eilert Ekwall established a specific chronology of English place-name usage. His monograph, *English Place-Names in '-ing'* (1923), refined the earlier observation by Kemble that such names referred to places occupied by the earliest emigrants from the Continent. Furthermore, Stenton's series of papers on "The Historical Bearing of Place-Names," and the more general conclusions in *Anglo-Saxon England*, had as their foundation Ekwall's seminal work. The volumes of the English Place-Name Society and Ekwall's *Oxford Dictionary of English Place-Names* represent more advanced stages of research which came to full maturity with the

---

[8] I. R. Hodder, "Locational Models and the Study of Romano-British Settlement," pp. 887–909; and A. Ellison and J. Harriss, "Settlement and Land Use in the Prehistory and Early History of Southern England: A Study based on Locational Models," pp. 911–62; in David C. Clarke, ed., *Models in Archaeology* (London, 1972).

[9] C. C. Taylor, "The Study of Settlement Patterns in Pre-Saxon Britain," pp. 109–13, in P. Ucko, G. W. Dimbleby, and R. Tringham, eds., *Man, Settlement and Urbanism* (London, 1972).

[10] Brian K. Roberts, *Rural Settlement in Britain* (Hander, Conn., 1977).

appearance of works by Cameron and Meaney at the beginning of the 1960s. Here were presented the conclusions of this generation of philologists, with a chronology based upon those place names assumed to be earliest. Those with *ingas* and *ingaham* added to a man's name represented the first and second movements of settlement by Anglo-Saxon war bands. With occupation came the names of pagan sites, then those with words or personal names considered to be archaic in Old English usage. Finally, names appeared that referred to a type of settlement (e.g., by function, as barton/*beretun*: a barley farm) as opposed to topographically related names (e.g., Fordham) which were assumed to have a later origin.[11]

These views, however, have been altered by place-name scholars following the publication since 1966 of papers by a new generation of philologists: J. McN. Dodgson, Margaret Gelling, Barrie Cox, and Margaret Faull. The revised toponymic chronology is not really a new paradigm, but rather a qualification of many earlier points. Both the *ingas* names and those bearing an archaic personal name are now judged just as likely, if not more so, to be based on the name of a late owner of the manor than on the name of an earlier warrior chief. Similarly, pagan worship sites most probably received their names when such worship was the exception, and not in the early centuries of Anglo-Saxon settlement. The earliest types of toponyms are now thought to be those with a *ham* suffix and certain of those with a topographic element. Margaret Gelling and Gillian Fellows Jensen have stressed the close connection between place names and settlement history. Gelling herself has found a particularly noteworthy pattern in some areas of Berkshire where topographical settlement names are "regularly used for the main settlement in large conglomerate estates, within which there may be a number of less important settlements with habitative names."[12]

---

[11] Eilert Ekwall, *English Place-Names in '-ing,'* (Lund, 1923). For Stenton's series of papers on "The Historical Bearing of Place-Name Studies," see *Trans. Royal Hist. Soc.* 4th ser., Vols. 21–25 (1939–43). Eilert Ekwall, *The Concise Oxford Dictionary of English Place-Names* (Oxford, 1936); the 4th edition, of 1960, does not include any of the revised chronology and should be used with caution. K. Cameron, *English Place-Names* (London, 1961). P. H. Reaney, *The Origin of English Place-Names* (London, 1961). The synopsis of the earlier paradigm is taken from Margaret Gelling, *Signposts to the Past: Place-Names and the History of England* (London, 1978), pp. 106–107.

[12] This account has been based on Gelling, *Signposts*, pp. 123–25. Seminal works by new philologists include: J. McN. Dodgson, "The Significance of the Distribution of the English Place-Name in *-ingas, -inga-* in South-east England," *Medieval Archaeology* 10 (1966), pp. 1–29, and "Place-Names in *-ham* in the Midlands and East Anglia," *J. English Place-Name Soc.* 5 (1972–3), pp. 15–73; M. L. Faull, "The Semantic Development of Old English *Wealh*," *Leeds Studies in English*, new ser. 8 (1975), pp. 20–44; M. Gelling, "Place-Names and Anglo-Saxon Heathenism," *Univ. of Birmingham Hist. J.* 8 (1961), pp. 7–25, and "English Place-Names Derived from the Compound *Wicham*," *Medieval Archaeology* 11 (1967), pp. 87–104. Recent reviews of toponymic studies have been presented in Gelling, *Signposts*; and Gillian Fellows Jensen, "Place-Names and Settlement History: A Review," *Northern History* 13 (1979), pp. 1–26.

Since its inception, medieval archaeology has served to augment documentary history. A general review of the information that archaeology contributed to rural studies was undertaken in 1962 by David Wilson, who gave a traditional interpretation of medieval society and land use.[13] Ten years later, Peter Fowler re-examined the literature, with strikingly different results. He concluded that "the single outstanding achievement of this branch of study has not been the resolution of basic problems but the development of an appropriate topographical methodology . . . ."[14] Fowler detailed the new methodological approaches, particularly the reliance by archaeologists upon the services of specialists. Chemists, botanists, and zoologists contribute to the analysis of archaeological finds, and the work of physicists has led to the electronic examination of unexcavated sites. Moreover, the techniques of aerial reconnaissance are now a fully accepted tool of archaeological research and have proven to be a major source of data in the study of settlement and land use.

The value of aerial photography was first shown in O.G.S. Crawford's seminal work, *Wessex from the Air*, and the technique was later used to great effect by Maurice Beresford in *Lost Villages of England* and in *New Towns of the Middle-Ages*. In *The Uses of Air Photography*, the leading practitioner of the technique, J.K.S. St. Joseph, synthesized the approaches and applications of a difficult process. A 1974 symposium held by the Council for British Archaeology reviewed developments in aerial reconnaissance in Europe, and the publication of papers presented there constitutes the most recent methodological review.[15] Increased aerial survey has led to the formation in England of several depositories of aerial photographs. The foremost is the Center for Aerial Photography at the University of Cambridge. The most interesting results of its works are published on an annual basis by its founder/director, J.K.S. St. Joseph, in *Antiquity*. In addition, there are the archives of the Air Photographs Unit, Department of the Environment, and those of the Royal Commission for Historic Monuments, which has similar archives in its National Monuments Record.

---

[13] David W. Wilson, "Anglo Saxon Rural Economy: A Survey of the Archaeological Evidence and a Suggestion," *Agricultural Hist. Rev.* 10 (1962), pp. 65–79.

[14] P. J. Fowler, "Farming in the Anglo-Saxon landscape: An Archaeologist's Review," *Anglo-Saxon England* 9 (1981), pp. 263–80. More recent is John M. Steane, *The Archaeology of Medieval England and Wales* (Athens, Georgia, 1984), a work that does include Anglo-Saxon material (e.g., pp. 143–45, 149–53, 258–60), excluded from Colin Platt, *Medieval England: A Social History and Archaeology from the Conquest to 1600 AD* (New York, 1978).

[15] O. G. S. Crawford and A. Keiller, *Wessex from the Air* (Oxford, 1928); Maurice Beresford, *The Lost Villages of England* (London, 1954), and *New Towns of the Middle Ages: Town Plantation in England, Wales and Gascony* (London, 1967); J. K. S. St. Joseph, ed., *The Uses of Air Photography: Nature and Man in a New Perspective* (London, 1966); *Aerial Reconnaissance for Archaeology*, D. R. Wilson, ed. (London, 1975). See also O. G. S. Crawford, *Air Survey and Archaeology* (London, Southampton, 1924), pp. 342–66; and M. W. Beresford and J. K. S. St. Joseph, *Medieval England: An Aerial Survey* (Cambridge, 1958).

Excavation and fieldwork by medieval archaeologists not only have made well-known contributions to the changing perceptions of urban development and daily life, but also have had a primary role in the debate over the nature and structure of the medieval village. Much effort has been given to the problem of the late medieval desertion of villages throughout England, and the results of many years of work were brought together in Beresford and Hurst's authoritative *Deserted Medieval Villages*.[16]

The scientific investigation of village remains revealed that the typology of village forms established by geographers was valid for only the final (or present) stage in the development of a village. Repeated findings from all types of settlement site thoroughly repudiated the concept of the medieval village as a static entity. Houses within the village had been rebuilt, often with a changed location, perhaps every generation. Villages grew outward with population increases, moved laterally over time, and often underwent at least one major reorganization of plan and structure.[17]

C.C. Taylor examined the plans of villages with more than one nucleus, tracing them back documentarily to ca. 1100. He theorized that the "polyfocal" village reflects an incomplete process of settlement centralization from an Anglo-Saxon hamlet grouping. Noting that the distribution pattern of polyfocal settlements was similar to the Romano-British settlement pattern, Taylor argued for a continuity of site preference, if not permanent occupation. He further suggested that the so-called secondary medieval settlement in wood and heath lands was actually the hitherto undocumented part of an Anglo-Saxon dispersed settlement pattern.[18]

Studies of early medieval settlement patterns have revealed a wide variation of form and morphology. Noteworthy among these studies are those undertaken by Barry Cunliffe in eastern Hampshire, C.J. Arnold in Sussex and the Isle of Wight, Peter Wade-Martens in East Anglia, Margaret Faull in Yorkshire, W.J. Ford in Warwickshire, and Alan Everitt in Kent.[19]

---

[16] Maurice Beresford and John Hurst, *Deserted Medieval Villages* (London, 1971). See particularly Hurst's "Review of Archaeological Research," pp. 76–144. Annual reports of all excavations appear in *Medieval Archaeology*.

[17] The evidence for these formations is best reviewed in J. G. Hurst, "The Changing Medieval Village in England," pp. 531–40, in *Man, Settlement, and Urbanism*. The type site for the study has been Warram Percy, Yorkshire, excavated by Hurst, but other sites have yielded evidence for major changes in village plans; see, e.g., Eric Klingelhöfer, *The Deserted Medieval Village of Broadfield, Herts*. British Archaeological Reports 2 (Oxford, 1974).

[18] C. C. Taylor, "Polyfocal Settlement and the English Village," *Medieval Archaeology* 21 (1977), pp. 189–93; and "The Anglo-Saxon Countryside," pp. 5–15 in Rowley, *Anglo-Saxon Settlement and Landscape*, particularly pp. 9–10.

[19] Barry Cunliffe, "Saxon and Medieval Settlement-pattern in the Region of Chalton, Hampshire," *Medieval Archaeology* 16 (1972), pp. 1–12; C. J. Arnold, "Early Anglo-Saxon Settlement Patterns in Southern England," *Journal of Hist. Geog.* 3:4 (1977), pp. 309–15;

Some studies have stressed the relationship of medieval village locations to early estates, revealed by the boundary clauses attached to
many surviving Anglo-Saxon land charters. This procedure has been
followed by A. E. Brown for estate boundaries in Northamptonshire, and
Bonney and Hill in separate studies of estate and parish bounds in Wiltshire and Hampshire.[20] These scholars concluded that some at least of
the parish boundaries of medieval England existed from the earliest days
of Anglo-Saxon occupation, and are likely even older, as there is increasing evidence for the considerable continuity of land use and territorial division within the countryside.[21]

A familiarity with Welsh laws and agricultural arrangements led
G.R.J. Jones to advance the theory that the multiple estate was a major
factor in medieval rural development. His argument that the pattern of
multiple settlements of bondsmen within a larger territory of seigneurial
control was Celtic in origin may be an extreme extension of claims that
the Roman villa estate was the basis for landholding that later evolved
into the medieval manor. Jones's theorizing, however, went far beyond
the question of the medieval manor. He speculated that these Celtic
territorial units could be taken back to an even more remote past. In the
Domesday records of some mainland manors (primarily along the Wiltshire Avon) with attached lands on the Isle of Wight, Jones saw a connection to the use of resources by the builders of nearby Stonehenge,
and he suggested that the organization of multiple estates was already
established in southern Britain during the early and middle part of the
second millennium B.C.[22] Professor Jones has more recently examined

Peter Wade-Martens, "The Origins of Rural Settlement in East Anglia," pp. 137–57 in P.
J. Fowler, ed., Recent Work on Rural Archaeology (Bradford on Avon, 1975); Margaret Faull,
"Roman and Anglian Settlement Patterns in Yorkshire," Northern History 9 (1974), pp. 1–
25; W. J. Ford, "Some Settlement Patterns in the Central Region of the Warwickshire
Avon," pp. 274–94 in Medieval Settlement; Alan Everitt, Continuity and Colonization: The
Evolution of Kentish Settlement (Leicester, 1986).

But see also W. L. D. Ravenhill, "The Form and Pattern of Post-Roman Settlement in
Devon," Proc. Devon Archaeology and Exploration Soc. 28 (1957), pp. 83–94; P. J. Fowler,
"Small Settlements and their Contexts in Western Britain, First to Fifth Centuries A.D.,"
Proc. Royal Irish Acad. 76c (1976), pp. 191–206, for the West; and C. Phythian-Adams,
Continuity, Fields and Fission: The Making of a Midland Parish (Leicester, 1978), for an exacting
study of a small area.

[20] A review of the methodology is Peter Brandon and Roger Millman, eds., Recording
Historic Landscapes: Principles and Practice (London, 1980). For a good example of the process,
see Geoffrey Hewlett, "Reconstructing a Historical Landscape from Field and Documentary
Evidence: Otford in Kent," Agricultural Hist. Rev. 21 (1973), pp. 94–110. It must be noted
that the "Hooper hedgerow analysis" is not yet a widely used research procedure; see
Cyril J. Johnson, "The Statistical Limitations of Hedge Dating," Local Historian 14:1 (1980),
pp. 28–33.

[21] The material is extensively reviewed in P. J. Fowler, "Agriculture and Rural Settlement," pp. 23–48 in A.A.S.E.

[22] G. R. J. Jones, "Settlement Patterns in Anglo-Saxon England," Antiquity 35 (1961),
pp. 221–32; "Early Territorial Organization in England and Wales," Geografiska Annaler 43
(1961), pp. 174–81. Surviving charters give no indication of an earlier "pairing" of estates
between mainland Wessex and the Isle of Wight. In fact, the logical origin of the arrangement is the late seventh-century conquest of Isle of Wight by Caedwalla of Wessex, the
extinction of the local dynasty, and the giving out of its lands to the conquering warriors.

the forms into which the early medieval multiple estate evolved. In Wales, Sussex, and Northumbria, he found evidence for the early existence of complex forms of estates, which contained lands of deliberately mixed natural resources. He proposed that such amalgamations were created for local self-sufficiency rather than for tribute to a central authority.[23]

Thus, settlement studies are concerned with the physical components of a rural community—its anatomy, as it were—but the broader study of rural history concerns the functioning of that community—its biology—the basis of which is agriculture.

The first major publication on English medieval agricultural methods was H.L. Gray's *English Field Systems* (1915). Gray was often forced to use late sources, but from them he was able to delineate regions in which certain types of field systems were most common. The three-field system he associated with the "classic" medieval manor. He placed its general use in the middle of the country, while the eastern and western areas followed practices based upon the two-field rotation of the infield-outfield system. The three-field arrangement was generally restricted to land best suited for more constant ploughing, and its presence or absence was not, he reasoned, due to any ethnic difference. Gray went so far as to suggest origins for the open field, the village, and the manor. The open field was the result of enclosing fallow land for an extra crop, following fiscal or population pressure; the village was a community of shareholders, brought into being by the necessarily common agricultural effort of the open-field system; and the manor was the physical embodiment of lordship, the result of economic dependence and political protection—following Maitland's theory of a peasantry which gradually lost its freedom to the late Saxon lord.[24]

In 1938, Charles and Christabel Orwin published *The Open Fields*, a study of much wider scope than its title suggests, for it dealt with the full extent of the medieval agrarian economy. They analyzed the mechanics of the open-field system, adding to documentary sources information from practicing agriculturalists. The Orwins concluded that the area of England with nucleated villages was also that which had open fields. These fields, they believed, were necessitated by the increased need to balance production with preservation of resources, that is, the conversion of wood and pasture to arable land had to be balanced by the availability of grazing and fodder for the increased number of plough teams for the enlarged arable. They found the open-field system to have been "common in England by the time historical records of land tenure begin," and they considered it to have become a perfectly bal-

---

[23] G. R. J. Jones, "Multiple Estates and Early Settlement," pp. 15–40 in *Medieval Settlement*.

[24] Howard Lee Gray, *English Field Systems* (Cambridge, Mass., 1915), pp. 77, 365.

anced but static system that underwent no change until "new crops and more productive methods developed" at the end of the Middle Ages.[25]

The same year, Evert Barger presented a review of agrarian historical research to date, to which he added an interpretation of early medieval farming that extended Seebohm's "villa" theory. Barger claimed that the heavy plough was the main agricultural tool of the Romano-British villa, and with it the heavy clays were first cleared and worked. He argued that the Anglo-Saxon settlers could not have been responsible for this clearance because their settlements on the heavy clay lands are well known, and it would put a "severe strain upon the laws of historical probability" to suppose that any conquering people would prefer un-cleared forest to abandoned cultivated lands. Referring to a similar ev-olution under the Carolingians, Barger argued that the Roman villa was the homestead farm (*Einzelhof*) from which communal village (*Gewann-dorf*) agriculture developed in England.[26]

In more recent years, field studies have been the object of renewed interest. In 1964 Joan Thirsk presented a revised dating for the estab-lishment of the common fields.[27] She claimed that Gray's division of England into areas of dominant field systems was not relevant, because pastoral agricultural systems were found in the uplands and in certain areas of lowland less suited to intensive cultivation. Moreover, she con-sidered evidence for the common use of pasture in the early laws of Wessex to prove only that some neighbors had cooperative rights over certain parcels. The later presence of open fields, she contended, should not necessarily prove the existence of common fields, if they developed via partible inheritance from the former. She suggested that the final formation of landholding took place only in the thirteenth century in some areas, but in others it was never complete, and the latter are gen-erally thought to have been the earliest enclosed.

Thirsk's position was soon questioned by J.Z. Titow who primarily criticized her methodology. He held that the explanation of "co-part-ners" suggested by the early laws was an assumption with no external evidence. Moreover, Thirsk had to hypothesize two redistributions of land, the first to create the open fields with no uniformly owned strips, the second to arrange the strips into a three-field pattern. Titow added a note of caution: arguing from the records of large estates can be mis-leading because several settlements were often treated as one manor in the documents, "with the demesne as a single unit," rather than spread among a cluster of separate field systems.[28] Moreover, H.S.A. Fox has

[25] Charles and Christabel Orwin, *The Open Fields* (Oxford, 1938), pp. 60–62.

[26] Evert Barger, "The Present Position of Studies in English Field Systems," *Eng. Hist. Rev.* 58 (1938), pp. 385–411. The reference here is pp. 406–407, 410, 411.

[27] Joan Thirsk, "The Common Fields," *Past and Present* 23 (Dec. 1964), pp. 3–25.

[28] J. Z. Titow, "Medieval England and the Open Field," *Past and Present* 32 (Dec. 1965), pp. 82–102.

expressed doubts about the importance of a movement from two-field to three-field systems in the later Middle Ages. He observed that three fields may actually require the same amount of ploughing as two, and that the three-crop rotation may just as readily entail only two fields, resulting in a mixed pattern that most likely dates back to the Saxon period and is related to the introduction of spring-sown grain.[29]

The use of common grazing land was examined by W.G. Hoskins and Dudley Stamp in 1963, in a work based upon the Royal Commission on Common Land.[30] They asserted that common grazing rights first had only a regional basis, such as the eastern *Andredeswald* to the men of Kent, or the New Forest to Jutes of Hampshire. This stage was followed by a division of summer pasturage among individual villages, but the practice of inter-commoning between villages, they believed, was older than the manorial organization because it was based upon the vill, not the manor.

To these discussions, Alan Baker and Robin Butlin have applied their detailed survey of the field systems of Britain, analyzing them according to properties common to all systems: structure, equilibrium, and change. They set up an evolutionary model based on the premise that the infield-outfield system had been practiced throughout primitive northwestern Europe. Population increase caused hamlets to coalesce into villages. In the "hamlet" stage, furlongs (small blocks of strips) were rotated, but when the land was reorganized for village agriculture, the furlongs were broken down into strips, and larger blocks were rotated for crop use. Pasture land was reduced, and arable land was made to serve pastoral purposes by means of communal grazing.[31] Since then, Richard Hoffmann has written that the goal of the medieval European peasant was the maximum self-sufficiency of each household. The common field system was therefore "the response by individual farmers to increased population and fixed agricultural technology, combining already existing agricultural cooperation and communal institutions of law and order."[32]

On the other hand, Shimon Applebaum, a specialist on Roman

---

[29] H. S. A. Fox, "The Alleged Transformation from Two-field to Three-field Systems in Medieval England," *Economic History Review*, 2nd ser. 39 (1986), pp. 526–48. Fox's main argument, however, is that there was no clear economic advantage to convert from one field system to another, at least until the early modern period, and in fact the late Middle Ages display "inertia" rather than agricultural revolution.

[30] W. G. Hoskins and L. Dudley Stamp, *The Common Lands of England* (London, 1963).

[31] Alan R. H. Baker and Robin A. Butlin, eds., *Studies of Field Systems in the British Isles* (Cambridge, 1973). See particularly those portions by Baker and Butlin: "Introduction," pp. 1–41, and "Conclusion: Problems and Perspectives," pp. 619–56. Their views should be compared to the more traditional ones of Slicher van Bath, *Agrarian History*, pp. 54–74.

[32] Richard C. Hoffmann, "Medieval Origins of the Common Fields," pp. 23–72 in Hoffmann, ed., *European Peasants and their Markets. Essays in Agrarian Economic History* (Princeton, New Jersey, 1975). But for a differing view of English "peasant" farming, see Alan Macfarlane, *The Origin of English Individualism* (Oxford, 1978).

Britain, has sought evidence for the survival of the villa estate, if not the building site, as a basis for Anglo-Saxon agriculture. He theorized that toward the end of the Roman period heavy imperial taxation and a worsening climate ruined the free farmer, who turned his person and his land over to the villa owner. The very large estates, however, were unprofitably worked as single units by large teams of slaves and so were split into colonate holdings. When the villa was finally abandoned, the tenantry survived, and so did the estate boundaries. These the Germans found and took over intact, Applebaum argued, because they had no reason to change a viable system. He further suggested that the new settlers found strip fields already in England, as may also have been the case in Roman villa fields near Coblenz. According to Applebaum, the standard rural agricultural unit in Britain when the Saxons arrived may well have been the bond-hamlet with its open fields, a typical "medieval" arrangement.[33]

Thus, for generations of scholars of early English rural history the great question has been that concerning the manor and the village: which was the formative unit of rural life? Even when solutions to this problem have been worked out, there remain numerous unresolved social and political questions which the manor/village problem does not address. Rural development was affected by institutions and conditions such as land tenure, the growth of towns and trade, the hundred and the manor, agricultural technology and population change, the ethnic origins of regional groups, and soil conditions and climatic fluctuation. A synthesis of these factors establishes where and under what conditions the peasants and their lords lived and worked during the early medieval period, and puts in perspective two conflicting, perhaps contradictory themes of medieval rural life: the tradition of village stability in the face of population growth and finite local resources, and the changeable pattern of landownership resulting from the haphazard formation and disintegration of estates.

MICHELDEVER HUNDRED

Micheldever Hundred's location in the core of rural Wessex, and its wealth of documentary and archaeological resources, make it an important subject for the study of early medieval settlement and land use. Lying ten miles north of Winchester, the 12,200 acre manor of Michel-

---

[33] S. Applebaum, "The Pattern of Settlement in Roman Britain," *Agric. Hist. Rev.* 11 (1963), pp. 1–14; and "Roman Britain," pp. 3–282 in *A.H.E.W.*, particularly the discussion of continuity of field boundaries at Great Wymondley, Herts., pp. 90–94, and Ditchley, Oxon., pp. 260–62.

dever was a *villa regalis* (the king's "tun" of a royal manor).[34] In 900, Edward the Elder gave it to the New Minster of Winchester (later Hyde Abbey) in honor of his father, Alfred the Great. Except for a brief confiscation by William the Conqueror, the monastery retained the lands until its dissolution, at which time the Wriothesley earls of Southampton acquired the bulk of the estate. It has remained intact to the present day, with only two further changes in family ownership.

Micheldever lies in an area rimmed by the Hampshire uplands at the approximate center of southern England, equidistant from the Thames estuary and the Bristol Channel, and as far from the middle Thames as from the Solent and Isle of Wight (Fig. 1.1). There is, therefore, no obvious directional bias in external relations. The specific geography of central Hampshire is a two-level basin, formed by the catchment areas of the Test and Itchen rivers. The northern, upper part of the basin is a single environmental zone of wide chalk uplands and deep fertile valleys, with moderate soil conditions and climate. As the southern portion of the basin was occupied by an ethnically different population, the northern half may be considered a more or less integral area, extending from the Itchen valley realignment in the south to the Hampshire "downs" (upland ridges) in the north, where the central ridge separates the Thames valley drainage from that descending to the Channel.

The locality is also free from the effects of urbanism. Northern Hampshire does not contain a Roman urban site between Winchester and Silchester (though the road connecting the two *civitas* capitals could have influenced the areas through which it passed). Moreover, the upper Hampshire basin was not the site of a Saxon *burh*, although market towns appeared in the later middle ages. Its inhabitants no doubt dealt with Winchester, the nearest city, but there was no obvious "suburban" development in the hundred.

The historical sources are based upon the many pre-Conquest charters for the locality. For the Micheldever lands there are five charters with bounds, and ten others give the boundaries of adjacent manors. There are several copies of the late medieval Hyde Abbey cartulary, one of which, the *Liber de Hyda* chronicle, was published in the Rolls Series (45) in 1866.[35] Two Hyde Abbey cartularies remain unpublished, and two other related items survive from the monastery: an abbey "miscellany" and King Edgar's illustrated New Minster charter of refoundation.[36] In

---

[34] See Chadwick, *Institutions*, pp. 256–57, for a brief discussion of early references. For the size of the manor, see Francis Henry Baring, *Domesday Tables* (London, 1909), pp. 192–93.

[35] Edward Edwards, ed., *Liber Monasterii de Hyda*, Rolls Series 45 (London, 1866). This manuscript was abridged by Stowe as B. M., Lansdowne 717.

[36] The four cartularies are *Liber de Hyda*; the Lansdowne MS; B. M., Cotton Dom. A xiv; and Harley 1761. For B. M., Cotton Dom. A xiv, see Sir William Dugdale, *Monasticon*

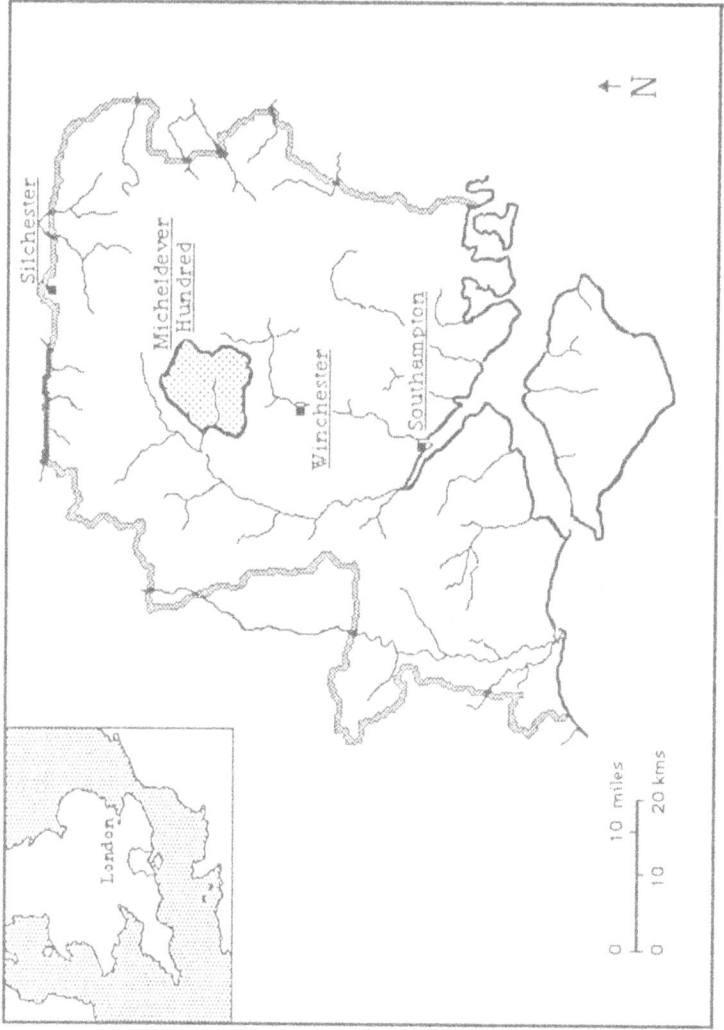

Fig. 1.1 Micheldever Hundred in Hampshire

addition, there are some late medieval and post-medieval estate documents held by the Hampshire Record Office.

The Micheldever area is well served by other disciplines contributing to rural studies. Hampshire has received serious archaeological attention: in the field as long ago as J.P. William-Freeman's 1915 *Introduction to Field Archaeology, as Illustrated by Hampshire*: from the skies by camera in Crawford's 1928 *Wessex from the Air*; and beneath its modern cities of Winchester and Southampton, as detailed in Martin Biddle's *Winchester Studies* and a series of reports on Southampton.[37] Besides the work of the two urban archaeological groups, other discoveries are reported and compiled by the Hampshire County Museum Service, while the Wessex Archaeological Committee oversees all the state-sponsored excavation. In addition to the archaeological resources, the Hampshire Record Office contains an unpublished study of Hampshire place names and the full series of early nineteenth-century, large-scale maps of all parish lands for the Tithe Award Commission. Hampshire localities have also been the object of settlement studies; the parishes of Chalton on the eastern edge of the county and King's Somborne near the west, as well as the area immediately around Winchester, have yielded details of Anglo-Saxon settlement patterns and manorial boundaries.[38] The chalk areas of the Hampshire upland north of Winchester have been designated a research area for the Royal Commission on Historic Monuments, with concentrated air photography and detailed analysis by its Air Photography Unit, National Monuments Record. This area has already been the subject of some initial publication, and two of the illustrations included in the report of the Symposium on Aerial Reconnaissance were in fact sites by Micheldever Wood.[39]

Helen Cam has praised the "soundness of the piecemeal method in evoking the contributions of philology and topography to history," and Peter Fowler has asserted that the "new topography" based on a "combination of techniques and directed toward a variety of source materials"

Anglicanum, ed. John Caley, Henry Ellis, and Bulkeley Bandinel, Vol. II (London, 1819), pp. 432–34. *A Catalogue of the Harleian Manuscripts in the British Museum* II (1808), pp. 205–207, provides a listing of each of 88 entries for the B. M., Harley 1761 cartulary. The miscellany is Stowe Park MS Ecclesiastica ii. 32, and the Edgar charter is Cotton MS Vespasian A viii. For a brief commentary, see G. R. C. Davies, *Medieval Cartularies of Great Britain: A Short Catalogue* (London, New York, 1958), p. 121.

[37] J. P. Williams-Freeman, *An Introduction to Field Archaeology, as Illustrated by Hampshire* (London, 1915); Crawford, *Wessex from the Air*; M. Biddle, ed., *Winchester in the Early Middle Ages*, Winchester Studies I (Oxford, 1976); Colin Platt and Richard Coleman-Smith, *Excavations in Medieval Southampton. 1953–1969* (Leicester, 1975); and Philip Holdsworth, "Saxon Southampton; A New Review," *Medieval Archaeology* 20 (1976), pp. 26–61.

[38] Cunliffe, "Chalton"; Hill, "Parish Boundaries"; M. Biddle and D. J. Keene, in Biddle, ed., *Winchester in the Early Middle Ages*, pp. 255–71. But see also S. Applebaum, "The Distribution of the Romano-British Population in the Basingstoke District," *Proc. Hampshire Archaeol. Soc.* 18 (1953), pp. 126–27.

[39] Wilson, *Aerial Reconnaissance*, pp. 110–11, 119.

was the "single outstanding achievement" of recent rural studies. The present author has found Micheldever Hundred and its setting in middle Hampshire a good subject for employing those techniques. The time period for the study, A.D. 700 to 1000, saw the passage in English history from conversion to Christianity to conquest by the Normans. As such, it included the early documentation of the late seventh-century laws of Ine of Wessex, and, at the other end of the study, the details of the Domesday Book for 1066 and 1086.

The Micheldever project was planned and carried out with five goals: (1) to establish field systems and other physical features of the medieval landscape of Micheldever Hundred, from documentary references, place names, and archaeological sources; (2) using the above, to determine manorial boundaries and other territorial divisions; (3) to correlate the spatial evidence with that for settlement date, size, and form; (4) in all three contexts, to establish the change or continuity in the pattern of settlement and land use, and to compare them to each other and to the surrounding areas of Hampshire; (5) to relate the observed forms and changes to the institutions of manor, village, and hundred and to the social, political, and economic circumstances that produced them.

The reconstruction of the rural development of a locality, and by extension, a region, presents the opportunity to test and evaluate in a precise and "real" setting the concepts of the multiple estate, the village community, and the territory of the "folk." The findings of the study of Micheldever Hundred bear upon such historical questions as innovation in agricultural practices, the level and direction of the early medieval economy, and the complex relationships among manor, village, and hundred.[40]

---

[40] The full range of research is presented in "Micheldever," while Anglo-Saxon rural institutions in the Micheldever region are discussed in Eric Klingelhöfer, *Manor, Vill, and Hundred: The Development of Rural Institutions in Early Medieval Hampshire* (Toronto, 1991).

II. THE CONTEXT OF EARLY MEDIEVAL MICHELDEVER

The context of the Micheldever area in the early Middle Ages is best examined in several ways: political, geographic, and economic. The political history comprises four periods: Roman, post-Roman and early Saxon, late Saxon, and eleventh century. Geographic considerations include geology, topography, pedology, hydrology, climate, flora, and fauna. The transportation system, agriculture, commerce, and industry are the aspects of the economic evaluation.

POLITICAL HISTORY

Britons and Romans in Hampshire

In many ways, Britain under Rome was similar to India under Britain: both were imperial administrative and economic systems that governed basically unchanged native populations. Religion, language, social institutions, and many occupations were only partially altered among the urban population and perhaps not at all among the large number of rural dwellers (*pagani*). Yet the parallel is a crude comparison; the specifics are in many ways different, significantly so in the manner in which imperial control ended in each country.

The century before the coming of the Romans witnessed substantial changes in southeastern England. A Celtic tribe from the Continent, the Belgae, had crossed the Channel and settled in large numbers south of the Thames. The Belgae did not occupy the hillforts typical of the early Iron Age, but rather constructed and defended large settlements, *oppida*, on more agreeable terrain, often at river crossings, as at the sites of later Canterbury and Winchester. In Hampshire, Belgic occupation appears to have extended no farther than the Test river. Farther west they may have formed an overlord class only.[1] The dominant Belgic powers on the eve of the Roman conquest were the Atrebates and the Regnenses,

---

[1] Sheppard Frere, *Britannia: A History of Roman Britain* (London, 1967), pp. 23–51. It has been replaced by Peter Salway, *Roman Britain* (Oxford, 1981), pp. 10–16. This and J. N. L. Myers, *The English Settlements* (Oxford, 1986), as Volume I A and B of the Oxford History of England, have replaced R. G. Collingwood and J. N. L. Myers, *Roman Britain and the English Settlements* (Oxford, 1937), which was out of date.

who were organized by the Romans into cantons with capitals respectively at Silchester and Chichester. West of these tribes, in present-day
Hampshire and Wiltshire, were independent Belgae. The Roman *civitas*
(canton) of these Belgae, with its capital of Venta Belgarum (Winchester),
was an ethnic "agglomeration of petty groups."[2] Stretching from the
Isle of Wight to the Bristol Channel, its geography discouraged internal
cohesion, and what economic and political base it may have had would
become further polarized by the growth of Bath (Aquae Sulis) in the
next centuries. Roman authorities may have simply created this canton
from all territories not occupied by unified and powerful neighboring
kingdoms.

The border between the cantons of the Belgae and the Atrebates is
not known precisely, but it probably lay along the high ground forming
the watershed of the upper Hampshire Basin, marked by the site of the
modern city of Basingstoke.[3] The Itchen and Test rivers and their tributaries (including the Micheldever stream) lay entirely within the Belgic
canton. Venta Belgarum was a city of the second rank, with a population
of perhaps 3,000.[4] Smaller Roman towns can be identified: the walled
port and possible naval station of *Clausentum* (Bittern, by Southampton)
at the mouth of the Itchen; *Onna* (Nursling) at a crossing near the mouth
of the Test; *Brige*, probably on the Test near Broughton; and an unnamed
defended settlement at Neatham.[5] The number of large and small Belgic
towns is typical for southern Britain.

In fourth-century Britain, villas enjoyed a new era of opulence that is
evident in their luxurious appointments and the treasures of recent discoveries.[6] Sheppard Frere held that this fourth-century prosperity was
not necessarily achieved at the expense of the towns, but reflected rather
the overall wealth of the curial class.[7]

Romano-British prosperity stemmed from a surplus of agricultural
production, plus a certain amount of exported tin, slaves, and wool
products. There were three types of agricultural operation: the Celtic
farmstead or hamlet, with work organized around an extended family
and its dependents; the private villa, typically a single enterprise with
lands worked by slaves, wage laborers, or sharecroppers; and the im-

---

[2] Frere, *Britannia*, pp. 51, 52.

[3] The border of the Belgae is depicted in Frere, *Britannia*, fig. 1, p. xvi.

[4] Ibid., p. 202.

[5] For Brige, Neathan, Clausentum, see David E. Johnston, "Hampshire: The Roman
Period," pp. 46–55 in *Archaeology of Hampshire*. Other sites are depicted on the *Ordnance
Survey Map of Roman Britain* (2nd ed.), 1956.

[6] In the 1970s two important late Roman silver treasures came to light; both have been
exhibited and published: K. S. Painter, *The Mildenhall Treasure, Roman Silver from East Anglia*
(London, 1977); and K. S. Painter, *The Water Newton Early Christian Silver* (London, 1977).

[7] Frere, *Britannia*, p. 254. Frere noted that Britain sent builders to repair Autun around
A.D. 300, and in 359 the army on the Rhine received 600 barges of grain from Britain: p.
280. Peter Salway presents a more circumspect view: *Roman Britain*, pp. 328–29, 371–73.

perial estates, usually extensive tracts with managers' villas and multiple communities of dependent workers. Mixed farming was practiced everywhere to a certain extent, and the large villas and imperial estates conducted large-scale cultivation of arable land and stock raising. The British woolen industry seems to have specialized in production of a heavy rug and a waterproof cloak, and an imperial weaving factory was sited at *Venta*, often identified as Winchester. The standing army in Britain would have provided a constant demand for regular supplies of grain, meat, and goods of leather and wool.[8]

The prosperity was a source of strength, but also a magnet for raiders from beyond the Empire. Although city walls first appeared at the time of the political troubles in the third century, these fortifications proved insufficient after the mid-fourth-century civil wars, when Britain suffered fifteen years of incursions by Irish, Picts, and Saxons, culminating in the great *Conspiratio Barbarica* of 367. Immediately afterward, the defences of Britain were reorganized and strengthened. Even small towns were fortified, while larger cities received artillery emplacements along their walls, and an expensive series of forts was constructed along the east coast, the "Saxon shore" of the raiders. Some British tribes were given special status and frontier duty, and Germanic mercenary *laeti* were brought in to provide the manpower for the new defences.[9]

Post-Roman and Early Saxon Hampshire

In 451 the Patrician Aetius prevented the Huns from conquering the northwestern provinces of the Empire and incorporating them into the dominions of Attila. The political murder of Aetius one year after the death of Attila released these lands from the nominal authority of the Roman Empire as well. Northern Gaul fragmented into its constituent power blocs: in the west were independent Amorican Celts; an enclave of "Roman" authority under Syagrius survived north of the Loire and in the Paris basin; pagan barbarians, Franks and Frisians, controlled the lands to the east; and Christian Alemanni, Burgundians, and Goths held everything to the south.[10]

The same fragmentation into successor states, divided among Celtic, German, and sub-Roman powers, seems to have taken place in Britain. That the arrangement in Gaul lasted only a generation does not mean that it could not have continued elsewhere for a much longer time. The

---

[8] Shimon Applebaum, "Roman Britain" in *A.H.E.W.*: grain surplus, p. 206, 207; weaving, pp. 215–18; rural economy, pp. 223–49. See also his "Peasant Economy and Types of Agriculture," pp. 99–107 in *Rural Settlement in Roman Britain*, Charles Thomas, ed., CBA Research Report 7 (London, 1966).

[9] Frere, *Britannia*, pp. 335–59; Salway, *Roman Britain*, pp. 374–412.

[10] These divisions are discussed in A. H. M. Jones, *The Decline of the Ancient World* (New York, 1966), pp. 80, 92, 96.

end of Roman Britain was a lengthy process, one perhaps due as much to economic and demographic problems as to the dubious value of mercenary barbarian troops brought to a region unable to pay for them. Nevertheless, barbarian troops were in Britain, and had been stationed at strategic positions since the late fourth century. The native *laeti* forces were no longer thought sufficient, and the fifth century saw the introduction of "allied" *foederati* tribesmen of Germanic and Irish origin.[11] Britons no doubt faced the same crisis as the peoples of the upper Danube and elsewhere in the West: the troops revolted when they were not paid.[12] In some areas, the revolts were crushed by other troops who would then demand *their* payments. Elsewhere, lands were forcibly occupied, and where federate tribes were already settled on the land, the cities were seized. Where first money, then food payments, were not forthcoming, the military simply took over the agricultural base.

A few details emerge through dusk of the twilight world of sub-Roman Britain. It is certain that most areas of eastern Britain were no longer part of Romano-British society. Yet western Britain had never been fully Romanized; under new influences from the Irish and Picts, Celtic customs revived. At the same time Christianity spread along the shores of the Irish Sea through the efforts of St. Patrick and later St. Columba. The primitive Britons, like their counterparts in Gallic Amorica, reverted to a Celtic political community of rival petty principalities.[13] The east coast was largely under the control of independent, amorphous Germanic tribal states, similar to the many groups of Frisians and Franks inhabiting the lower Rhine, and just as strongly pagan.

The center of Britain remained a core of slowly eroding Romano-British territory, made up of independent groups of cantons or fragments of cantons, perhaps only briefly united under a Syagrius-like leader of the provincial aristocracy, the shadowy Ambrosius Aurelianus (who may have been the Celtic legendary hero, Arthur, "the Bear"). It is generally agreed that around A.D. 500 Germanic expansion was decisively halted, and may even have retreated before a renewed effort on the part of a unified "Roman" leadership, forcing some Anglo-Saxons to re-emigrate to the Continent. But the second half of the sixth century saw a sudden reversal of fortunes. By 600, the English had taken or neutralized all the surviving cities of central Britain. John Morris summed it up: "The British collapsed because their states were rotted and hollow." He attributed this to the internecine warfare among the sub-Roman cities, and to the inability of the economy to support a central authority.[14]

---

[11] Frere, *Britannia*, pp. 360 passim.

[12] See Jones, *Ancient World*, pp. 217–75. The areas of revolt in Britain are delineated in J. N. L. Myres, *Anglo-Saxon Pottery and the Settlement of England* (Oxford, 1969).

[13] John Morris, *The Age of Arthur. A History of the British Isles from 350 to 650* (New York, 1973), p. 304.

[14] Ibid., pp. 222–24.

Morris did admit to another factor in the rapid decay of British power. Because they still lived in towns and continued a tenuous trade with the Mediterranean, the British suffered the full effects of the mid-sixth-century plague. Their contact with the barbarians had been minimal, and this isolation from the contagion kept the pagan English strong while the British weakened. Parallel situations may have existed in North Africa, where healthy Berber troops were repulsed only by imperial reinforcements unavailable to Britain, or perhaps in the second-century struggles of Marcus Aurelius, when the empire was struck by its first plague, but the barbarians across the Danube were not. "In Britain, the sixth-century plague infected a people who were already enfeebled and dispirited by the decay of their political institutions."[15] Even so, it must be remembered that the *civitates* of sub-Roman Britain were finally overrun by barbarians a full century or more after the other western provinces had been transformed into Germanic kingdoms.[16] The extra century of sub-Roman rule may help explain why the Anglo-Saxon kingdoms were behind their Continental counterparts in political development.

For central Hampshire, in the canton of the Belgae, the entire period A.D. 400 to 700 is poorly understood. Political changes and population movements are deduced from Germanic pagan burials of the fifth to seventh centuries. They occurred around Winchester in central Hampshire, but are rare west of the Test river. The burials testify to the presence of at least some Saxons. Fourth-century Germanic burials outside the walls are evidence for mercenary *laeti* and their dependents in late Roman Winchester.[17] Neighboring *civitas* capitals had dissimilar fates. Chichester, the capital of the Regnenses, soon fell to barbarians who would later be called South Saxons. Silchester of the Atrebates remained independent until ca. 600, and Dorchester was taken later in the seventh century.[18]

Traditions are vague about the origins of the kingdom of Wessex. Martin Biddle has proposed what can only be called a "Germano-British" state based upon Winchester, a "British community in which Saxon and Briton were being fused together."[19] Thus is explained the Celtic names borne by the earliest leaders of the House of Wessex (Cerdic and

---

[15] Ibid., p. 302.

[16] The latter half of the sixth century also saw the Visigothic reduction of imperial cities in Spain, and the Lombard occupation of north Italy. See E. A. Thompson, *The Goths in Spain* (Oxford, 1969).

[17] Martin Biddle, "Hampshire and the Origins of Wessex," pp. 323–41 in *Problems in Economic and Social Archaeology*, G. de G. Sieveking, I. H. Longworth, and K. E. Wilson, eds. (London, 1976), p. 337.

[18] Chichester: Martin Welch, "Early Anglo-Saxon Sussex: From Civitas to Shire," pp. 13–45 in *The South Saxons*, Peter Brandon, ed. (London and Chichester, 1978), pp. 27, 28; Dorset: *A.S.E.*, p. 65; Silchester: *A.S.E.*, p. 63.

[19] Biddle, "Origins of Wessex," ibid. For a more developed argument, see Myers, *English Settlements*, pp. 146–62.

Cynric), as well as the piecemeal entrance of the Anglo-Saxons in Berkshire, Hampshire, and Wiltshire. Such a political entity would have differed little from the Continental successor states of the empire, where the varied elements of the late imperial society were rearranged within the context of economic decay and demographic collapse. Biddle suggests that this state was formed by the remnants of the Belgic and Atrebatic cantons, and that the southern, Winchester (and Micheldever) part was detached early in the sixth century by Saxons invading the upper Avon valley. Alternatively, it is possible that each *civitas* made arrangements for its capital's survival. At Winchester that could mean drawing upon Germans, first soldiers, then immigrants, to preserve its independence. This arrangement would have resulted in a fused population before the collapse of British authority elsewhere in the late sixth century. At Silchester there are no pagan burials, no evidence for Germanic troops "settling in." Its defences may have been manned by Irish mercenaries, or at least by forces led by men of Irish ancestry whose names and script have been found there.[20] These two sub-Roman cities need not have formed a single state, but they often could have acted as allies, protecting their territories jointly against newcomers. In any case, Winchester's fusion of population would have permitted it to adapt to the political realities of the late sixth century. Soon after that time, in contrast, Silchester appears to have been abandoned.

In the half century between the "Justinianic" Plague and Augustine's mission, the sub-Roman entity in the center of Britain had come to an end, and the major states making up the Anglo-Saxon "Heptarchy" were established. A century later, the last center of paganism in Britain, the Isle of Wight, was forcibly converted to Christianity. This was accomplished by one of the expansionist kings of Wessex, Caedwalla, who claimed descent from Cerdic and whose name suggests a link with a Celtic forebear and the *Gewissae* of Winchester.[21]

The early promise of Wessex was not to be fulfilled, for it was Mercia that became the dominant power in southern England, reaching its peak

---

[20] The evidence is summarized in S. Frere, "The End of Towns in Roman Britain," pp. 87–100 in *The* Civitas *Capitals of Roman Britain*, T. S. Wacher, ed. (Leicester, 1966), pp. 95–96; and abbreviated in Frere, *Britannia*, p. 377. Morris, *Age of Arthur*, applied the Irish origin of Ebicatos of Silchester to Cynric of Winchester as identical to Cunorix of Wroxeter (p. 125). By claiming that the Irish "were ready to fight on either side," and that Cunorix was just such an example, he avoids a problem with his outline of events: that the late fifth-century ruler of the Belgae had enlisted barbarians, fought against Arthur, and perhaps also fought and fell in alliance with the English at Badon (p. 210).

[21] F. M. Stenton offers a good introduction to the term *Gewissae* and its historical context: *A.S.E.*, p. 69. Perhaps most scholars would agree with Biddle's use of *Gewissae* as the name for an authority which expanded first to the whole of southern Wessex and later as far as the Thames, "Origins of Wessex," p. 336. On less firm ground Biddle suggests its origin as a locational description of the sub-Roman state based on Germano-British Winchester. John Morris was the most recent proponent of the contrary view, that "Gewissae was the earlier name of the middle Thames Saxons," and had nothing to do with sub-Roman Hampshire: *Age of Arthur*, p. 294.

under Offa, a contemporary of Charlemagne. Mercia seized from Wessex the land along the Thames that would later become Berkshire, leaving Micheldever only fifteen miles from the Mercian border. Yet the Mercian hegemony failed to coalesce into a unified kingdom, partially because of the long established tradition of autonomy in the other kingdoms. Egbert of Wessex was able to take advantage of this weakness, and in 829 he thoroughly broke the power of Mercia. With Winchester now firmly its capital, Wessex controlled all the land south of the Thames. Its new status was recognized by the marriage of King Ethelwulf to a Carolingian princess in 856. The Wessex monarchy administered its other territories through under-kings, who were usually members of the ruling family, holding vice-regal powers. It was from this expanded base that Wessex was able to meet and withstand the Viking onslaught of the late ninth century, a storm that destroyed all the other English kingdoms and their ruling houses.

Late Saxon England

Hampshire had been the victim of several Viking raids in the mid-ninth century, but it lay far outside the occupied zone of most of eastern and northern England that came to be known as the "Danelaw." In the tenth century, Alfred of Wessex preserved independent English rule and forced the Danes to accept territorial limitations and conversion to Christianity. His son Edward resumed the war, extending his suzerainty over the Danes; Athelstan conquered the North; and Edgar was recognized as overlord by all the Celtic rulers of Britain. In four generations England had been at least superficially unified, and it seemed as if all of Britain might be, but that was beyond the means of tenth-century political or military skill. A series of succession struggles and regencies weakened royal authority to the extent that at the end of the century it was unable to defend itself adequately. England witnessed a prosperity without commensurate power, and so the dragon ships from the north returned to English shores.

The new prestige of "Wessex triumphant" included a particular interest in the arts and learning, especially by King Alfred. His will directed that certain religious establishments be founded. The most important of these was the New Minster, placed beside the cathedral minster in Winchester. A monastic church used by the royal family, the New Minster received a royal foundation grant that included the hundred hides of Micheldever and other smaller estates.

The Eleventh Century

The renewed assault of Viking attacks began at the end of the tenth century and ended when the Danish king himself invaded and conquered England.[22] The English response was a half-hearted military action by the magnates responsible for defence, and when that failed, the payment of tribute.[23] Hampshire was subjected to raids or campaigns in at least ten of the years between 980 and 1013, and in 994 it was the winter quarters for the Danish "host."[24] Abandoned by their ealdormen, the Anglo-Saxon kings were replaced in 1016 by a Danish dynasty; Canute married the recently widowed queen, Emma, who was also the sister of the duke of Normandy.

In Hampshire, little evidence for the Danish dynasty survives. Scandinavian names appear in the records of eleventh-century Winchester, as would be expected in the royal capital.[25] Place names in the vicinity may indicate local estates that were distributed by Danish kings to their countrymen, e.g., Bransbury.[26] Both the Old and New Minsters were extensively refurbished at this time, and Canute presented large gifts to the Winchester churches, the New Minster receiving the famous altar cross illustrated in its *Liber Vitae*, and an estate at Drayton at the west end of the Micheldever valley.[27]

Canute's dynasty did not prosper. Harthacanute was succeeded in 1042 by his half-brother Edward. The old House of Wessex was not truly restored, however; the absence of heirs, the political domination of the crown by powerful regional earls, and the regime's strong ties to Norman religious and secular authorities ensured that the reign of Edward the Confessor was but a prelude to a new dynasty. The year 1066 witnessed four kings of England. Edward's death in January was followed first by the hasty succession of Harold Godwinson, earl of Wessex, then by the short-lived victory and recognition at York of Harold Hardrada of Norway, and finally by William of Normandy's devastatingly thorough campaign leading to his coronation in London.[28] Charter witness lists and Domesday book entries show that twenty years after Hastings, Normans had substantially replaced Englishmen in positions of ecclesiastical authority; the political and military power, and nearly all the landed wealth, were held by the Norman aristocracy.[29] The eleventh

---

[22] See Lucien Musset, *Les invasions: Le second assaut contre l'Europe chrétienne (VIIe-Xe siècle)* (Paris, 1965).

[23] *A.S.E.*: failure of magnates, p. 384.

[24] This material is presented in David Hill, *An Atlas of Anglo-Saxon England* (Toronto and Buffalo, 1981), pp. 55–59.

[25] Olof von Feilitzen, "The Personal Names and Bynames of the Winton Domesday," pp. 143–210 in Martin Biddle and D. J. Keene, "The Early Place-Names of Winchester," pp. 231–40 in M. Biddle, ed., *Winchester in the Early Middle Ages*, Winchester Studies I (Oxford, 1976).

[26] "Micheldever," p. 478.

[27] *Liber Vitae* is B. L. Stowe 144, and the cross is reproduced in D. Talbot Rice, *English Arts 871–1100* (Oxford, 1952), pl. 81. For the Drayton gift of 1019, see *Liber Monasterii de Hyda*, Edward Edwards, ed., Rolls Series 45 (London, 1866), pp. 324–26.

[28] *A.S.E.*, pp. 538–44.

[29] F. M. Stenton, "English Families and the Norman Conquest," pp. 325–43 in *Prepa-*

century in general witnessed the decline of the old English noble *gesith* class: first during the reigns of the Danish kings; then in the generation of political struggle between the pro-Norman King Edward and the aggressive, Danish-related House of Godwin; and finally following the casualties of the two wars of 1066 and the successive failed rebellions thereafter.

By 1100 political and social processes were in motion which were to direct English life for the next several centuries. Because Norman feudal ties transcended the conflicting and ill-defined obligations of family and state, the followers of William were far better organized than any equivalent early medieval group, and they concentrated wealth and power to a degree unknown elsewhere in northern Europe. England's brief incorporation into Canute's Scandinavian empire had been a foreshadowing of the economic advantage it would gain from its commercial integration with Normandy and Flanders, and the subsequent creation of the most dynamic regional economy beyond the Mediterranean.[30] Norman castles may have frowned over English borough towns, but their garrisons increased the demand for goods and services, and the presence of French merchants meant freer access to Continental markets. The source (and even existence) of the prosperity of the late Anglo-Saxon and Anglo-Danish kingdom is a matter of some debate. It has been attributed to agricultural and tenurial developments, to the stable markets of the "borough system," and to the profit derived from a wool trade with the Rhineland.[31] Whatever the case, at the mid-eleventh century the population was still rising and urban life was as well developed in England as it was across the Channel. Norman military strength and political stability created conditions that enabled the English economy to expand still further, rather like Frank Barlow's description of the Anglo-Norman state—"On the whole it seems that William's monarchy was Edward's run at full power."[32]

Perhaps symbolizing the impetus of the new regime and the permanent changes it wrought was the rebuilding of Winchester Cathedral on a gigantic new scale, in a new architectural style. This enterprise was accompanied by the transference of the two-hundred-year-old New Minster from the center of the busy "capital" city to a location outside the city walls, Hyde Meadows, where it remained (known as Hyde

---

ratory to Anglo-Saxon England, Doris Mary Stenton, ed. (Oxford, 1968), repr. from *Trans. Royal Hist. Soc.*, 4th series XXVI (1944), pp. 1 ff.

[30] For a review of the Scandinavian trade, see *A.S.E.*, pp. 542–44.

[31] Peter Sawyer, "The Wealth of England in the Eleventh Century," *Trans. Royal Hist. Soc.* 5th series XV (1965), pp. 145–64. But see also R. Welldon Finn, *Domesday Studies: The Norman Conquest and its Effects on the Economy* (London, 1966).

[32] Quoted in Sawyer, "Wealth of England," from Frank Barlow, "The Effects of the Norman Conquest," in C. T. Chevalier, ed., *The Norman Conquest: Its Settlement and Impact* (London, 1966), no page given.

Abbey) until the Dissolution. Its Micheldever estates had been confiscated by William in 1066, when its last Saxon abbot, Harold's uncle, had fought and died at Hastings along with a body of the monks. The lands were later returned to a chastened abbey that soon became a center of Norman influence and a firm ally of the Norman kings.[33]

GEOGRAPHY

Geology

The great calcareous deposit formed in the seas of the Mesozoic Cretaceous Period is today a chalk belt stretching across southern England from the Cotswolds to the Cliffs of Dover. This former sea bed was uplifted in the Miocene Period by the action of the Wealden Anticline, which divides a "once continuous Tertiary basin of deposition into the London and Hampshire Basins."[34] The Tertiary (or Cenozoic) strata filling these basins and covering part of the Chalk consist of alternating beds of clay and sand, but where exposed on the upthrust chalk they have been removed by glacial weathering. Chalk is actually soft limestone, and in northern Hampshire it is Upper Chalk, whiter than the lower chalks and containing more flint nodules, which are a type of silica formerly in solution that has been deposited in small pockets and fissures in the chalk.[35]

In more recent geological time, gravel beds and alluvia have filled the bottoms of the major valleys in the Chalk belt. Two earlier types of deposit exist in places upon the chalk plateau surfaces—sarsen stones and Clay-with-Flints. Sarsens are the remnants of Eocene sands, cemented into compact hardness, and later broken into often fairly regular blocks. They are perhaps best known for their use in the megalithic monuments of Stonehenge and Avebury. These examples are particularly impressive specimens, but at one time sarsens from that size down to a pebble lay scattered throughout the Wessex chalkland. Man has since largely eliminated them from the landscape, primarily in field clearance, and secondarily as a source of construction material stronger

---

[33] Sir William Dugdale, *Montasticon Anglicanum*, Vol. II, J. Caley, W. Ellis, and B. Bandinell, eds. (London, 1819), p. 129.

[34] L. Dudley Stamp, *Britain's Structure and Scenery* (London, 1946), p. 181. For a more detailed view of these geological formations, see T. R. Owen, *The Geological Evolution of the British Isles* (Oxford and New York, 1976), pp. 139–44; and J. G. C. Anderson and T. R. Owen, *The Structure of the British Isles*, 2nd ed. (Oxford, New York, 1980), pp. 196–97.

[35] Stamp, *Britain's Structure*, p. 75; and Dorothy H. Rayner, *The Stratigraphy of the British Isles* (Cambridge, 1954), pp. 336–41. The Department of Scientific and Industrial Research, Geological Survey and Museum, has published the most pertinent information on the Hampshire Basin, in its British Regional Geology series: C. P. Chatwin, *The Hampshire Basin and adjoining Areas*, 3rd ed. (London, 1960).

and more permanent than chalk. C.P. Chatwin believed that the word—Saxon *sar* (troublesome) and *stan* (stone)—referred to their "hindrance to early clearers of the land." They were also called "greywethers," presumably because they looked like a flock of sheep from a distance.[36]

Clay-with-Flints comprises red and brown clays containing pebbles and sand. It is the result of two processes: the destruction of Eocene sand and clay strata, and the decomposition of the Chalk *in situ*, releasing its flint nodules into the secondary matrix. Clay-with-Flints once must have covered the Chalk entirely, but is now restricted to the tops of hills and ridges. The clays are acidic and act in solution upon the Chalk, resulting in sometimes deep solution holes, or "pipes," filled with Clay-with-Flints.[37]

Topography

In Hampshire, the Chalk is the dominant sub-surface material for the whole sloping terrain from the watershed divide to the Channel (Fig. 2.1). To the east of this slope are the Alton Hills over 700 feet above sea level, while to the north is the 900-foot-high ridge of the Kings Clere Syncline, and to the west is upland leading to the Salisbury Plain.[38] Within the Hampshire depression are many minor flextures, particularly the Winchester, Stockbridge, and Portsdown anticlines, east-west ridges formed of chalk. The Winchester Anticline is perhaps the most important, as this long ridge of chalk divides the Hampshire basin into two parts: an upper basin of high chalkland to the north, and a lower basin of Tertiary clays and sandy soils to the south. The latter land is fairly flat, with much alluvial deposition in the shallow river valleys. The chalkland to the north, however, has been deeply carved by erosion into long ridges cut by branching tributary valleys, many of which are now dry. This typical landscape of the Chalk upland throughout Wessex is due partially to excavation by Ice Age semi-frozen sludge, but mainly to normal river erosion of the soft chalk when the water table was higher during inter-Glacial periods.[39]

The middle Hampshire topography comprises a series of east-west valleys intersecting a series of north-south valleys. Just north of the basin-dividing Winchester Anticline are the east-west valleys of the Wallop, the Sombourne, the Headbourne, the Easton-Ovington course of

---

[36] Chatwin, *Hampshire Basin*, p. 92.

[37] Ibid., p. 76; Stamp, *Britain's Structure*, p. 76.

[38] Chatwin, *Hampshire Basin*, p. 91.

[39] For geomorphic structures see: Owen, *Geological Evolution*, p. 196; Reginald W. Hooley, "The History of the Drainage of the Hampshire Basin," *Proc. Hants. Field Club and Archaeol. Soc.* 9 Part 1 (1921–25), pp. 151–52. For valley formation: Stamp, *Britain's Structure*, p. 76.

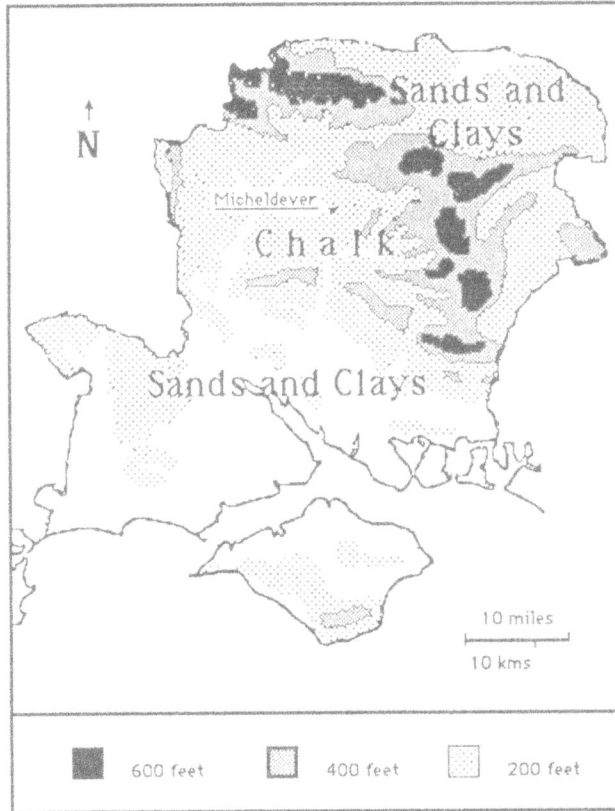

FIG. 2.1 Topography and Geology of Hampshire

the Itchen, and the Alre (once considered the Itchen). The next east-west system to the north is formed by the Anton and the Micheldever, extending east into the upper Candover Valley. To the north is a third system, containing the upper Test and the Bourne. The laterally running valleys are the main courses of the Test and Itchen, the lower Candover, and the Tichborne (presently called the Itchen).[40]

The rectilinear pattern is continued at a smaller scale, because minor folds exist within these valley systems, creating microtopographies. The valley of the Dever (as the Micheldever stream is known locally) is actually two parallel depressions, separated by a central ridge running from Northbrook via Norsebury to the high ground at Bullington. The Dever pierces this ridge at Sutton Scotney.

---

[40] The Tichborne turns at Cheriton to form a subsidiary east-west valley. This long, dry valley is technically a tributary of the upper Itchen and thus part of its catchment area, but because the land beyond Cheriton is high with poor soils and is physically removed from the areas of early settlement, it is not considered integral to this study.

The combined valley has a nearly rectangular shape, five miles wide and nearly twice that in length. The lower course of the Dever continues eastward into the valley of the Cranbourne brook, while side valleys lie north on each side of the Tidbury Ring promontory, and a major sub-valley leads south at Barton Stacey. East of this point, ridges and valleys repeat regularly on the south flank of the Dever. At Micheldever village, there is a three-fold division of valleys fanning out in a generally east-ward direction to drain the remainder of the Micheldever catchment area. The southerly one, bearing the name "Southbrook," is itself com-posed of three valleys that define and divide Micheldever and Dodsley Woods, and extend beyond them as far as Northington Down. The cen-tral course of the Dever passes across the Roman Road (present A33), and its valley continues east to drain the terrain north and west of the Candovers. Carrying the runoff from the 600-foot-high ridge between the Micheldever and upper Test valleys, the "Northbrook" heads north-east toward Woodmancott and the east side of Popham. Elevations along the central course of the Dever valley are 400 feet at its east edge, 260 feet at the Strattons, 180 feet at Bullington, and below 160 feet at the Test valley.[41]

Pedology

The Micheldever valley lies at the center of the Chalk belt, but even here other geological deposits affect soil conditions. Along the lengths of river valleys, there are spreads of alluvium and gravel, while at higher elevations patches of Clay-with-Flints are scattered over the downland. Maps plotting the surface, or "drift," geology are incomplete, because many areas of shallow clay have been unnoticed on the Chalk, and within the depicted zones of Clay-with-Flints the chalk stratum appears on the surface at intervals.[42] Figure 2.2 shows the surface (drift) geology for middle Hampshire, and it is apparent that the greatest occurrence of Clay-with-Flints is to the east and north—in fact, on the edges of the Test-Itchen watershed.

The apparently random scatter of Clay-with-Flints deposits actually seems to follow a pattern. In east-west valleys, the Clay-with-Flints ap-

---

[41] Topographic designations and elevations here and elsewhere are taken from the most recent Ordnance Survey maps. The relevant sheet is No. 168 of the one-inch scale map for northern Hampshire.

[42] J. P. Williams-Freeman, *An Introduction to Field Archaeology, as Illustrated by Hampshire* (London, 1915), p. 303. Fred Aldsworth's study also notes that recent road construction projects have found extensive Clay-with-Flints where none is marked on the soil survey maps, "Towards a Pre-Domesday Geography of Hampshire. A Review of the Evidence." Unpublished B.A. thesis, University of Southampton, 1974, p. 12. The maps used here are the Geological Survey of England and Wales, one-inch scale sheets 283, 284, 299, 300 (most recently revised, 1893), published by the Ordnance Survey, 1905.

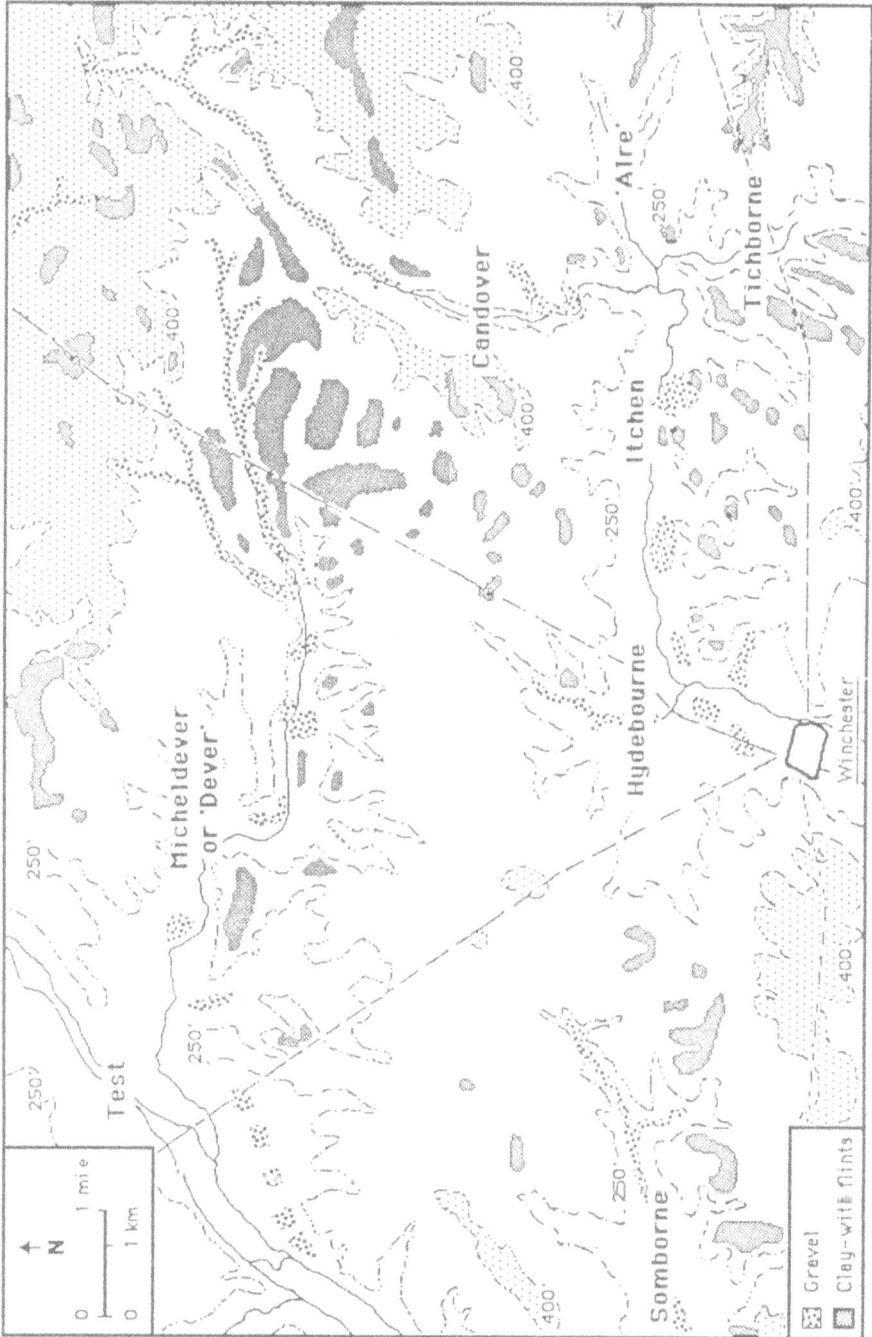

FIG. 2.2 Surface Geology of the Micheldever Area

pears to a markedly lesser degree on the northern slopes than on the southern ones. For example, there are no such deposits on the north flanks of the Somborne and the upper Tichborne. There are only a few recorded patches to the north of the upper Itchen and the Dever; along the Test, the north face has fewer deposits than the south. At one time all of Wessex was covered by Tertiary layers of sand and clay, later mixed to form Clay-with-Flints, much of which has been eroded by periglacial forces, but an indeterminate amount has been removed by ploughing.[43]

One may deduce several factors that contribute to the pattern appearing in middle Hampshire. First, the north slopes of the valleys are generally higher and steeper, reflecting the general topographic tilt of the Hampshire basin. Secondly, the north faces receive more sunlight and warmth; they thaw faster and may thus break down the clay over chalk more rapidly. The northern slopes also have a longer growing season, which permits earlier planting. Farming was probably more intensive there, with the result that the soil, then the subsoil, underwent more erosion. Surface geology dictated settlement and land use, but it remains to be seen if the pattern of Clay-with-Flints deposits in north-central Hampshire results from prehistoric and Roman agricultural activities, or medieval farming.

Pedologically, the soils of the Chalk are "rendzinas," as they have an abundance of lime. The more acid "podsols" would have formed on the wider patches of Clay-with-Flints.[44] Variations between the two soil types affect the agricultural potential of the land, and also determine whether the natural flora is calciphile or calciphobe.[45] Because the acid clay actively reduces the alkaline chalk, and when mixed they make a better soil than each alone is capable of forming, it has long been the practice for farmers to prepare their fields, perhaps once a generation, by "chalking" the clay and "marling" the sandy soils and the chalk with clay or marl. The result of this activity can be found in the numerous chalk pits and marl pits, most of which date from the eighteenth and nineteenth centuries. They dot the landscape today, especially where the Chalk is covered by clay. These manmade features have sharp sides as freshly dug pits, and can be more than twenty feet deep, but when abandoned they take a bowl-like shape, perhaps thirty yards wide. The surface appearance of abandoned pits is similar to that of naturally occurring "swallow holes," spots where the acid clay has dissolved and

---

[43] Stamp, *Britain's Structure*, pp. 76, 77. See also H. H. Lamb, *Climate, History, and the Modern World* (London, 1982).

[44] The Geological Drift Map also labels wide areas as "clayey soil" and "loamy soil." These are general indicators of surface types, and not accurate plots of deposits. These soils may be considered "heavy" and "rich" respectively, and their presence, as well as that of more definite geological types, must be taken into account when examining the uses to which land has been put.

[45] Stamp, *Britain's Structure*, pp. 91–97. Susan Limbrey, *Soil Science and Archaeology* (London, 1975).

partially filled a hole in the chalk.[46] Complementing the study of "natural" geology is recent work on sedimentation, in particular, that resulting from erosion of soil on the Chalk, caused by agricultural activities. L. Dudley Stamp noted that it was "easy to see the downward wash of fine soil particles in almost any sloping field after heavy rain. The much greater thickness of soil in most valleys, for example the dry valleys of chalklands, tell the same story."[47]

A review of studies on colluvial deposits in secondary valleys on the Chalk has shown that there was considerably more deposition associated with human activity than was previously believed. Intensified Romano-British farming and its concomitant "Celtic field" system of small rectangular fields with strongly defined banks or lynchets, may therefore come at the *end* of a long period of soil loss on the Chalk. The Celtic field may not have been the result of soil movement forming these lynchet deposits, but rather a system devised to prevent further erosion of a soil that was already overworked.[48]

In prehistoric times, if not later, the fertility of the chalkland soil steadily regressed. Susan Limbrey examined this pedological transformation in some detail. She concluded that the continued ploughing of land containing Clay-with-Flints caused both erosion and leaching (the downward passage through the soil of nutrients in solution), making the soil impossible to work with the ard, a simple scratch plough.[49] The upper ploughsoil was more liable to erode, and the lower ploughsoil became more clayey and harder to work. A true plough, however, turned the soil and prevented leaching; it eventually worked down to the lower soil, adding calcium, other nutrients, and body to the soil. Limbrey thus reaffirmed the older view that the Celtic field system was cultivated by the ard, but this was true only for light soils. The clays could not have been successfully worked at any level of intensity without the true plough.

Even limited use of the clay lands by Romano-British farmers may have had important secondary results. Karl Butzer noted that even though the organic components of the soil can be rebuilt by abandonment, the loss of mineral nutrients through cultivation/erosion, particularly phosphorous and potassium, have "long term deficits that affect all kinds of vegetative forms, even dominant woodland forms."[50]

---

[46] For chalk pits see Stamp, *Britain's Structure*, p. 98. For swallow holes, see Williams-Freeman, *Field Archaeology*, pp. 293–94.

[47] Stamp, *Britain's Structure*, p. 101.

[48] Martin Bell, "Valley Sediments and Environmental Change," pp. 75–91 in *The Environment of Man: The Iron Age to the Anglo-Saxon Period*, Martin James and Geoffrey Dimbleby, eds. (Oxford, 1981); Karl W. Butzer, *Archaeology as Human Ecology: Method and Theory for a Contextual Approach* (Cambridge, 1982), pp. 123–45.

[49] Limbrey, *Soil Science*: erosion and leaching, p. 94; use of the ard, p. 181; unsuitability of clay soils, p. 188.

[50] Butzer, *Archaeology as Human Ecology*, pp. 145–46.

Hydrology

The principal element of hydrology is rainfall. In the Hampshire basin (Fig. 2.3) variations in the amount of annual rainfall received by different localities from 1941 to 1970 form a discernible pattern.[51] Rainfall patterns may have altered with the overall climatic conditions, but it may be assumed that these patterns are determined not only by the principal direction of rain movement, but also by unchanging geographic considerations (e.g., topography or proximity of the English Channel). The area of heaviest rainfall (over 900 mm.p.a.) occurs on the hills at the north and east edges of the basin. A generally dryer belt (under 800 mm.p.a.) appears along the Test valley and connects to the generally dryer south Hampshire lowlands. Two discrete localities of lighter rainfall exist in the vicinity of Micheldever Hundred. One is the lower course of the Micheldever valley itself, from Sutton Scotney to the Test. The other is a small area at the Worthies where the land is apparently shielded from southeastern storms by the high ground of the Winchester Anticline. In years of heaviest rainfall, the fields in these areas could be expected to suffer the least. Similarly, crops there could be harvested slightly earlier than elsewhere. Dendrochronology gives the history of rainfall, but cannot distinguish between two nearby localities, except under extraordinary circumstances.[52]

Rainfall patterns may indicate the suitability of land for arable production, but the location of springs is a major determinant of settlement. The most important aspect of the Hampshire Chalk is its porosity. While it is less susceptible to waterlogging or early spring freezing, it also makes for a landscape with few courses of running water. Figure 2.3 shows the present hydrology of the Hampshire Basin. It assigns few springs to the Chalk. Most lie just off it, at the interface of the Chalk with the clay beds. Water percolates through the Chalk to accumulate at the actual aquifer and the deep-bottomed river valleys. These rivers and the secondary rivulets, like the Dever and the Candover, are fed seasonally by "winterbournes," intermittent streams that are dry most of the year, but in winter carry rain and snow-melt that the ground is unable to absorb.

---

[51] The hydrological data are based upon the *Hydrological Map of Hampshire and the Isle of Wight* (1979) produced by The Hydrological Unit, The Institute of Geological Sciences, under grant from the Department of the Environment. The relevant material is presented in the insert map "Relief and average annual rainfall (1941–1970)." The data plots are similar to, but do not duplicate, the pattern of rainfall 1868–1902, of pl. I, in William Whitaker, *The Water Supply of Hampshire* (London, 1910). Whitaker shows a similar pattern in the Test valley, but there are discrepancies in the figures for the low readings near Southampton and at the Worthies. The more recent readings, however, have the authority of greater frequency and accuracy, and the rainfall patterns that they depict bear a more consistent relationship to the topography.

[52] For an introduction to dendrochronological techniques, see John G. Evans, *An Introduction to Environmental Archaeology* (New York, 1978), pp. 97–100.

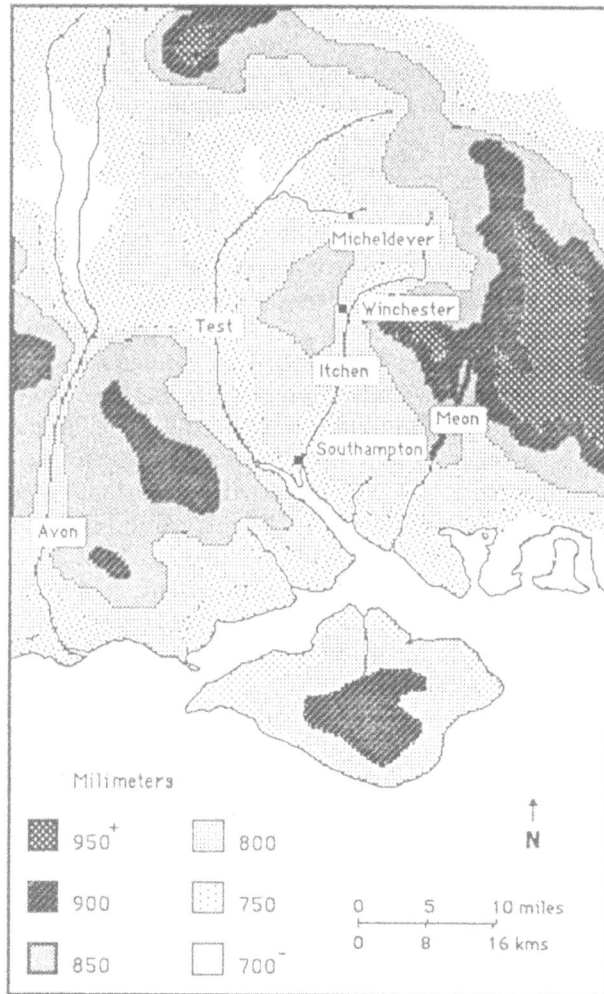

Milimeters

950+   800

900   750

850   700-

N

0   5   10 miles

0   8   16 kms

Fig. 2.3 Hydrology of Hampshire

The river system of the Hampshire Basin is composed of the Test, the Itchen, and their tributaries, plus the south Hampshire minor rivers of the Meon and Hamble east of Southampton Water, and west of it the several small streams in the New Forest. In the upper Hampshire Basin, all the rivers are chalk streams, with much of their water entering the system not from spring-fed streams, but rather from the aquifer through the chalk or gravel bottoms of the deep valleys. Here, for much of the year the major rivers are rarely more than three or four feet deep, and often they are composed of several channels in a fluctuating zone less than fifty yards wide. Their valleys are often one mile wide and over 150 feet deep to the water level. The two tributaries that are of direct concern to Micheldever Hundred are the Candover and Micheldever rivulets, which flow into the Itchen and the Test, respectively. The 1910 survey of the water supply of Hampshire remains the most extensive source for descriptions of these tributaries. It is often based upon reports by T.W. Shore, a Hampshire naturalist and antiquary who commented upon the Dever rivulet:

The Micheldever stream . . . which joins the Test before the junction with the Anton (near Bransbury) is supplied by springs which may be seen among the watercress beds near Northbrook, a little north of Micheldever village, and by the footpath to East Stratton. The highest occasional source of the stream is at the south of Stratton Park. The Micheldever receives a branch which is fed by the springs above Bullington, the highest of which is near the Stockbridge and Basingstoke road, at an elevation of about 217 feet.[53]

Although the perennial source of the Candover is now considered to be at Totford, at the turn of the century it rose at Chilton Candover at 300 feet, and in wet seasons at Preston Candover at 324 feet. It was noted that at that time no stream had started at Axford for at least sixty years, although early spring flooding often took place there.[54]

The original appearance of an entire countryside of intermittently running winterbournes, or "lavants" as they are also known, has been a matter of concern to scholars, starting with J.P. Williams-Freeman's early observations on Hampshire and in particular the conditions on the upper Test.[55] There he found an area drained by two small chalk streams which in winter rose from five springs, but there were seven further tributaries which ran rarely, perhaps once in twenty years. He noted that in six cases out of the seven, they rose by the site of old manors, and he concluded that those sites had been chosen in Saxon times, before the drop of the water table by fifty or sixty feet. This was the same drop in water table that General Pitt Rivers had found in Roman wells in similar terrain in Dorset, during his pioneering archaeological explorations of 1887.[56]

Williams-Freeman believed that this fall in water level was due to the agricultural improvements made in the landscape by clearing the woodland and draining the valleys.[57] Shimon Applebaum, however, used the

---

[53] Whitaker, *Water Supply*, p. 28. Shore wrote numerous articles and monographs on nearly all aspects of Hampshire archaeology and natural history. Most of these were published in local newspapers, and in the *Papers of the Hampshire Field Club and Archaeological Society*. His keen eye and good common sense make his notes invaluable to all researching local history.

[54] Whitaker, *Water Supply*, p. 31.

[55] Williams-Freeman, *Field Archaeology*: local terminology, p. 124; Test river tributaries, pp. 117–19. It should be noted that 1840 was the end of the last wet period (1820–40).

[56] Lieut.-General A. H. L.-F. Pitt-Rivers, *Excavations at Cranbourne Chase* I (London, 1887), p. 27.

[57] Williams-Freeman, *Field Archaeology*, p. 117.

same instances of water table change to argue for a Roman and early
Saxon climate that was wetter than the present. He cited the Roman
occupation of now waterless sites to augment his evidence for increased
peat formation in northern England from A.D. 400 to 600. Applebaum
did note that "improved modern drainage" might have caused him to
overemphasize this claim, and that Pitt-Rivers's observation could have
been affected by "some purely local geological factor."[58]

Whatever the cause, a general drop in the water table in parts of
southern England has been accepted by archaeological and hydrological
authorities. F.G. Aldsworth's research on the pre-Domesday geography
of Hampshire has provided a critical re-examination of the evidence.[59]
He concluded that the earlier assumptions about the water table were
too generalized. Comparing the sites of springs on the Anglo-Saxon
charters to the present heads of water courses reveals that "the spring
line on the fringes of the central chalk belt has altered little since the
late-Saxon period, while in the central area a considerable lowering has
taken place."[60] Spring locations have moved down along water courses,
dropping as much as two hundred feet in altitude. Aldsworth produced
a linear graph showing the fall in the water table in relation to the al-
titudes of the springs. He proposed that this graph would permit the
reconstruction of ground-water contours, and therefore the water
courses, of central Hampshire in the late Saxon period.

Aldsworth's discovery appears at first glance to explain the conflicting
conclusions on the drop in water level. The chalk uplands of Northern
Hampshire do seem to be a "purely local geological factor," i.e., the
difference between spring lines on and off the Chalk. Aldsworth argued
that because the off-chalk springs continued to flow, the cause of the
drop was restricted to the chalk soils only. But these springs on the
fringe of the Chalk are formed where the water of the permeable Chalk
is forced horizontally because its descent is blocked by less permeable
clays. No matter what was occurring at the surface of the Chalk— aside
from arctic or desert conditions—the chalk/clay interface could not
change its location. If there had been a reduction in rainfall since the
early medieval period, it would certainly have reduced the amount of
water flowing through the peripheral spring line, and a number of the
springs might even have dried up, but they would not have moved
regularly downhill.

For the present, all one can say is that the lowered water table may

---

[58] Shimon Applebaum, "Roman Britain," pp. 3–277 in *A.H.E.W.* Vol. I, Part II, p. 6.
He disagrees with Lamb's 1966 proposal that the Roman Period became drier and warmer,
perhaps similar to today's, arguing that there was insufficient evidence for lower rainfall.
[59] Aldsworth, "Pre-Domesday Geography," p. 14, refers to R. A. Pelham's contribution
"Hydrology in the Past," pp. 101–104, in *A Survey of Southampton and the Region* (Southampton, n.d.).
[60] Aldsworth, "Pre-Domesday Geography," p. 16.

have had two causes: climatic change, leading to reduced rainfall; and/ or manmade clearance of the vegetative ground cover, resulting in the dehydration of the upper surface of the Chalk. Even if evidence were available on the flow from the peripheral springs, only documentation of the woodland clearance could prove that the drop was due to manmade causes rather than climatic change. Both the causes and the (equally problematic) effects of lowered water table on the Chalk are addressed in this study, but until many more data on the water table at post-Roman and early medieval sites are forthcoming, all conclusions must remain tentative.

Climate

H.H. Lamb has recently summarized climatic variation in world history.[61] After a late Iron Age that brought harsh weather to northwestern Europe, the Roman Empire in the first centuries A.D. enjoyed a climate not dissimilar to that of the present, evidenced in the limits of vine and olive growing. The weather appears to have become increasingly warm and dry until the very end of the fourth century. By this time, a high sea level had put parts of the British coastline (e.g., Somerset Levels, The Fenland) under water, and it also flooded the North Sea coast where the Germanic tribes of the Saxons, Angles, and Jutes were settled. Wetter summers and colder winters in the fifth century onward caused rivers to freeze over more often and Alpine glaciers to advance. By the eighth century, the cold climate of the post-Roman period was being replaced by a dryer climate, with warmer summers and dryer winters. The ninth century seems to have been one of fluctuation and even regression, a factor that no doubt encouraged Scandinavian emigration. The tenth century was dry again, leading up to the warm climate of the central Middle Ages, which dramatically dissipated after 1300. In this early medieval "optimum" Arctic ice again melted, returning the shore line to near what it had been in the late Roman period.

The variations in sea level would not have affected central Hampshire, beyond changes in the sites of port facilities at river mouths, but weather conditions control agriculture everywhere. The growing season is determined not so much by the coldness of the winter, as by the dates of the first and last frosts, and the amount of moisture in the soil during ploughing and sowing times.[62] Similarly, crop yields are affected by the

---

[61] H. H. Lamb, *Climate, History and the Modern World* (London, 1982), pp. 156–87. Lamb's basic contribution to the field is *The English Climate* (London, 1954, rev. 1964). The most recent review of the archaeological perspective on medieval climate is J. M. Steane, *The Archaeology of Medieval England and Wales* (Athens, Georgia, 1984), pp. 174–78.

[62] See Emmanuel Le Roy Ladurie, *Times of Feast, Times of Famine: A History of Climate Since the Year 1000* (Garden City, N.Y., 1971), pp. 289–92. But see the review of this work by John D. Post, "Meteorological Historiography," *Journal of Interdisciplinary History* III: 4 (1973), pp. 721–32.

amount of rainfall during the growing season, and they can be seriously reduced by the mildew that follows a rainsoaked harvest. According to the nineteenth-century Hampshire agricultural writer and social reformer, William Cobbett, a warm late spring is the most important factor in a successful crop, noting "the old remark of the country people in England, 'May makes or mars the wheat;' for it is in May that the ear and grains are formed."[63]

Flora

The Country where the soil is stiff loam upon chalk is never bad for corn. Not rich, but never poor. . . . . It is a country for sheep, which are always sound and good upon this iron soil.

So wrote William Cobbett about the Micheldever-Candover area in 1822.[64] Middle Hampshire is now an area of large farms based on the cultivation of cereals, primarily barley for the brewery trade. In the nineteenth century there was a common rotation of barley, sheep pasture to rest the soil, and a legume crop to restore the nitrogen. In recent years, artificial fertilizers have added nutrients to what is generally a thin soil, susceptible to wind and water erosion and the leaching out of minerals.

Agricultural production is determined in part by climatic conditions and in part by the properties of the soil. The latter are both inherent in its geomorphology and inherited from past vegetative growth upon it. Specialists in pollen analysis recreate floral history by comparing relative amounts of pollen collected from samples dated by archaeological or geological deposit, or more precisely by radiocarbon dating techniques. To the general background provided by the pollen are added the details of specific plant or seed remains from archaeological contexts.[65]

The history of the vegetation on the Chalk is one of varying proportions of woodland, pasture, and arable land, a constantly changing ratio reflecting commodity demand, climatic conditions, and the uses to which the land had earlier been put. This may be true of much of lowland Britain. Once totally forested, the clearance of woodland for Neolithic arable land was followed in later prehistory by an increase in grazing land, perhaps because more fertile areas were cleared for cultivation.[66] The Romans appear to have greatly increased cereal production in

---

[63] William Cobbett, *Rural Rides* (London, 1853, repr. 1931), p. 61 (19 June 1822).

[64] Ibid., pp. 75–76.

[65] See Evans, *Environmental Archaeology*, pp. 13–26, for an introduction to pollen analysis and other plant studies.

[66] Sir Harry Godwin, *The History of British Flora: A Factual Basis for Phytogeography* (Cambridge, 1975), p. 474. Godwin's 1956 edition was the pioneer work in phytogeography, and subsequent research has been directed to amending and expanding his findings.

Britain, even exporting it to the Continent.[67] After a renewal of forests on abandoned Roman farms, the early Middle Ages witnessed an expansion of arable fields at the expense of woodland, and later the pasture land as well, as agriculture tried to keep pace with a greatly expanding population.[68]

The vegetative history of the Roman and Saxon periods has recently been examined by Judith Turner.[69] "By the end of the Roman occupation forest may well have been almost as scarce in some parts of Britain as it is today," but some areas of lowland, particularly in the east of England, "appear to have retained their woodland nature." The Anglo-Saxon period saw a reduced pressure on the land; "pollen diagrams indicate a regenerated forest and lower proportion of arable and pasture lands, being maintained for several centuries, some times until the Viking invasions or later."[70] One may conclude that the Romans and their predecessors inaugurated unprecedented forest clearance, while the early Anglo-Saxons were rarely able to maintain the Roman level of agriculture, as considerable tracts of land fell to waste and the woodland re-established itself.

The techniques by which pollen analysis help establish vegetative history unfortunately cannot be applied with facility to the chalklands of Hampshire. Research by Keith Barber of the University of Southampton has shown that pollen grains within the valley peat of the chalk rivers have been extensively destroyed by microbes and oxidation. The peat dries out during the summer months when pollen is deposited, even though the wet autumns preserve fallen leaves and other plant material. Unlike other parts of Britain, no pollen diagrams have been assembled for Hampshire, and what pollen has been found there under waterlogged conditions is associated with urban sites (Porchester, Winchester, Southampton). It is likely that sites adjacent to the Chalk, but on the poorly drained clay, could preserve a pollen history, but thus far none has been located. Consequently, a reconstruction of early medieval flora in Hampshire is presently tentative, being based largely on seeds and other plant remains that are more readily preserved on archaeological sites.[71]

---

[67] See Winifred Pennington, *The History of British Vegetation* (London, 1969), pp. 97–98.

[68] Alan H. R. Baker and Robin A. Butlin, *Studies of Field Systems in the British Isles* (Cambridge, 1973), p. 655.

[69] Judith Turner, "The Vegetation," pp. 67–73 in *The Environment of Man*; quote on p. 70.

[70] Ibid., pp. 71–72. Turner does cite pollen analyses from northwestern England that show little change, or even an increase in farming from Iron Age levels, but these are not relevant to the southern England development.

[71] K. E. Barber, "Pollen-analytical Palaeoecology in Hampshire: Problems and Potential," pp. 91–92 in *The Archaeology of Hampshire, from Palaeolithic to the Present*, S. J. Shennan and R. T. Schadla-Hall, ed., Monograph No. 1, Hants. Archaeol. Soc. (Winchester, 1981). Barber's efforts to locate preserved pollen in the chalk streams of the upper Hampshire basin met with failure. He cautions that the absence of a detailed history of the flora does

In lieu of an account of the historic vegetation specific to Hampshire, one must extrapolate from descriptions of southern England in general, and reject evidence for plant presence in areas geographically dissimilar to Hampshire. First, Roman and Anglo-Saxon agriculture are examined, then the methods of silviculture of the same periods.

Romano-British agriculture was dominated by cereal cultivation, and according to current opinion, bread and club wheats extensively replaced the prehistoric emmer and spelt varieties. It is no longer thought that barley dominated bread wheat during the Anglo-Saxon period, although barley certainly became more common. The more typically medieval crops, oats and rye, have been proven to be more limited than earlier supposed, and both may have served primarily as a source of fodder. Beans and peas appear on Roman and early Saxon sites, and were probably garden rather than field crops until the late Saxon period. The Romans are believed to have introduced the grape, mulberry, walnut, fig, plum, pea, radish, and the herbs fennel and dill. Cabbage may have been indigenous, but beet and carrot appear first on Saxon sites. There is also a wide assortment of berries and fruits that are thought to have been grown in early medieval hedgerows, not in orchards or gardens.[72]

Not all the crops were foodstuffs for man or animal; there were also fiber crops. Flax had been grown since prehistoric times, and linen was commonly used for shifts and undergarments. Hemp was widespread by the late Saxon period. It was the prime material for rope-making, and was probably also used for sacking, both items necessary for early medieval commerce. The pollen record suggests that these two crops were grown in association—one would think as local cash crops—because flax is too demanding a plant to be grown continuously on the same ground, and new fields would have to be sought for it, leaving the old fields for hemp.[73]

William Cobbett's description of central Hampshire around Micheldever continued with a consideration of its woods:

---

not permit the use of such earlier attempts at landscape reconstruction as Leslie Grinsell's *Archaeology of Wessex* (London, 1956), where "the equation of soil and vegetation types with geology . . . is of course ecologically untenable."

[72] This material is drawn from F. J. Green, "Iron Age, Roman and Saxon Crops: The Archaeological Evidence from Sussex," pp. 129–53 in *Environment of Man*. For Roman wheat, pp. 132–33; for Saxon grain, pp. 139–40. For Roman garden crops, see Pennington, *British Vegetation*, pp. 97. Compare with Richard Roehl, "Patterns and Structure of Demand 1000–1500," pp. 107–42 in *The Fontana Economic History of Europe: The Middle Ages*, Carlo M. Cipolla, ed. (New York, 1972), esp. pp. 114–15, 120.

[73] For evidence of hemp and flax, see Green, "Iron Age, Roman and Saxon Crops," in *Environment of Man*. Green added without citation that flax and hemp had been imported into southern England in the Roman and medieval periods. It is not clear if he meant that they were not imported in the Saxon period, nor is it clear if "import" means from the Continent or from northern England.

The trees grow well, where there are trees. The woods and coppices are not numerous, but they are good, particularly the ash, which always grows well, upon the chalk. The oaks . . . are by no means stunted; and some of them are very fine trees . . . The underwoods here consist, almost entirely, of hazel, which is very fine, and much tougher and more durable than that which grows on soils with a moist bottom. This hazel is a thing of great utility here. It furnishes rods wherewith to make fences, but its principal use is to make wattles for the folding of sheep in the fields . . . Chalk is the favorite soil of the yew-tree . . . .[74]

The Micheldever area of Hampshire has not changed significantly since 1822, as most copses have been retained for sport shooting. The make-up of several of the large woods has been drastically altered, though, where the Forestry Commission has replaced the mixed oak forest with faster growing fir, thus inadvertently destroying the information that intact woodland has to offer about its past use.

During the first millennium A.D., the sylvan ecology changed as well. The historically established trees of southern England are primarily the oak, beech, and birch. The pedunculate oak is common to clay lands, and the sessile oak favors the lighter and thinner soils of the uplands. Beech trees are now very common on calcareous soils, but had not been part of the original landscape. The beech is believed to have extensively colonized overworked farmland in the late Iron Age and Roman periods. Before that time the lighter soils were under continual use, and the thick oak-dominated forests on the heavier clays could not be penetrated by the beech.[75] Similarly, hawthorne, dogwood, holly, and ivy were the primary forest flora, but on the Chalk the dominant species became hawthorne, juniper, dogwood, and blackthorn. Hedges contain not only shrubs, but trees as well. Some may have been planted, others are more likely colonized, but some hedges are the remnants of old woodland borders, the rest of the wood having been removed. In the Micheldever valley, hedge trees are oak, hazel, elder, sycamore, maple, and hawthorn, while ash and holly are rare.[76]

To the argument that the Romans cleared most of the prehistoric woodland, depleting the timber that fueled their pottery and iron in-dustries, an authority on silviculture, Oliver Rackham, responded that the Romans would not have been able to supply fuel to their cities (and baths) and their industries by the continued felling of virgin forest.[77]

---

[74] Cobbett, *Rural Rides*, p. 76.

[75] Pennington, *British Vegetation*, pp. 103, 104. There is difficulty in assigning the ap-pearance of the beech as the dominant wood species on the Chalk downs to the late Roman period (p. 94), because the rise in beech pollen begins in the Iron Age. It would seem to have been a lengthy process, perhaps increasing in momentum during the more intense agriculture under the Romans.

[76] D. E. Allen, personal communication, 20 November 1982.

[77] Oliver Rackham, *Trees and Woodland in the British Landscape* (London, 1976), pp. 49–52. But see also Russell Meiggs, *Trees and Timber in the Ancient Mediterranean World* (Oxford, 1982), p. 102, for Roman exploitation practices.

Outside the water routes, the Roman transportation system in Britain did not have the logistical capability to move the necessary tonnage the appropriate distances to the centers of population. Rackham argued that the Romans must have established programs of managed woodland to renew their supply of firewood and timber. He even suggested (and it is not impossible) that certain individual stands of managed trees may go back to Roman woods management. He would look back even farther, to the fairly standard sizes of poles making up prehistoric corduroy trackways across logs, as evidence for the great antiquity of some sort of managed woodland.[78]

Rackham believed that nearly all the woods in England until the past century had been managed woodland for at least a millennium. Certainly, in the Middle Ages, wood had multiple uses. First, it was typically the major source of fuel, as logwood or charcoal, to heat homes, cook food, and fire industries. Secondly, it supplied timber for posts and beams, scantling and poles for walling, and split shingles for roofing, as well as for furniture and transportation. Thirdly, woodland was a source of pasture for domestic stock and was home for the animals of the hunt. All woods had some of these uses, and some had all of them. The importance that woods had in the early medieval period appears in the late seventh-century laws of Ine of Wessex, where replacement values for trees were given at 30 and 60 shillings. These penalties were the same for certain types of theft, and the same (at 60 shillings) for a slave's wergild.[79]

The mechanics of woodland management result in an appearance different from that of the present English woods. According to Rackham, many of the trees were "coppiced," that is, cut off near ground level on a regular basis, perhaps every five years. Most species grew again rapidly, having the larger root system to draw on. Larger or straighter trees were kept for timber, but rarely for more than a century because the quality of wood sharply decreases upon the onset of "old age." Trees at places that were substantially, rather than occasionally, given over to pasture would also be cropped by "pollarding," removing the trunk at a height of eight or nine feet, above the browsing level of cattle. So too were trees in hedgerows, resulting in the stubby appearance which managed hedgerows on the Continent still have. It was perhaps only in purely pasture land that the value of a tree was less for firewood or timber than it was for sheltering cattle and for retarding water evaporation in the pasture. Such trees might then be allowed to grow un-

---

[78] Rackham, *Trees and Woodland*, p. 48. The resulting "crop" of poles may not have been intentional, if the agriculture was organized in a "long fallow" rotational system, with woodland growth on the fields for five years or so.
[79] The laws of Ine: 43,44. *Gesetze* I, pp. 88–123; *E.H.D.* I, p. 369.

trimmed to old age, and the resulting landscape became the English "parkland."[80]

In England, medieval and post-medieval population pressure transformed substantial amounts of woodland into arable land, either directly through assarting, or indirectly via woodland-pasture, then pasture-arable. Yet the worsening climate of the late Middle Ages may have had little overall effect on woodland, for the cooler, damper weather that created a greater demand for heating fuel by the stable post-Black Death population would also have been beneficial for tree growth. Rackham emphatically denied the assumption by historians that the English woodland was destroyed for fuel before the modern period, as may have been the case in Mediterranean countries. He argued logically that "a wood need no more be destroyed by felling than a meadow is destroyed by cutting a crop of hay."[81] But to this analogy one must add the observation that by the late fifteenth century coppices in Hampshire were scarce and their plantation was encouraged by the Crown.[82] This replanting may not have been associated with population growth or industrial need, but may have simply made up for an earlier immoderate clearance of woodland, or was perhaps associated with the reorganization of farmland incidental to the enclosure of the open fields.

Fauna

Man shares the countryside with wild animals, whose numbers and make-up are often dependent upon human use of the land. At one end of the land-use spectrum is virgin woodland, where the larger animals are hunted and trapped for meat and fur. At the other end are arable fields, which support large numbers of smaller animals, primarily rodents, and their predators as well. Wildlife indigenous to the fields, and the foraging depredations of deer, feral goats, etc., only serve to reduce the agricultural objective—a stable food supply.

A variety of wild animals inhabited the upper Hampshire basin in the early medieval period.[83] Red deer and roe deer were the largest herbivores; they no doubt did the greatest amount of damage to crops, but they also provided the best game. Wild boar preferred deep woods, as did badger. Otter were local to river banks, though the beaver had been

---

[80] Rackham, *Trees and Woodland*, pp. 66–95; Meiggs, *Trees and Timber*, pp. 267–68.

[81] Rackham, *Trees and Woodland*, p. 93.

[82] See H. L. Edlin, "Silviculture in the New Forest," pp. 104–19 in *The New Forest* (London, 1966), especially p. 108.

[83] This account of animal presence and introduction is drawn from G. B. Corbet, "The Distribution of Mammals in Historic Times," pp. 179–202 in *The Changing Flora and Fauna of Britain* (London, New York, 1974); and Juliet Clutton-Brock, "The Animal Resources," pp. 373–92 in *A.A.S.E.*

hunted to extinction in this area of Britain several centuries before. Predators like the polecat and the pine marten avoided men, but the stoat, weasel, and fox were no doubt frequent visitors to the farmyard. Bears roamed the higher elevations of western Britain, and the wolf continued to threaten English flocks for centuries.

Until the rabbit was introduced to Britain in the twelfth century, hares and feral goats had been the major cause of garden damage. Red squirrels enjoyed an undisputed ecological niche because the gray squirrel did not appear in England until Victorian times. The common house mouse had crossed the Channel before the Romans, but the rat's arrival is harder to date. The brown rat is an eighteenth-century phenomenon; the black rat may have entered England as early as the Roman period.[84]

In early medieval animal husbandry, every animal had multiple uses, both alive and dead. No aspect of the domestic animal was wasted. Alive, they gave their labor or products like milk and eggs, plus body heat to warm peasant huts and valuable manure for the fields and gardens. Dead, they supplied flesh for meat, bones for utensils from ice skates to combs and rings, and organs for materials from bladder bags to the membrane coverings of storage jars. The modern species of domesticated animals were well established by this time, though there is some uncertainty over their relative importance, e.g., sheep versus cattle.[85]

The most expensive animal to maintain was the horse. The nobility kept it to fulfill their military and administrative service, but it also served as a status symbol and a hunting mount. The horse was eaten, though perhaps more rarely with time, and its hide was strong and handsome. It served as a pack animal along with the mule, but its use as a plough beast in the early medieval period is a subject of controversy.[86] Certainly it was sometimes used for such work in the eleventh century. The Bayeux Tapestry shows a mule drawing a plough and a

---

[84] J. F. D. Shrewsbury, *A History of Bubonic Plague in the British Isles* (Cambridge, 1970), pp. 11, 12, argues that, while Italy had rats in the sixth century, there is no evidence for their presence in Britain until the drawing of one in the ninth-century Book of Kells, and the word first appears in Aelfric's *Vocabulary*, ca. 1000, as *raturus*. See J. Rackham, "Rattus rattus: The Introduction of the Black Rat into Britain," *Antiquity* 53 (1979), pp. 112–20.

[85] Reviews of domesticated animals in the early Middle Ages have been used as sources: Clutton-Brock, "Animal Resources"; Mark Maltby, "Iron Age Romano-British and Anglo-Saxon Animal Husbandry—A Review of the Faunal Evidence," pp. 155–203 in *The Environment of Man*; M. L. Ryder, "Livestock," pp. 301–410 in *A.H.E.W.*, Vol. I; and Jennie Coy, "Animal Husbandry and Faunal Exploitation in Hampshire," pp. 95–103 in *The Archaeology of Hampshire*.

[86] A full investigation of the introduction of the workhorse to medieval English farming is in John Langdon, *Horses, Oxen, and Technological Innovation. The Use of Draught Animals in English Farming from 1066 to 1500* (Cambridge, 1986). At the time of the Norman Conquest, the horse seems to have been little used for ploughing (pp. 37, 38).

horse pulling a harrow; there is no reason to doubt the authenticity of these scenes of the late eleventh century.[87]

The most common large investment in livestock was in cattle. They had a multitude of uses: carting, ploughing, logging, and the more direct benefits of milk and meat products. Horns went into lanterns and windows, and skins became cowhide or were converted to leather. Cattle had been a measure of wealth in the Iron Age, and in the Middle Ages they continued to be the principal element in the agrarian economy, evidenced by the interest that the Domesday Book took in the number, even fractions, of plough teams. The larger the number of cattle, the greater the amount of land that could be cultivated, but also the greater the need for pasture and fodder. This demand explains the arrangements for common stubble grazing and the Book's interest in fodder-producing meadows.[88]

The pig was the staple meat of the Anglo-Saxons. Not kept in the village or in special sties, pigs lived in herds in woodland, often a considerable distance from the home village or manor. The Domesday Book took an interest in pork production; the measurement of woodland by the number of pigs it could support was a common entry. Pig manure was unobtainable in the woods, and the pig did no real service to the medieval farmer, except perhaps to keep down the growth of bushy underwood in areas where deer had been hunted out. While the pig may have been appreciated mainly for its meat, it was also rendered into the valuable byproducts of lard and tallow.

Until recently, sheep were ubiquitous upon the Hampshire downland, and had been so in the past. Sheep yielded meat, wool, and dairy products; their manure on fallow ground was helpful in restoring strength to the soil. Even their "knuckle bones" were used regularly in gaming. The goat was less common but perhaps more versatile. While mutton or lamb may be preferable to goat's meat, the goat not only supplied meat, plus milk, cheese, and wool fiber, but also could serve as a beast of burden. The goat could fend for itself better on scrubland, but, like the sheep, it needed a fold for protection at night.

Beekeeping, the sole source of sweetener, was commonly practiced in forest glades and upland meadows, and some sort of fish rearing must have taken place in the large number of mill-ponds recorded in the Domesday Book. The goose is thought to have been the dominant barnyard bird of the early Middle Ages.[89] Simple shelters would have

---

[87] The tapestry was made in southeastern England, most likely for Odo, earl of Kent and bishop of Bayeux. C. H. Gibbs-Smith, *The Bayeux Tapestry* (London, 1973), fig. 3; Lynn White, *Medieval Technology and Social Change* (Oxford, 1962), pp. 57–68.

[88] This was pointed out by the Orwins in *The Open Fields* (Oxford, 1938), but in a static system, not the dynamic model proposed in Baker and Butlin's *Field Systems*, pp. 630–32.

[89] Clutton-Brock, "Animal Resources," pp. 387–89.

sufficed to protect the birds from the elements, though raised structures would have prevented predators from burrowing in. It is not known if dovecotes were already a seigneurial phenomenon, like coney warrens or deer and boar parks, which were considered an aristocratic privilege, obtainable by royal license.

Even a poor man had a right to a hunting bird or dog. Used primarily as a protector of livestock and property, the dog remained a scavenger, living off scraps and refuse. Unlike the Celts, the Anglo-Saxons did not eat dogs. Cats were kept to prevent vermin from destroying vulnerable foodstuffs, especially the grain supply. The cat and dog were the only common animals that did not add to the overall agricultural product, but they did ensure that it was not diminished by wildlife depredation.

The analysis of faunal material from archaeological sites and its evaluation by statistical techniques have made specific contributions to the study of the agricultural economy of the late Roman and early medieval periods. Although much of the fourth century was a time of rural prosperity, the ties between town and villa were first strained, then severed. Markets dwindled, and farm life turned away from the town economy. A change in diet included new amounts of venison. Evidence for hunting has appeared at some late Roman sites, where the increased amount of deer bones is seen as an "indication of disruption to an established agricultural system."[90] At Exeter most of the cattle bones of the fourth century were from immature animals. But stock enclosures appeared within the city walls, suggesting that a breakdown of the cattle trade serving the city was here offset by "home-grown" beef.[91]

As the details of sub-Roman adjustments to economic regression are revealed by faunal analysis, so too the earliest Anglo-Saxon meat trade is shown to have been rudimentary, but certainly greater than has been assumed for the eighth and ninth centuries.[92] At Hamwic (Southampton) at the mouth of the Itchen and at other sites, faunal analysis revealed that a majority of the butchered cattle were immature males, indicating that cattle not needed for dairy or breeding stock were the basis of a regular supply of beef for the town.[93] The bones appear in large numbers, tens of thousands, during a site-life of less than two centuries (more than at any other excavated Anglo-Saxon settlement), and a significant

---

[90] Annie Grant, "The Significance of Deer Remains at Occupational Sites of the Iron Ages to the Anglo-Saxon Period," pp. 205–213 in *The Environment of Man;* quote on p. 208.

[91] Maltby, "Animal Husbandry," p. 182. Note that the example is in one of the most remote and least Romanized *civitates*. In more highly developed areas of Britannia and other provinces, sophisticated provisioning systems may have continued, but they also may have been disrupted by military requisitioning for troops and their dependents.

[92] Among others, *A.S.E.,* pp. 55–58, 525–27.

[93] Maltby, "Animal Husbandry," p. 183. But see also P.C. Buckland, P. Holdsworth, and M. Monk, "The Interpretation of a Group of Saxon Pits in Southampton," *Journal of Archaeological Science* 3 (1976), pp. 61–69.

number of them had been used for industrial and craft purposes. A long-range, permanent cattle market is suggested by the fact that animals in such numbers must have been brought some distance through the poor soils and broad woodland of the Southampton area, and also by the fact that regular slaughtering was required to supply raw material to a large artisan population.

A complex early medieval economy is also suggested by studies of sheep bones. Applebaum contended that in late Roman Britain there were concentrations of sheep being reared for wool, but if so, limited to certain localities only, because the present evidence indicates that the Romans in Britain raised sheep primarily for meat.[94] In the Anglo-Saxon period, the kill-off pattern was radically altered, with a great increase in the number of sheep kept until maturity. This is considered evidence for "a large scale increase in the importance of wool production to enable extensive wool and cloth trading to take place."[95] Other findings have noted substantial numbers of wethers (gelded rams), which have heavier fleece, again pointing to an emphasis on wool production.[96]

Regional differences may prove that wool specialization was not country-wide, but the Hampshire sites are among those yielding this faunal evidence. Thus, while early medieval animal husbandry was mixed, as was farming in general, certain activities such as cattle and sheep raising could take advantage of growing markets located nearby, e.g., Hamwic. The Anglo-Saxon commercial system operated with a minimal amount of proper coinage (especially in the eighth and ninth centuries); thus evidence for the size of this trade has come to light only recently, with the development of palaeo-environmental studies and the application of computer analysis to archaeological bone remains.

ECONOMICS

Three aspects of the early English economy are important to an understanding of rural development at Micheldever: (1) the physical survival of the Roman road system and the uses to which it was put by the Saxons of Hampshire; (2) the important transformation of agriculture from a subsistence economy to one of surplus production, and the possible influence that contemporary climatic conditions had upon it; and (3) the role of trade and crafts in the countryside, especially the demand for rural products.

---

[94] Maltby, "Animal Husbandry," p. 175; Applebaum, "Roman Britain," pp. 214–218.
[95] Maltby, "Animal Husbandry," p. 178.
[96] Clutton-Brock, "Animal Resources," pp. 380–81.

The Transportation System

Before the Romans came to build their roads, there already existed ancient "ridgeways," long-distance trackways running along watershed divides. Some ridgeways went for hundreds of miles across Britain. But less noticeable were the smaller tracks that served farmsteads, hamlets, and fields, and that linked them to the larger settlements. Like the ridgeways, the traceable paths sought routes of better drainage and avoided the valley bottoms where possible. This has given rise to the belief that river valleys largely comprised difficult, marshy ground. It is possible that some valley bottoms had become unsuitable for both agriculture and habitation because of the great amount of silt eroded from the ploughed fields.[97] There is no reason to doubt that most major tracks survived into the Roman period and beyond. The future site of Winchester was a confluence of major Iron Age roads, and immediately south of the Micheldever valley ran a ridgeway connecting the lands east of the Candover with those west of the Test. This track survives in several places across the central chalk downs, and by Micheledever it is called the Lunway or the Alresford Drove.[98]

Construction of the Roman road system through Britain was an expensive undertaking, taking several generations to complete. Ditches on either side supplied the material for the raised bed or agger. Stone rubble was added, usually in several layers. It was topped with gravel and cambered to drain off water. According to Ivan Margary, the primary roads could be up to thirty feet wide, with secondary ones less than twenty feet wide, and some minor roads little more than ten feet wide.[99]

The Roman road system was founded on the need to move troops as rapidly as possible from one strategic point to another. It was not really constructed for animal use, and indeed many slopes of ascending roadways would have been hard going for a laden draught animal.[100] Despite the technical difficulties, the system did encourage rapid communications and commerce among the Romano-British towns, and between the hinterland and the ports. Thus, while one series of roads converged on the capital and metropolis, *Londinium*, another pattern was formed by a series of nearly parallel roads leading southeast to the Channel ports.

The efforts of Margary and others have revealed the extent of the

---

[97] See Bell, "Valley Sediments," in *Environment of Man*.

[98] For prehistoric ridgeways in central Hampshire, see C. F. C. Hawkes, et al., "St. Catherines Hill," *Proc. Hants. Field Club and Archaeol. Soc.* XI (1930), p. 4, fig. 3. See also R. H. Cox, *The Green Roads of England* (London, 1914, repr. 1948), pp. 94–95.

[99] Ivan D. Margary, *Roman Roads in Britain* I (London, 1955), p. 15. The revised edition (London, 1967) has no changes affecting Hampshire.

[100] See Albert C. Leighton, *Transport and Communication in Early Medieval Europe*, A.D. 500–110 (Newton Abbott, Devon, 1972), pp. 48–52.

imperial road network in Britain. The record is still far from complete; in fact, portions of the system appear never to have been finished. But the imperial roads were only part of the transportation system in the first millennium A.D. One must also take into account the pre-existing long-distance routes, and on a local level, the paths and trackways of the Romano-British countryside. These surfaces no doubt bore more actual traffic than the Roman-made roads because travel for most of the population was strictly inter-village, or even villa-village, rather than inter-city. Consequently, the emphasis on the well-made (and easier to locate) Roman roads suggests an unfortunate bias on the part of scholars overly familiar with long-distance travel, associated with the Georgian turnpikes and modern motorways.

In Hampshire, Roman roads radiate from Winchester, as from most *civitas* capitals, like the spokes of a wheel (Fig. 2.4).[101] The road system by the Micheldever valley is well established. The Cirencester road flanked it to the west, and the Silchester road cut through it from the northeast. Passing along the far side of the Test was the Silchester-Sarum road. Filling the interstices of this triangle were local village and farm tracks of the central chalk downs, as well as the ancient ridgeways passing through the area.

The Roman road system no doubt suffered in the fifth century, though in most places it would take centuries of disuse for its presence to be forgotten.[102] As Margary pointed out, the wooden bridges were the weakest part of the system. After only a few years of neglect, permanent breaches in the system could occur at river crossings, where local traffic sought alternative routes.[103] The late Roman authorities appear to have lodged German *foederati* at strategic points by the imperial road system. Upon the barbarization of the provinces, however, there was no administrative necessity for clear lines of communication. Indeed, local communities may have been more secure away from the highways.[104]

A new network of roadways serving early medieval villages and their fields often replaced Roman roads and Celtic secondary tracks. Aerial photographs most vividly depict how the roads that survived were those that fulfilled local functions: carrying crops to a central location for rendering dues or for exchange at a rudimentary market; or bearing soldiers most rapidly between early medieval strategic locations. In Anglo-Saxon charters, the larger roads used by the military were called *straet* (from the Latin *stratum*, "paved") and *herepath* (army road), and minor roads

---

[101] Margary, *Roman Roads*, pp. 81–83, 89–93.

[102] Brian Hindle took a more sanguine view of Roman road continuity in "Roads and Tracks," pp. 193–217 in Leonard Cantor, ed., *The English Medieval Landscape* (Philadelphia, 1981).

[103] Margary, *Roman Roads*, p. 18; Leighton, *Transport*, pp. 59, 60.

[104] See Myers, *Anglo-Saxon Pottery*, pp. 74–77, 103.

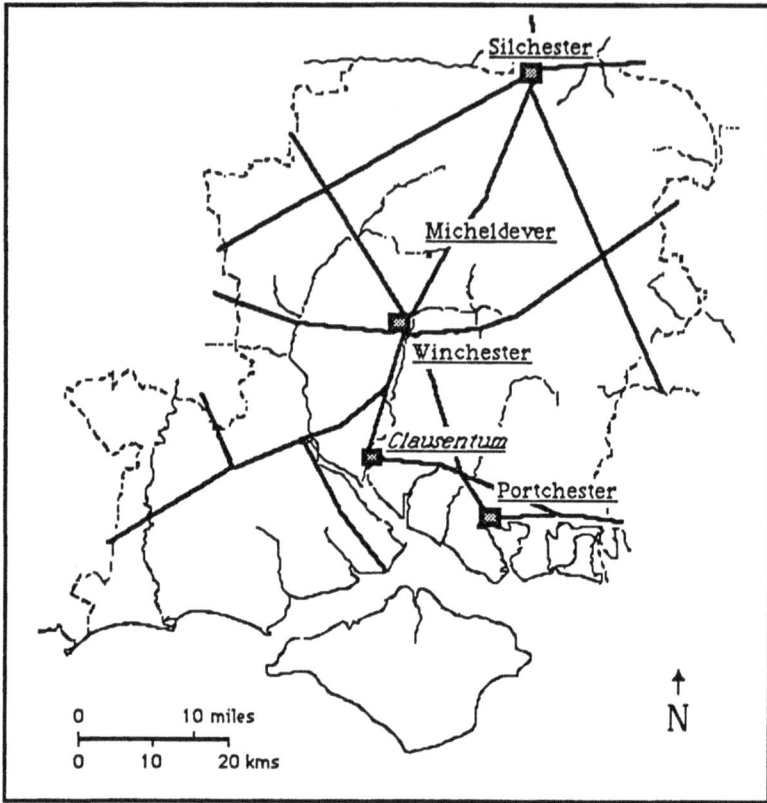

FIG. 2.4 Roman Roads in Hampshire

were given descriptions such as the "foul way" and the "stubby way."[105] It took centuries to create the medieval pattern of villages and to develop the medieval field system, so it was also with the new communication system established by the Germanic possessors of the land. In fact the long duration of this process may have ensured the continued survival of some of the Roman roads, because, as this study will demonstrate, the medieval landscape firmly coalesced at the same time as urban activity and the associated need for long-distance communications returned to England.

Agriculture

The first conversion of woodland to arable land was for Neolithic cultivation; it was restricted to river gravels and calcareous limestone

---

[105] L. A. G. Strong, *The Rolling Road*, (London, 1956); cited in Leighton, *Transport*, p. 52, n. 6; Stenton, "The Road System of Medieval England," pp. 234–52 in *Preparatory to Anglo-Saxon England*, particularly p. 235.

and chalk areas. By the time of the Roman conquest, there were some Celtic settlements on heavier soils, and Romano-British sites have yielded remains of weeds typical of clay soils, suggesting that some activity was taking place on heavier and damper soils. Under the Romans, if not before, agriculture seems to have moved slowly beyond the lighter soils, a movement which intensified under the Anglo-Saxons.[106] The clear division between Celtic chalk and Anglo-Saxon clay cultivation is no longer valid, and one may propose a transitional period when much of the primaeval forest was cleared and the clays were cultivated with initial success. This hypothesis is presented as a tentative solution to the problem of transition. As the heavy plough was developed in stages, so its effectiveness would have increased in stages.

The technological innovation of the heavy plough was the catalyst for the movement onto different soils. The simple, light ard of the ancient world was not capable of handling the heavy clays. The introduction of the heavy plough has been attributed to the Belgic peoples of the first century B.C., the Romans in the first or third century A.D., the Anglo-Saxons in the fifth century, and the Danes in the ninth century.[107] Certainly its development was a lengthy process—the eight-ox team seems to have been adopted only a few generations before Domesday Book.[108]

Just as the forests are likely to have been cleared in stages of increasingly difficult soils (gravel and chalk; clayey loam; heavy clay), so the medieval plough and team was the final stage in a series of technological adaptions. The eight-ox team was necessary for the heavy clays, but unnecessary for the lighter soils. It is likely that medieval farmers applied different ploughs and teams to different soil types, and that the eight-ox heavy plough was typical only of areas like the English Midlands or the Ile de France.[109] A type of heavy plough was probably in limited use in later Roman Britain, and was one of those developments of the late antique world that in mature form was widespread in the early medieval period, like the heavy cavalry, the codex, and the watermill.

In the early Saxon period, agriculture was at a subsistence level that

---

[106] Martin Jones, "The Development of Crop Husbandry," pp. 95–104 in *Environment of Man*, especially pp. 111–12.

[107] Lynn White, Jr., *Medieval Technology and Social Change*, treats the conflicting dates in some detail (pp. 51–52). He concludes that the Scandinavians introduced the heavy plough in the late ninth century (p. 53). But note Applebaum, following Thomas, with a strong case for the plough in Roman times, "Roman Britain" in *A.H.E.W.*, pp. 83–87. For the older view of a Celtic heavy plough, see Edward Hyams, *Soils and Civilization* (London, 1952, 1976), pp. 247–48. Georges Duby contends that the Romans found an advanced agricultural technology in the hands of the northern barbarians, but "they did not adopt it for themselves": *The Early Growth of the European Economy: Warriors and Peasants from the Seventh to the Twelfth Century* (Ithaca, N.Y., 1974), p. 16.

[108] For the confusion wreaked in the Domesday Book by differing plough teams, see *D.B.B.*, pp. 417 ff.

[109] *A.S.E.*, pp. 515–16.

altered the landscape minimally. The catalyst for the shift in agricultural productivity may have been the technological innovation of the heavy plough, but the mere presence of this implement should not be proposed as the cause of the massive outlay of human energy expended in clearing trees from the clay lands.

The middle centuries of the first millennium A.D. did not experience population pressure, economic expansion, or governmental land programs. It was instead a time of substantially reduced population levels, economic decay, and ineffective governmental authority. The unfavorable climate of the late and post-Roman periods had a regional role in socio-economic developments and should have retarded the clayland expansion of agriculture.[110] In a wetter climate, the heavy clays became even more difficult to work. A plausible alternative explanation is that the farmers in southern England were forced onto the clays because the lighter soils were exhausted.

Clearance of the chalk and gravel soils had begun in the fourth millennium B.C., and these lands had been under increasingly intensive arable farming during the Roman centuries. The characteristic Celtic field pattern may well have evolved as a system for combatting soil erosion.[111] With minimal opportunity for manuring the fields, and with a limited variety of crops (given the Roman demand for cereal production), the farmers of Roman Britain may have been faced with a steady impoverishment of the soil, as its mass was eroded and its nutrients leached out.[112] The suggested late Roman creation of extensive tracts of imperial sheep farms on the chalk downs of southern England may not be evidence of an imperial bureaucracy's priority for clothing for its troops,[113] but rather the appropriate use of exhausted cropland as pasture.

The region of Hampshire-Wiltshire chalk upland did not convert *en masse* from mixed arable production to livestock rearing in the late Roman period. According to Applebaum, the rural economy collapsed for a variety of reasons.[114] Climatic deterioration after the second century

---

[110] Lamb, "Climate from 1000 B.C. to 1000 A.D.," pp. 57, 60. For a good summary of varying opinions, see K. Greene, *The Archaeology of the Roman Economy* (Berkeley, 1986), pp. 81–86.

[111] See Bell, "Valley Sediment and Environmental Change."

[112] The Romans did advocate fallowing and fertilizing with farmyard dung, practices which would have extended the fertility of the chalk soils, but there is as yet no evidence that they were employed in Hampshire. See K. D. White, *Roman Farming* (Ithaca, N.Y., 1970), pp. 118, 125.

[113] Sheep farms and cattle ranches are discussed in R. G. Collingwood and I. Richmond, *The Archaeology of Roman Britain* (London, 1969), pp. 179–81; Applebaum, "Roman Britain," pp. 232–34; Frere, *Britannia*, p. 300.

[114] It was formerly believed that southern Britain underwent a late Roman conversion from arable land to livestock production; Collingwood and Myers, *Roman Britain*, p. 223. C. C. Taylor has convincingly challenged many elements of this theory, "Late Roman Pastoral Farming in Wessex," *Antiquity* 41 (1967), pp. 384–86. Peter Salway, *Roman Britain*,

meant that autumn-planted wheat would suffer from slow ripening and mildew, though spring-planted barley would do well. Much of the agrarian wealth of Roman Britain had come from the villa clearance of clay lands, but worsening weather made them increasingly unproductive. The presumed demand by the late Roman government that villas on the chalk downs join in the heightened production of wheat over the more appropriate summer cereals (barley) eventually destroyed the efficiency of the villa system. The same demand upon native farming communities for a crop that was planted in the autumn meant a substantial reduction in land available for pasture on winter stubble, resulting in the over-grazing of available common pasture.

There is evidence to support this hypothesis in the Micheldever area. Grain-drying ovens appear in Britain in the second and third centuries; alternative explanations of their purpose, preventing mildew and crop rot in wetter weather or preparing barley in beer making, are both related to difficulties or reductions in wheat production.[115] One such drying oven has been found in the Dever valley, on the east side of Bullington parish.[116] Evidence for a difficult and inefficient production of wheat is also present in those Clay-with-Flints areas that have been under continuous woodland since Roman times. Field survey shows that in the Micheldever area villas had indeed expanded their arable range into the heavier soils.

In addition to the problems of ploughing and susceptibility to crop damage that came from planting the wrong crop in the wrong climate, another result of the much-reduced woodland was a scarcity of fuel for the inhabitants of the estates of middle Hampshire. The wholesale clearance of woodlands also left cropland more exposed to wind damage, and by reducing the absorption rate and raising the run-off rate, it may also have had the double effect of lowering the water table and increasing the potential for erosion of topsoil.[117] All these factors were magnified by a climate that deteriorated throughout the late and sub-Roman periods. The once populous Hampshire downland may have been

---

pp. 627–28, stresses the financial rewards that mixed farming earned in the "villa-economy." Shimon Applebaum, "Roman Britain," in *A.H.E.W.*, pp. 232–34, argues that Hampshire may indeed have been a sheep-rearing area, but an increase in grazing land at the expense of native cultivation cannot be proved; on pp. 244–47, he presents his argument for the fifth-century economic collapse.

[115] For ovens, see Frere, *Britannia*, pp. 278–79; Collingwood and Richmond, *Archaeology of Roman Britain*, p. 151; Salway, *Roman Britain*, pp. 458–59; and Greene, *Roman Economy*, p. 76.

[116] At Ordnance Survey sheet SU44SE, coordinates 464417, as noted in the Hampshire County Manning Office. The unexcavated site lies between the "bath house" on the Dever and the Roman buildings in Tidbury Ring, which have yielded Constantinian coins.

[117] Compare with Hyams, *Soil and Civilization*, pp. 250–58. While examining a Celtic origin for the heavy plough, Hyams observed that the collapse of the Roman Empire saved the soils of northwestern Europe from being over-exploited. He went on to suggest that it was the slow medieval development of the rich soils of northwestern Europe that gave an agricultural base sufficient for industrialization and worldwide expansion.

largely deserted by the end of the fifth century, the elegant villas serving as shelters for herdsmen and their flocks.

With the end of Roman rule, the transformation was complete. The lighter soils of Wessex, perhaps once the "bread basket" of Britain, and the center of its most flourishing and highly developed villa system, could no longer support the export of grain to the Continent. The long-term clearance of the clay soils may have freed these lands for either pasture or cultivation. With a heavier plough, a Romano-British grain-producing population was no longer restricted to the light soils, but cultivation remained limited because the clay soils underwent a leaching process of "iron pan" formation after only five or ten years. The early medieval introduction of the moldboard, however, enabled the farmer to turn over the topsoil, reversing the leaching process. The clay lands retained their tilth and could be permanently cultivated.[118] It was the double technological development of first the heavy plough and then the moldboard, combined with an increasingly mild climate during the eighth century, that created the dynamics of population growth and economic expansion of the early Middle Ages.[119]

Commerce and Industry

During the early Middle Ages, the exchange of produce and craft goods progressed from a local to a regional level. Surpluses in agrarian production permitted an increase in secondary rural production—more livestock and commercial crops. There is palynological evidence for a rise in hemp and flax growing to a level beyond the needs of any single community or local group.[120] Similarly, animal bones from Saxon sites reveal a kill pattern that suggests to archaeologists that some commercial specialization was taking place.[121] This could only have taken place under a revival of commerce and industry, a situation where grain production and animal husbandry had expanded faster than the needs of the local population. In some parts of England it was becoming more profitable to raise fiber crops than to increase food crops. The exploitative value of livestock had also increased, not just for meat and dairy products, but also for the raw materials for craft work which they provided: wool, leather, organs, horns, and bones.

As the supplies of raw materials grew, so did the production of craft

---

[118] Limbrey, *Soil Science*, pp. 169–71, stresses that wetter weather would make clay soils unworkable. The same argument should apply to areas on the Chalk covered by Clay-with-Flints.

[119] Here I apply to Anglo-Saxon England Lynn White's argument that the heavy plough brought about a rise in the population of Germany and Scandinavia: *Medieval Technology*, p. 54.

[120] See Green, "Iron Age, Roman and Saxon Crops," in *Environment of Man*.

[121] See Annie Grant, "Significance of Deer Remains," and Maltby, "Animal Husbandry."

goods made from them, and the markets by which they were exchanged. David Wilson has presented a detailed account of Anglo-Saxon industry; he covered the production of glass, metals, iron, textiles, leather, basketry, as well as working in bone and horn, wood, and stone.[122] Pottery making and other container and "packaging" industries were necessary components of early medieval enterprise, as were the food-processing trades (milling, butchery, baking). The increased commerce in exchanging these goods brought a growth in transport. As noted above, some Roman roads and Celtic tracks survived into the Middle Ages, while new roads connected most Anglo-Saxon settlements. Packhorses needed ostlers and harness makers, and carters needed carpenters and wheelwrights.[123] The tolls charged in Domesday indicate that the packhorse carried four times the load of a man, and each ox attached to a cart drew twice the load of a packhorse.[124] Permanent containers consisted of tubs, barrels, and chests. Baskets would have been used for much produce; other material was conveyed in coarse sacking, or even leather containers: pouches, flagons, or hard leather casks, but pottery vessels less often. All conveyances needed leather thongs, straps, and belts, and of course rope and cording. Some of the hemp production went into rope making for land transport, but water traffic had an obvious demand for rope as well. Both coastal and marine shipping called for the services of shipwrights and the wood, pitch, and iron ware they used. Sails needed large quantities of canvas cloth, which was made from those Anglo-Saxon cash crops of flax and hemp.[125]

The level of economic activity in the eighth and ninth centuries still involved few real markets and long-distance trade routes, nor were there numerous foreign merchants. Even so, it now appears to have been more developed than was assumed twenty-five years ago.[126] Recent archaeological evidence supports Peter Sawyer's claim for an economic "take-off" some centuries earlier than had been thought. Sawyer has suggested that England's growing wealth in the tenth century was based on the wool trade, and that markets for this wool in the Rhineland opened up with the German discovery and exploitation of silver mines in Saxony.[127] He would thus have the source of English prosperity in the late Middle Ages also serve as the source of its wealth in the early Middle Ages. At present there seems no better explanation for the huge amounts of silver in the late Anglo-Saxon economy, as reproduced in

---

[122] David M. Wilson, "Craft and Industry," pp. 153–82 in *A.A.S.E.*

[123] Leighton, *Transport and Communication*, p. 41.

[124] Leighton, ibid., citing *The Domesday Survey of Cheshire*, J. Tait, ed., Chetham Society, New Series, Vol. 75, pp. 217–25.

[125] "Canvas" is defined as unbleached cloth made of hemp and flax, and its etymology is derived from *cannabis*, "hemp": *The Oxford English Dictionary* (Oxford, 1971), p. 331.

[126] *A.S.E.*, pp. 525–28; and Philip Grierson, "Commerce in the Dark Ages: A Critique of the Evidence," *Trans. Royal Hist. Soc.*, 5th Series, Vol. 9 (1959), pp. 123–40.

[127] Sawyer, "The Wealth of England," pp. 145–64.

the Danegeld figures.[128] Certainly, Charlemagne's concern for the specifics of English woolens as shown in his letter to Offa should indicate that the English textile industry had regular overseas markets in the eighth century.[129]

If Sawyer's hypothesis is correct, how would it affect Hampshire and Micheldever? Winchester has been identified as the center of the Roman wool area,[130] and if so, it could have continued as such into the medieval period. One might then conclude that Wessex survived the Viking attacks in part because of its durability as the center of the English export trade, with Hamwic (Southampton) as its port. The existing evidence, however, cannot support the argument. There is no definite proof that the imperial weaving factory at Venta was situated in Winchester (Venta Belgarum), nor is there an indication that the area around it specialized in sheep rearing. There is circumstantial evidence that the recorded imperial weaving mill was located at Venta Icenorum (Caister-by-Norwich) in East Anglia, the great sheep-rearing area of the later Middle Ages.[131] And it is eastern England, not the Hampshire Downs, where Sawyer would put late Saxon wealth.[132] Wessex, it would seem, had neither the blessing of the German wool trade, nor the curse of Danish conquest, which elsewhere meant the near-total destruction of political and religious institutions.

Hampshire nonetheless took part in the general early medieval economic expansion, and was itself the most prosperous southern region west of Kent. Its urban centers consisted of two large towns and several smaller settlements that offered purely local markets. The towns were Winchester and Southampton, which together appear to have met the definition of a city for the eighth century, but individually may not have achieved a fully developed urban form until the growth of boroughs in the tenth century.[133] Even after that, the towns continued to show an imbalance in character, with Winchester the political, ceremonial, and religious center, and Southampton the commerce, manufacturing, and shipping entrepôt.

Southampton's origin lies in the Roman fortified port of Clausentum on the Itchen near its mouth.[134] There is no evidence that this site was

---

[128] See Michael Dolley, "The Coins," pp. 349–72 in *A.A.S.E.*, esp. p. 370; David M. Wilson, "The Scandinavians in England," pp. 393–405 in *A.A.S.E.*, pp. 401–402; and Gwyn Jones, *A History of the Vikings* (Oxford, 1968), p. 364.

[129] *A.S.E.*, p. 221.

[130] Collingwood and Myers, *Roman Britain*, pp. 239–40.

[131] Applebaum, "Roman Britain," in *A.H.E.W.*, pp. 217–18.

[132] Sawyer, "The Wealth of England," pp. 145–64.

[133] See Martin Biddle, "Towns," pp. 99–150 in *A.A.S.E.*, esp. p. 114.

[134] The most detailed accounts of the Southampton port development are: L. A. Burgess, *The Origins of Southampton* (Leicester, 1964); P. V. Addyman and D. H. Hill, "Saxon Southampton: A Review of the Evidence," *Proc. Hants. Field Club and Archaeol. Soc.* 25 (1968), pp. 61–83; 26 (1969), pp. 61–96; and Philip Holdsworth, "Saxon Southampton; a New Review," *Medieval Archaeology* 20 (1976), pp. 26–61.

occupied beyond the early fifth century, but excavations there have been generally uninformative. By A.D. 700 low-lying land across the river from Clausentum was the site of renewed activity. During the early eighth century (perhaps under the strong monarchy of Ine), it developed into a booming commercial settlement, called Hamwic, Hamwih, or Hamtun. It had a population of perhaps 3,000, and was clearly the major port along the south coast, probably dominating the trade with the Seine. Saxon Southampton was one of the North Sea entrepôts, a dozen or so centers of international commerce spread from the English Channel to the Baltic.

At pre-Viking Hamwic, as at the other trading towns, there is evidence for nearly every sort of craft, but material from some activities is more permanent than that associated with others. There is a preponderance of evidence for iron and metal working in cinders, slag, "sprue" residue, and broken bone or stone molds. For boneworking there are large quantities of discarded fragments, as well as finished or partially finished combs, pins, knife handles, etc. Horn cores testify to horn products, lanterns, and window "panes." According to the excavators, this site was similar to contemporary Dorestadt in Holland, with many thousands of items of waste material suggesting a truly large-scale center employing hundreds of craftsmen. The archaeological evidence is less firm for the industrial use of fibers, oils, and skins. The manufacture of cloth, bedding, rope, unguents, pigments, and leather goods is thus hard to measure, as is the slightly more obtainable evidence for woodworking, carpentry, and boat building. The demand for most of these materials would have surpassed the resources of the lower Hampshire Basin and the Isle of Wight. Produce from north Hampshire and Micheldever would have found in eighth- and ninth-century Southampton one of the few centers of demand, and it is probable that livestock and fiber commodities of wool, flax, or hemp were drawn from northern Hampshire to the craftshops and port at the mouth of the Itchen.

When Alfred reorganized Winchester as a fortified *burh* ca. 880, it had been less an urban entity than a collection of private estates within the Roman walls, smaller versions perhaps of the royal and episcopal establishments.[135] Late Saxon Winchester was a true city, with typical burghal tenements and a regular street plan imposed by Alfred. The expanded authority of the kings of Wessex was no doubt accompanied by a greater political establishment attached to the Court. The tenth century also saw an enlarged ecclesiastic presence, through new foundations made by Edward and Edgar especially, and by the greater role the clergy played in the affairs of state during the latter's reign. The

---

[135] See Martin Biddle and D. J. Keene, "The Early Place-Names of Winchester," pp. 231–40, "Winchester in the Eleventh and Twelfth Centuries," pp. 241–48, and "General Survey and Conclusion," pp. 449–508 in *Winchester in the Early Middle Ages*.

royal, episcopal, and monastic population of the tenth century drew
upon their estates' demesnes, but were otherwise served by merchants
and craftsmen, the markets of which would have attracted produce from
all the upper Hampshire Basin. The names given to the Anglo-Saxon
streets are known, and many refer to commercial or craft activities that
took place there: fleshmongers (butchers), tanners, shoemakers, shield-
wrights, perhaps goldsmiths and cloth bleachers, and later, parchment
preparers. A full complement of medieval trades is represented in the
survey of properties and their occupants taken ca. 1110, which apparently included information from a previous list made in the 1050s. From
these exceptional records, Martin Biddle and Derek Keene have reconstructed the details of a fully developed city of the early twelfth century,
concluding that Winchester was not only a major metropolis, the capital,
one might say, of the "Norman Empire," but that it had been "a major
regional centre in the pre-Conquest period."[136]

Agriculture in the north Hampshire villages of Micheldever Hundred
was probably affected by late Saxon urban growth. The villages were
certainly close enough to profit from the market opportunities that
Winchester's population created. "Provisioning the city and the distribution of its products implied a good deal of traffic with the surrounding
countryside, and it is in this trade that markets outside West Gate and
inside North Gate may have been especially important from an early
date [the late ninth century]."[137] The development of the estates and
settlements of the Micheldever valley may have been hastened by the
proximity of Winchester, but there is no reason to believe that their
pattern of evolution was abnormally altered in any way. The late Saxon
foundation of borough towns meant that most settlements in southern
England were a day's journey from a permanent marketplace, and in
this context urbanism stimulated further pre-Conquest rural development.

SUMMATION

In the heart of the southern Chalk belt, Micheldever from 700 to 1100
was a locale that had suffered a great drop in both population and productivity at the end of the Roman period. The soil, it seems, was no
longer able to support the intensive agrarian regime of the Roman authorities and villa owners, and the deposits of Clay-with-Flints could
not be broken by the light and not kept fertile by the heavy plough
without a moldboard. A generally drier and warmer climate after the
seventh century increased the growing season, and made clay areas less
difficult to work. The drier weather may also have been an important

---

[136] Ibid., p. 461.
[137] Ibid., p. 460.

element in the general lowering of the water table in the central Hampshire chalkland around Micheldever.

In the early medieval period, the heavy plough and large plough team converted clay soils into productive grain fields, giving new life to the agriculture of the depleted chalk regions. At Micheldever, all but the most intractable deposits of Clay-with-Flints were then available for cultivation. The open chalk downs surrounding the Dever valley were no longer necessary for arable use nor were they able to support it adequately; they would have been given over to pasture, especially for the production of wool. Wooded areas were unsuitable for sheep rearing, though they did support swine herds and animals for the hunt. At the same time, more cattle were needed for the population and manufacturing center at Southampton. It is likely, then, that partially wooded areas were used as pasturage for rearing livestock.

Technical innovation in arable production and an ameliorating climate, therefore, permitted a mixed agricultural regime, which at Micheldever likely involved an expanded wheat crop, with flax for linen, swine for local consumption, and cattle and wool as commodities that had a regular market if not at the royal city of Winchester, then at the busy industrial and commercial center of Southampton.

III. EARLY MEDIEVAL SETTLEMENT

The scarcity of readily identifiable early medieval settlements has led archaeologists to employ an analytical technique used by prehistorians and geographers—the study of settlement patterns.[1] This involves the compilation of maps depicting settlement distribution and the search for significant patterns in that distribution.

The "dynamic relationship between man and terrain" underlies settlement studies.[2] For early medieval Micheldever Hundred and its region, topography forms the fundamental element in a series of factors determining rural settlement and land use. The terrain of middle Hampshire is typical of the Wessex heartland: high chalk downland of rolling hills and plateaux, intersected by narrow, dry valleys. The topography of the Micheldever region generates two distinct patterns of settlement. An "upland pattern" is based upon the broad upper valley slopes and flat ridges, with habitations often found near the spring line. The other type of settlement, a "valley pattern," displays strongly linear elements based upon the valleys of rivers and major streams.

Drift (surface) geology can alter both types of topographically based pattern. Habitations tended to avoid localities where the easily worked chalk subsoil was covered by a thick, intractable deposit of Clay-with-Flints. On such sites, extensive woodland was to survive often into the later Middle Ages. At the other extreme, easily drained spreads of valley gravel always attracted farmers, particularly when climatic conditions made spring planting difficult.

It is, however, the effect of other variables upon a more or less static geographic background that determines a specific pattern of local settlement.[3] In examining the location and nature of the settlements around Micheldever in the Roman, early Saxon, and late Saxon periods, one

---

[1] For an introduction to the study of settlement patterns, see Irving Rouse, "Settlement Patterns in Archaeology," pp. 95–107 in P. Ucko, G. W. Dimbleby, and R. Tyingham, eds., *Man, Settlement and Urbanism* (London, 1972). The seminal work in these studies is by Michael Chisholm: *Rural Settlement and Land Use. An Essay in Location* (London, 1962). He employed the techniques of economic geography first used by Johann Henrick von Thunen, especially the principle of commodity transportation in determining "Economic Rent." See particularly pp. 114–23 for factors that determine village location, and pp. 124–34 for settlement patterns. Settlement in early England is discussed in Brian K. Roberts, *Rural Settlement in Britain* (Folkestone, Kent and Hamden, Conn., 1977), pp. 52–81.

[2] Donald A. Davidson, "Terrain Adjustment and Prehistoric Communities," pp. 18–22 in Ucko, et al., *Man, Settlement and Urbanism.*

[3] See Brian C. Bluet, "Factors influencing the Evolution of Settlement Patterns," pp. 3–15 in Ucko, et al., *Man, Settlement and Urbanism.*

must ask: how was settlement distribution affected by changing soil conditions, climate, and population density? The relevant data for the Micheldever valley and adjacent portions of the Candover and upper Itchen valleys are collected in a series of maps (Figs. 3.1–3.4).[4] Each map has a background format showing physical topography, surface drift geology, and the courses of Roman roads.[5] These maps illustrate the distribution of settlement, divided by period into Roman, early Saxon (eighth century), and late Saxon (eleventh century). A fourth map depicts changes in the early medieval settlements as indicated by archaeology and place-name chronology. It should be noted that these maps are concerned with settlements only, and not with the nature and morphology of the territories and populations which the settlements served, topics that are explored in later chapters.

THE ROMAN SETTLEMENT PATTERN

The four centuries in which southern England was under Roman rule have left their mark unevenly upon the landscape. The straight, gravel-surfaced Roman roads of the imperial transportation system have often survived as present trunk or secondary roads, farm tracks, and field boundaries. Other features of the Romano-British landscape, particularly the rural settlements, are rarely recognizable. Most are known solely through archaeological fieldwork and aerial photography.

The Micheldever valley lies in an area marked by the triangular shape of three major Roman roads.[6] One might expect Roman rural settlement

---

[4] Maps are basic tools for settlement studies. G. C. Dickinson declared for statistical mapping: "It must be treated as a highly specialized, often expensive (of time and labour) device which above all is an integral part of the task at hand": *Statistical Mapping in The Presentation of Statistics* (London, 1963), p. 8.

[5] The physical topography is taken from the Ordnance Survey map, 1" series (1 inch = 1 mile), sheet 168 (SU41), 1959 ed., rev. 1963. The drift geology is taken from *The Geological Survey of England and Wales*, 1" series, sheets 283, 284, 299, and 300, produced by the Ordnance Survey, 1905. The Roman roads are those routes depicted on figure 1 of Martin Biddle, "Hampshire and the Origins of Wessex," pp. 323–41 in G. de G. Sieveking, I. H. Longworth, and K. E. Wilson, *Problems in Economic and Social Archaeology* (London, 1976).

Many of the archaeological details can be found in the survey of sites undertaken by R. T. Schadla-Hall in 1974–1976, and published as *The Winchester District: The Archaeological Potential* (Winchester, 1977). The basic data are located in the files of the Winchester District Archaeologist, those of the Archaeological Officer of the Hampshire County Planning Office, and those of the Wessex Archaeological Unit, Salisbury. All three offices carry data from aerial photographs transferred to 6" series maps. Auxiliary material is in the Cope Collection for Local History at the Southampton University Library.

Secondary sources contain some of this material: Alfred B. Milner, *History of Micheldever* (Paris, 1924); Audrey Meaney, *Gazetteer of Early Anglo-Saxon Burial Sites* (London, 1964); J. P. Williams-Freeman, *An Introduction to Field Archaeology as Illustrated by Hampshire* (London, 1915); and Fred Aldsworth, "Towards a Pre-Domesday Geography of Hampshire: A Review of the Evidence," unpublished B.A. thesis, Southampton University, 1974.

[6] Margary's Nos. 4, 42, and 43. See Ivan D. Margary, *Roman Roads of Britain*. Vol. I, *South of the Foss Way—Bristol Channel* (London, 1955).

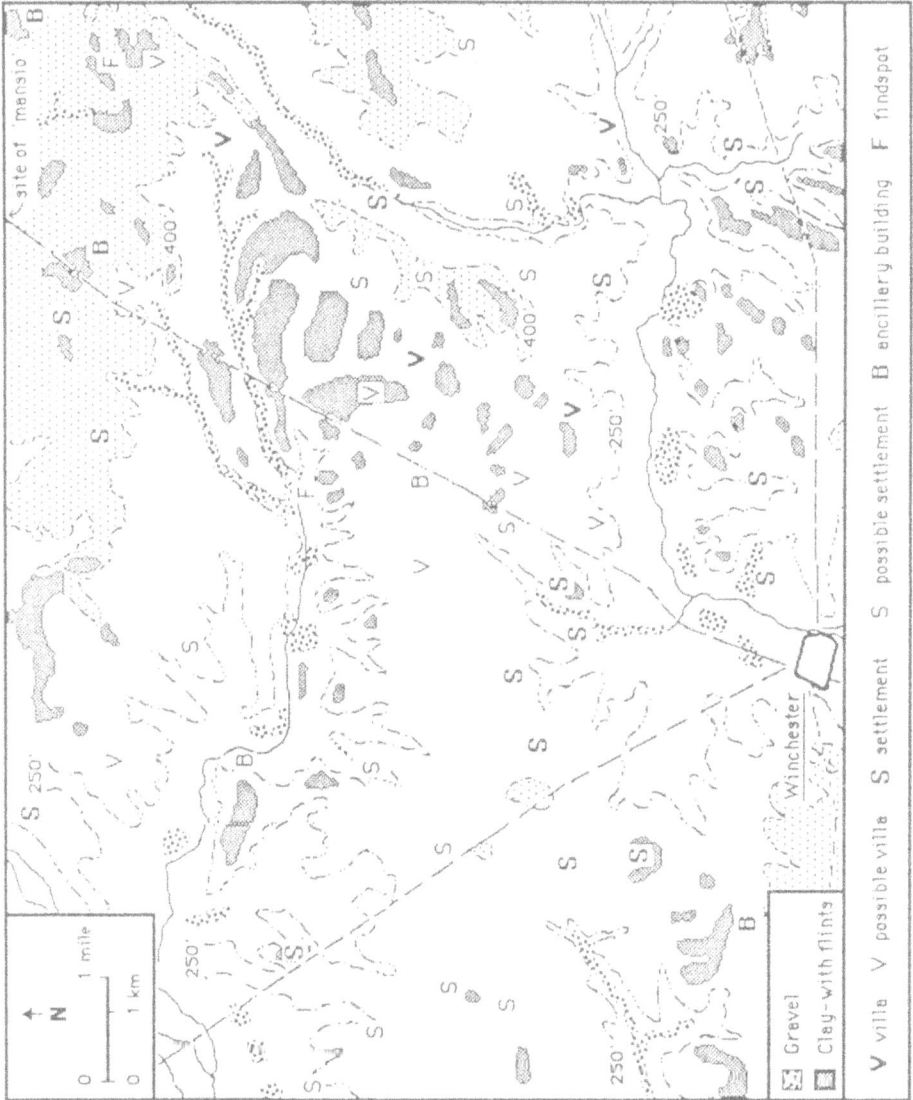

FIG. 3.1 Romano-British Settlement Pattern

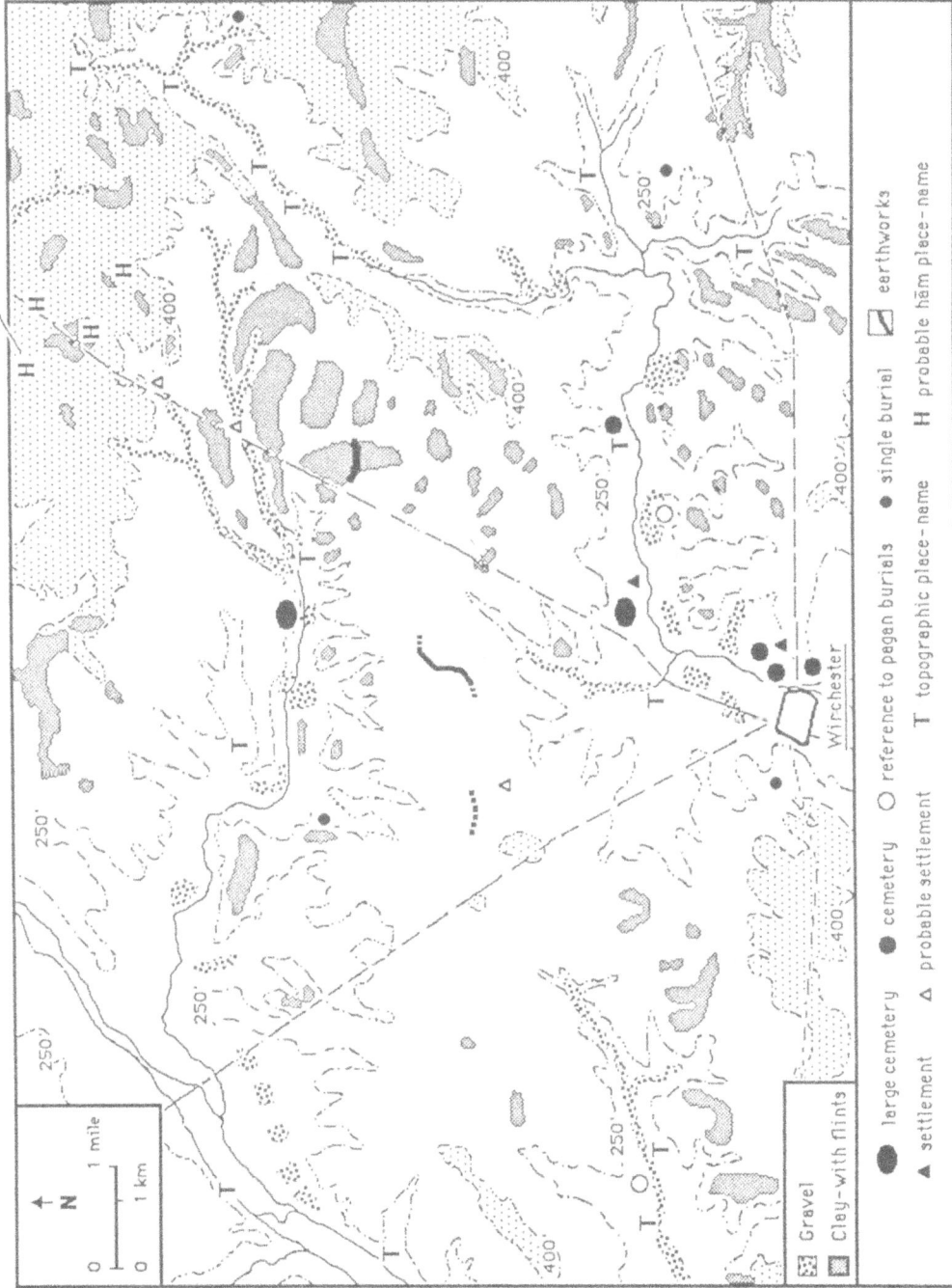

FIG. 3.2 Early Saxon Settlement Pattern

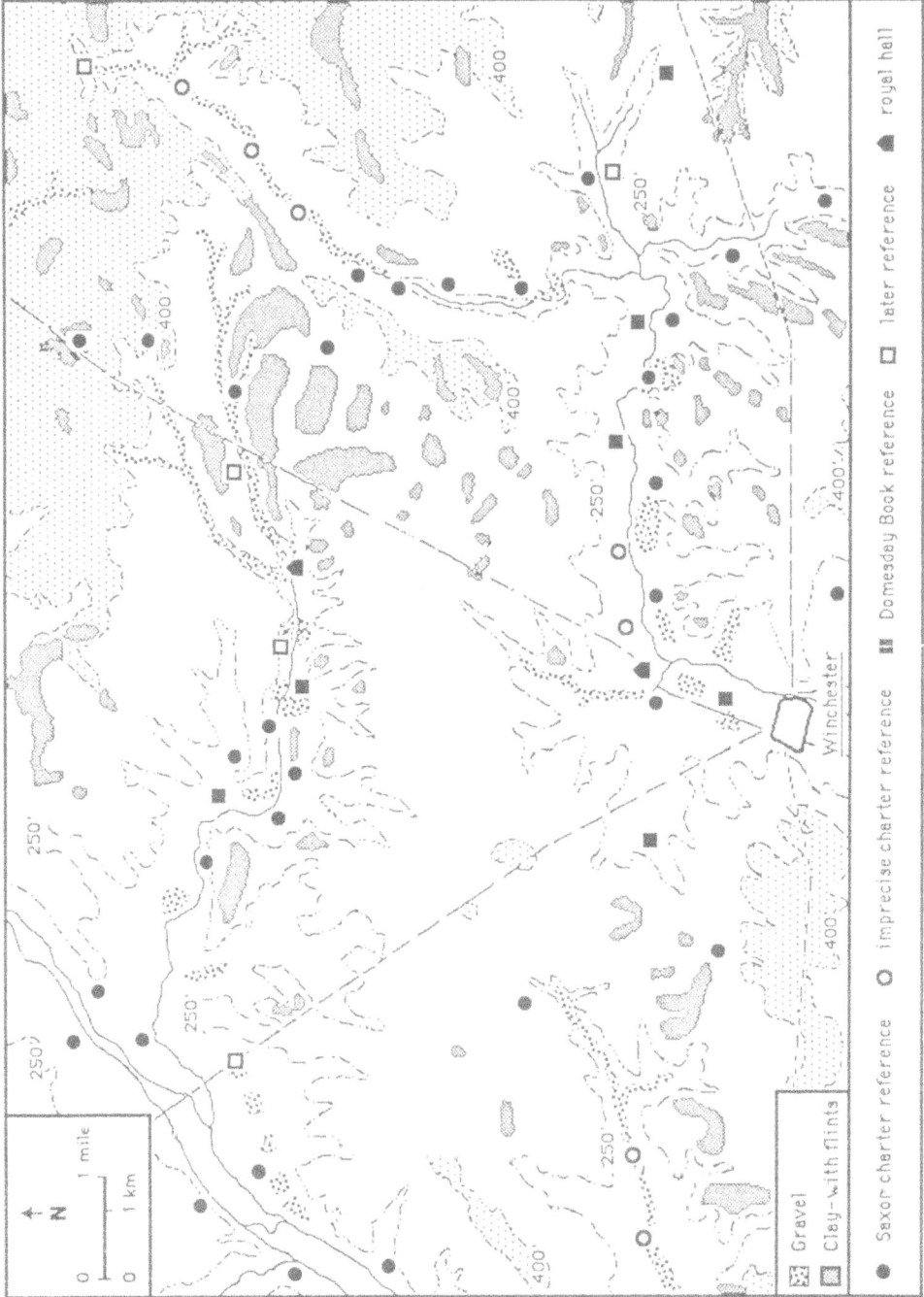

FIG. 3.3 Late Saxon Settlement Pattern

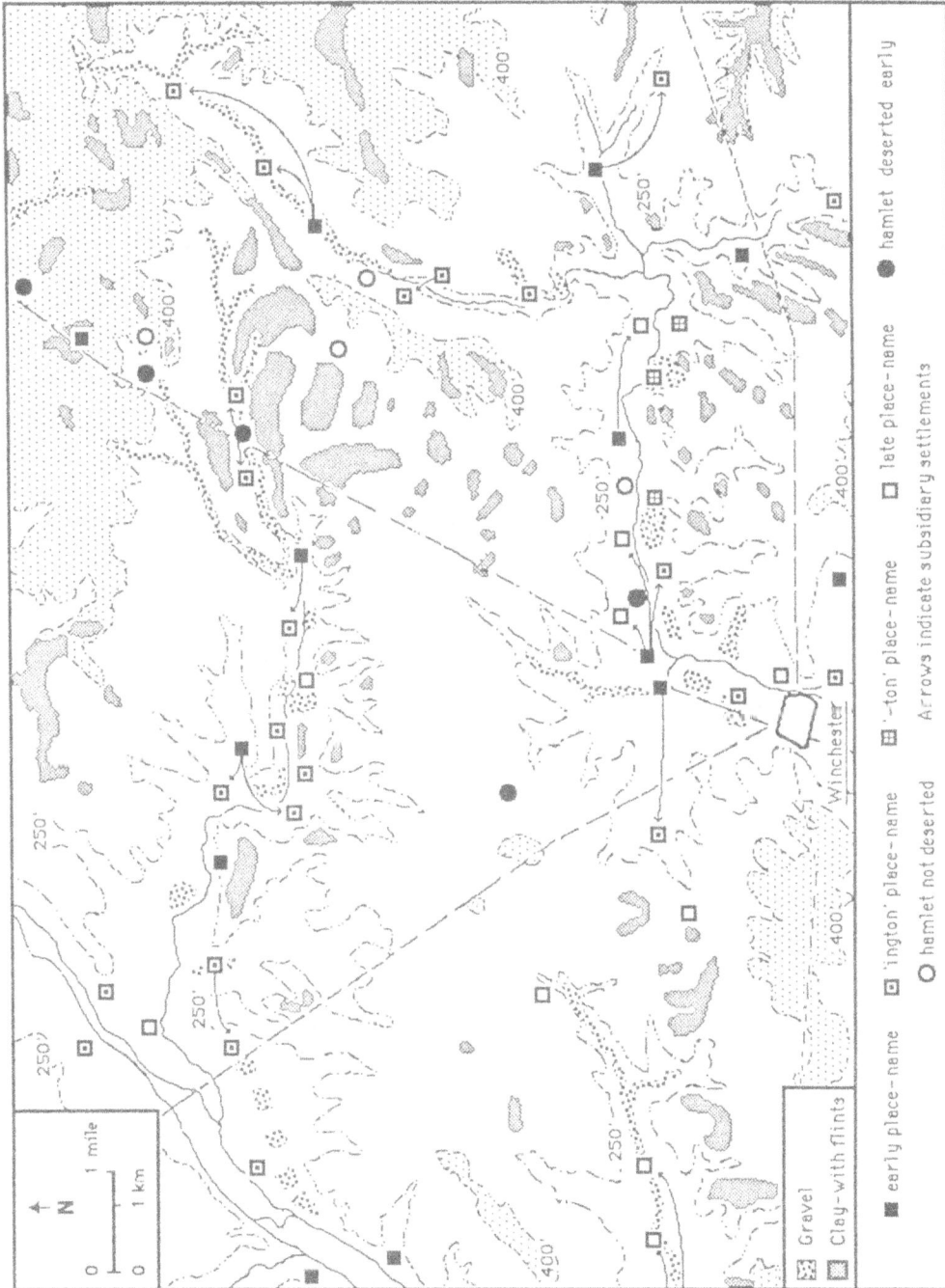

FIG. 3.4 Early Medieval Settlement Change

to have been affected by these roads, and also by the prehistoric track-ways that continued in use throughout the Roman period. The proximity of the cantonal capital of *Venta Belgarum* (Winchester) could also have influenced settlement. Different types of rural site (villa, hamlet, etc.) can sometimes be distinguished without extensive investigation. Since concrete dating is available for only a few of the Romano-British sites in middle Hampshire, all known sites of that period are presented on Figure 3.1.

Romano-British settlements in the Micheldever area are neither aligned along the courses of rivers and streams nor restricted to those ridges that divide the valleys. Sites occur in areas of Clay-with-Flints as well as in other areas. Perhaps surprisingly, the placement of settlements bears little relation to the Roman road system and also seems not to have been markedly influenced by the presence of the prehistoric routes.

Certain patterns appear. In the Itchen catchment area, no site was at an elevation below 250 feet (above sea level). Along the course of the Dever, a possible bath house was found near Bullington, and a number of Roman artifacts have been unearthed in Micheldever village, but in neither case is there definitive evidence for a habitation site. Thus the Micheldever valley also seems to have had no settlement below the 250-foot line. The absence of lower-lying settlements might be related to the spring line and water table, but these factors normally restrict occupation above a certain altitude, not below it.

Were valley bottoms simply unsuitable for settlement? Modern archaeology has discarded the older view that valley bottoms were untouched until the introduction of the heavy medieval plough. One might expect the valleys of Hampshire to have been used primarily for summer meadow and winter grazing, as they were organized during the Middle Ages. Bottom land in this fairly well-developed part of Roman Britain is unlikely to have remained covered by marshes or primaeval forest. Roman activity on the Dever indicates that the valley bottom there was not undeveloped. Furthermore, a site in the Candover valley (above the 250-foot contour) was placed directly beside the former course of the stream, which therefore was not unusable marshland at the time.

An alternate explanation for the pattern of Romano-British settlements may be found in their field systems. The settlements would rarely appear in the valley bottoms if they were normally sited in the center of their fields. The streams would have served as natural divisions between farms, just as ridge lines were the usual location of Celtic routes of communication. In order to work the land most efficiently, the sites of farmsteads, hamlets, villas, and even villages would have been set some distance back from the stream boundaries of the respective agricultural units. Until the Romano-British sites of middle Hampshire are defined with greater chronological precision, the sinuous local water courses will continue to obscure and confuse settlement distribution based upon agricultural units on the high ground between boundary streams.

Roman scholars have examined aspects of rural settlement in Hampshire, but it has recently been noted that only one villa—that at Twyford, south of Winchester—has been properly defined.[7] Nevertheless, Shimon Applebaum's study of Romano-British settlements in northern Hampshire proposed an "Andover group" type, in which fourth-century villas were surrounded by outlying agricultural settlements, British hamlets, and farmsteads. These villas were collection points for the produce of the servile occupants of the outlying dependencies. Applebaum further argued that the increased cereal production needed to fulfill the *annona* grain tax, combined with the deteriorating climatic conditions of the later Roman period, increased both ploughing and erosion, resulting in the loss of fertility of the chalk downland of southern England by the beginning of the fifth century.[8]

Another pattern to Roman settlement in Hampshire has been observed by Peter Fasham around the city of Winchester.[9] He noted an uninhabited zone on the north side of the city, while beyond it (at three miles out), there was a belt of "almost continuous settlement" near the Worthy villages. Beyond these were more fields, presumably belonging to the ring of settlements. In one location he found a series of large, long fields, eighty yards wide and perhaps ten times that in length. Their shapes were clearly unlike the square or stubby rectangular forms typical of the Celtic field. The length of the long rectangular fields north of Winchester might have called for professional surveyors, and it could indicate that a late Roman *territorium* of Venta extended this far.

Does the Roman settlement pattern of the Micheldever area support the views of Applebaum and others? The distribution of settlement at Micheldever has elements of both the Winchester and the Andover patterns, and may be a transition between the two. As Fasham noted, Romano-British settlements are absent immediately beyond the Winchester suburbs and cemeteries. Past this zone, at around three miles north of the city, there is a collection of farmsteads, hamlets, and larger settlements. Beyond this group lie villas about five miles out, interspersed with small settlements, the pattern observed by Applebaum. Only detailed archaeological excavation can fully explain these patterns, but an interpretation may be proposed at this stage. The empty zone around Venta was the land farmed by townsfolk. The group of small occupation sites beyond constituted the dwellings of farmworkers and tenants of small farms (with about one-half mile radius of attached land)

---

[7] David E. Johnson, "The Roman Period," pp. 46–65 in S. J. Shennan and R. T. Schadla-Hall, eds., *The Archaeology of Hampshire, from the Paleolithic to the Industrial Revolution*, Monograph No. 1, Hants. Archaeol. Soc. (1981), esp. p. 47.

[8] S. Applebaum, "Roman Britain," pp. 3–282 in *A.H.E.W.*, esp. pp. 241, 242. Applebaum further suggests that the Andover area of Hampshire was an imperial estate: p. 32.

[9] Johnson, "The Roman Period," pp. 54, 55. He is referring to the preliminary findings of P. J. Fasham, Director of Excavations for the M3 Archaeological Rescue Committee. Mr. Fasham has corroborated these findings in personal communication.

that were owned as investments by middle class citizens of Venta. The wider lands of the villas (with about one mile radius of attached land) were owned by the upper class and the state. In the "villa zone" were also the small settlements of dependents, either subholdings for specific economic functions (e.g., sheep rearing) or dispersed *coloni* settlements that increased in number over time.[10]

Besides the unoccupied zone of the Winchester pattern, there are other areas without Romano-British settlements. On the south bank of the upper Itchen only two Roman sites are known, suggesting an unusually low density of occupation. In the upper Micheldever valley there is no evidence for Romano-British occupation between the findspot of artifacts discovered in Micheldever village and the site of a villa four miles to the east (Fig. 3.1). As the Silchester road crosses the Dever at this point, the absence of settlement is conspicuous. Outside the compact group of suggested tenant farmsteads three miles from the city, nearly all the sites in the Micheldever region are five miles apart or two miles apart, the distances being, respectively, villa-to-villa and farmstead-to-farmstead.[11] The gaps in the expected pattern are the likely locations of undiscovered Romano-British settlements.

The Roman road from Silchester had no apparent influence upon the distribution of settlements near its course, and the other Roman roads also seem to have had little effect on the location of sites.[12] Similarly, aerial photographs of soil marks representing major field divisions or trackways that clearly relate to Roman sites often show no discernible relationship to the contemporary settlement distribution. Here again, the further archaeology of settlements should expose the effect that Roman roads had upon both the rural sites and their land units.[13]

---

[10] The argument that the Roman Empire witnessed a steady transformation of both free farmers and slaves into tied tenant farmers is put forward by M. I. Finley, *The Ancient Economy*, 2nd ed. (Berkeley, California, 1985), pp. 91–93.

[11] Both figures have a plus-or-minus value of 0.2 miles, but while there does seem to be a pattern to the spacing of these sites, the lack of adequate dating material for them discourages the employment of a historical geographic model. But see A. Ellison and J. Harriss, "Settlement and Land Use in the Prehistory and Early History of Southern England; A Study based on Locational Models," pp. 911–62 in David L. Clarke, ed., *Models in Archaeology* (London, 1972).

[12] The site of a probable *mansio* (posting station) lies just north of the survey area, in the grounds of a former coaching inn, in North Waltham parish. Such stations often attracted subsidiary settlement and grew into villages and even small towns, clearly dependent upon the road for their existence. See R. G. Collingwood and Ian Richmond, *The Archaeology of Roman Britain*, 2nd ed. (London, 1969), pp. 4–7.

[13] It is often difficult to discriminate from aerial photographs between wide ditches separating farms and villa properties, and the tracks that ran into, or through, these land units. A somewhat dated, but available synthesis can be found in the publication of conference papers in *Rural Settlement in Roman Britain*, Charles Thomas, ed., (London, 1966). Applebaum's contribution to *A.H.E.W.* is more recent (1972), but is a presentation of his own theories and conclusions.

THE EARLY SAXON SETTLEMENT

For the Saxon period, archaeological field survey and reconnaissance techniques are joined by a survey of place names of the Micheldever region.[14] Figure 3.2 illustrates how the pagan cemeteries, occupation sites, and early place names supplement each other in a consistent pattern. Distances between sites here are as close as one-half mile between the *hams* at Popham, and the one mile between sites near the Roman road by East Stratton. Although too little is known about the specifics of early Saxon habitation sites to make confident statements concerning population and density, the Saxon period saw a new distribution of settlements in the Micheldever region. Three factors together produced the early Saxon settlement pattern: the division of the chalkland into river valleys; the Roman city and early medieval royal center of Winchester; and the Roman roads.

The Valley Distribution

With one exception (Popham), the place names that contain toponymic elements thought to be among the earliest used by the Anglo-Saxon settlers belong to villages that lie near the valley bottoms. Settlements that bear wood names, e.g., Sparsholt, Wield, were most likely established in wooded areas long after the open land was settled. Woodmancote suggests a late rather than early origin, but the name itself is probably a replacement for the *Ticcesham* that appears on the Anglo-Saxon charter S360. At any rate, in spite of its altitude, Woodmancote/Ticcesham is not on a ridge, but lies in the upper reaches of the Northbrook valley, a tributary of the Dever.

Settlement sites in the main course of the Dever lay below the 250-foot contour, and in its upper reaches the sites were situated in the valleys, not up on the downs. Archaeologically attested habitation sites alone provide the evidence for early settlement in the Stratton vicinity, because there have been no discoveries of burials from Micheldever eastward to the Candover valley. The sites of burials that have come to light in the Dever valley correspond to the general settlement pattern, but with a difference. Although the two sites (one cemetery and one single "warrior's" burial) are above the 250-foot elevation—farther up the slopes than the settlements—they both lie closer to the valley bottom than to the ridge lines separating the watersheds. A likely explanation for the choice of these locations is that they lay at the early Saxon bound-

---

[14] The place names of the Micheldever region have been collected and their distribution patterns analyzed in Klingelhöfer, "Micheldever," Appendix A, pp. 453–92.

ary between land under cultivation and that used for grazing or retained as woodland.

The same pattern appears in the Candover valley, where settlements containing early place-name elements string along the valley bottom, while on a slope, at the 250-foot elevation, was an Anglo-Saxon burial. The Somborne valley has villages with early, topographic elements in their names, situated on the valley floor, while an Anglo-Saxon charter (S381) refers to "pagan burials" on its north slope. At the upper end of the Itchen, the Tichbourne and "Alre" valleys also contain early settlement names, and on the high ground between them was an Anglo-Saxon double burial. The course of the upper Itchen itself contains a large Saxon cemetery, and charters refer to more pagan burials across the river (S695, S699). Both sites are farther from the river than are the villages, though they are not as far up the slope as elsewhere. Nevertheless, the overall pattern for the Micheldever region is evident: a distribution of settlements along the valley bottoms, with cemeteries a short distance up the slopes.

Distribution near Winchester

The second factor determining early Saxon settlement was the presence of the former Roman city of Winchester. There were several burial sites outside the city, and some within it. The number of cemeteries discovered some distance from the city, on the east side of the Itchen, rather than by the Roman walls on the west, may suggest that there was a long-term settlement outside the east gate and bridge, one that could well have had its origin in the sub-Roman period. It is possible, too, that some of the land around Winchester was worked by inhabitants of the walled area, as in Roman times, but much of it must also have been attached to hamlets growing up in the formerly unpopulated zone surrounding the city. Archaeological findings indicate that at least two of medieval Winchester's suburbs had their origins in the mid-Saxon period, if not before, and it has been postulated that all the suburbs originated in Saxon villages distinct from the town.[15]

Distribution along the Roman Road

A third factor in settlement distribution was the survival of Roman roads. It is now thought that certain place names ending in the element *hām* were related to the Roman road system, and not to the "typical"

---

[15] See Martin Biddle and D. J. Keen, "Winchester in the Eleventh and Twelfth Centuries," in M. Biddle, ed., *Winchester in the Early Middle Ages*, Winchester Studies I (Oxford, 1976), p. 258; also the recent excavation at Winnal, *Medieval Archaeology* 31 (1987), pp. 140–41.

Saxon riverside pattern of settlement. One settlement in the Micheldever region is a likely candidate for inclusion in this *hām* group: Popham, on the north edge of the Dever drainage basin. Popham is the only medieval village in the area that is not situated in a valley, but stands on an exposed piece of high ground. It is located, however, ten miles from Winchester on the Roman road to Silchester, the line which is preserved for only three miles farther north. Beyond that point the Roman course to Silchester was replaced by the medieval road to Basing(stoke) and the London basin. Furthermore, Popham is situated on the high ground dominating the watershed divide. Could barbarians have been planted there to protect the Dever-Candover-Itchen valleys, and ultimately sub-Roman Winchester?[16]

The archaeological excavation of a prehistoric site one mile south of Popham on the Roman road recovered post-Roman pottery, suggesting the nearby presence of an early Saxon settlement. Farther south, Stratton took its name from the Roman road (*straet*) that passes between East and West Stratton. Archaeological fieldwork on the course of the road there located potsherds datable to the mid-Saxon period, and it is expected that future excavation will uncover the settlement itself. Down in the Itchen valley the Roman road lies close to the pagan cemetery at Abbots Worthy, and then crosses through the village of King's Worthy, the probable site of a royal hall. No further sign of settlement has been found along the other Roman roads from Winchester. Thirteen miles northwest of Winchester, however, a large pagan Saxon cemetery has recently been excavated near Andover, at the crossroads of the Winchester-Cirencester and Silchester-Sarum roads. This site has an even greater strategic potential than Popham.[17]

Few anomalies mark the distribution pattern. The two recent discoveries of Anglo-Saxon pottery on the line of the Roman road across the Dever valley are tied not only to the "Roman road" pattern, but to the "valley" pattern as well. Earlier this century, Anglo-Saxon pottery reportedly was found at a spot northwest of Winchester, in the upper reaches of the Headbourne valley, over a half mile from the Cirencester road.[18] If correctly identified, the pottery should indicate the presence of a settlement, or perhaps a cemetery. Both kinds of sites have been found elsewhere in the Micheldever vicinity, but only in valleys, by

---

[16] On the other hand, it is possible that it guarded the upper Test valley, and the few miles from there to Silchester, from attack from the south.

[17] The sites along the Roman road at Micheldever are recorded in the files of the M3 Archaeological Rescue Committee, held by the Wessex Archaeological Unit, Salisbury. The Andover site is discussed briefly in Biddle, "Hampshire and the origins of Wessex," p. 328; a preliminary note is in *Medieval Archaeology* 19 (1975), p. 222.

[18] This site is listed in Schadla-Hall's gazetteer, p. 140. The sherds were discovered during excavation of an Iron Age site: R. W. Hooley, "Note on a Hoard of Iron Age Currency Bars found on Worthy Down, Winchester," *Proc. Hants. Field Club and Archaeol. Soc.* 10 (1929), pp. 178–93.

Roman roads, or as satellites of Winchester. It is possible that this site was related to the presence of the Roman road, but had to be situated some distance from it for a particular reason, perhaps the availability of resources (water, wood, good soil) or the presence or absence of earlier settlement at the site. Documentary evidence may even offer an identification of the site. It could be the settlement that had as its northern boundary the southern edge of the lands of Wonston, marked by the feature described as the *fritheling dic* (S374).

Earthworks datable to the early Saxon period are also rare. Fieldwork in Micheldever Wood has established one such bank-and-ditch, which spans the wood and the wide area of Clay-with-Flints that nearly matches the present limits of the wood. It intersected Roman earthworks and was in turn cut through by medieval woodland banks and ditches. The function of this feature is not known for certain, but it may once have marked the northern edge of the wood, which was known as Papenholt throughout the Middle Ages and extended at least one mile south of the earthwork.[19]

Aerial photographs reveal the twisting line of another earthwork used in part as a post-medieval field boundary, and appearing as such on the early nineteenth-century Tithe Award map for Wonston.[20] It was certainly a feature of the medieval landscape, even if it were of prehistoric origin. Charter bounds again suggest an identification; it may have been the "lynchet" referred to in the Micheldever grant (S360).

Summary

Early Saxon settlement in the Micheldever region was affected to some degree by the presence of Roman roads and the old Roman city. By far the most important factor, however, was the course of the river valleys, in which ran the major lines of communication and the settlements connected by them. These settlements invariably lay close to the stream beds, while their cemeteries were farther uphill, but not placed far back on the downland.

The confinement of most early Anglo-Saxon settlement to the valley bottoms is in stark contrast to the Roman settlement pattern. This dichotomy is common in Britain, and the few points of similarity between the distribution of Roman and Saxon settlements are sought as evidence for continuity.[21] At other sites in Hampshire, early/mid-Saxon settle-

---

[19] On the Saxon earthwork and other archaeological features, see P. J. Fasham, "Fieldwork in and around Micheldever Wood, Hampshire, 1973–1980," *Proc. Hants. Field Cub and Archaeol. Soc.* 39 (1983), pp. 5–45.

[20] H.R.O., Tithe Award Collection: *Wonston Tithe Award Map* (1838).

[21] For an early assessment of the generally observed pattern of river settlement, see H. J. Fleure and D. E. Whitehouse, "The Early Distribution and Valleyward Movement of Population in Southern Britain," *Archaeologia Cambrensis* 16 (1916), pp. 100–40.

ments have recently been found not in the valleys, but upon the chalk downs. These sites were abandoned perhaps by the eighth century, and their presence adds an important element to the history of settlement and land use.[22] One such site may have already been located near Micheldever—the possible "Fritheling" between Wonston and Headbourne Worthy—but others have not yet appeared. The cemeteries of the Hampshire downland sites surprisingly have not yet come to light; the pagan cemeteries of the Micheldever region are on the valley slopes. It may be that in the early Saxon period there were occasionally farmsteads and even villages upon the high Wessex downland, supplementing the overall pattern of valley settlement. Popham would be another example in the Micheldever area, serving this occasional "infilling" pattern as well as the pattern of *hām* place names along Roman roads. Indeed, these downland sites could have been sited originally for strategic purposes, either local or regional, which when no longer operative would lead to the desertion of such high and exposed locales.

The rarity and brevity of Anglo-Saxon occupation of the upper elevations of Hampshire downland reflect a general abandonment of those areas for the more productive valley bottoms, a movement that Applebaum attributed to an impoverishment of soil on the chalk downs. The ruin of the villa economy and the basis of Roman life in central Wessex was brought about, according to Applebaum, by an overworking of the land in response to increased imperial demand for payment-in-kind taxes to support the huge and expensive late Roman military structure.[23] One could further argue that the soil was made more susceptible to depletion and denudation by a climatic deterioration in the late Roman period, which not only meant greater run-off and erosion, but also caused shorter growing seasons that led to a demand for winter planting, exposing the land even further to the effects of harsh weather.

A lowering of the water table may explain the change in settlement pattern from a Roman downland occupation to a Saxon valley occupation. Climate alone is unlikely to have caused such a drop in the fourth through sixth centuries, when western Europe was actually wetter than in succeeding centuries. On the other hand, the overworking of the downland, including the near total clearance of woodland and the hard-panning (formation of mineralized horizons that obstruct percolation) of subsoil over Clay-with-Flint deposits from the overuse of a shallow

---

Peter Warner has recently written on a similar abandonment of Roman occupied lands in valleys at Blything Hundred, East Suffolk; he also suggested that enough Roman features remained to cause Saxon manors to evolve within the boundaries of Roman estates. *Greens, Commons, and Clayland Colonisation: The Origins and Development of Green-Side Settlement in East Suffolk,* Univ. of Leicester, Dept. of Local History, Occasional Paper, 4th ser., no. 2 (Leicester, 1987).

[22] For a review of these sites, see D. A. Hinton, "Hampshire's Anglo-Saxon Origins," pp. 56–65 in Shennan and Schadla-Hall, *Archaeology of Hampshire.*

[23] Applebaum, "Roman Britain," pp. 231–32, 246–47.

plough, could have led to less water absorption and more run-off and erosion. The abandonment of wide areas of arable land, and its eventual return to woodland, should have raised the water table again, but this might have coincided with the early medieval drier climate and the clearance of regrown forests.

The Britons

The absence of the British population from the early Saxon landscape remains one of the major problems of early medieval research. There had been heavy population loss in late Roman times, and emigration to Brittany probably came from central southern England as well as from the Severn estuary.[24] This population loss was probably further exacerbated by the sixth-century plagues that are known to have reached Britain. There is no evidence, however, that the Saxons were affected by any epidemic until the plague of 664, as recorded by Bede.[25] This discrepancy may well be a major factor in the replacement of the British rural population by an Anglo-Saxon one during the period 550–700 A.D., but it does not explain why there is as yet little or no physical evidence for the presence of the British population after the first decades of the fifth century.

The major tool of the archaeologist, pottery, is missing from the sub-Roman settlements. The few sherds that have been found (comprising soft, crude, handmade grass-tempered wares) have been categorized as Germanic, along with the more typically Germanic types of pottery from cremation cemeteries.[26] The grass-tempered wares may indeed have been made by Anglo-Saxons, but they may also have been made by Britons, perhaps as much-needed replacements for their dwindling supplies of Roman pottery, following the collapse of the Romano-British ceramic industries in the early fifth century or earlier. Such a notion would necessarily imply a degree of interaction between the British and Germanic populations that appears nowhere in the sources, but which could have concerned only those Britons actually in the English-controlled territories (which by A.D. 600 included most of latter-day England). Further, the exchange of domestic goods and methods of their production, and the necessary fraternization with pagan Anglo-Saxons, may have concerned only non-Christian Britons, who also have left no trace in the records. Indeed, these two groups could well have been mutually supportive, even bringing a renewed vigor to cult practices

---

[24] John Morris, *The Age of Arthur. A History of the British Isles from 380 to 650* (New York, 1973), pp. 249–60.

[25] *H.E.*, III, 30; IV, 14; V, 24.

[26] For a brief comment on these wares, see Biddle, "Hampshire and the Origins of Wessex," p. 326.

and worship at old Celtic sanctuaries, perhaps often with new names and incorporating a new mythology. Some portion of the surviving Celtic population could even have viewed the Saxon settlers as protectors of open-minded paganism against the threat of the proselytizing and doctrinaire Church and its Christian kings and tyrants.

That the origin and use of grass-tempered pottery are attributable to a surviving Celtic population seems more plausible than the alternative assumptions that the Britons either completely abandoned most of the island or that they used only utensils of wood, metal, and leather— anything but pottery.[27] That some Britons did co-exist with the Anglo-Saxons, in cooperation or by coercion, may be seen in the survival of Celtic and Latin place names in areas of early Germanic settlement. Celtic place-name elements are particularly strong in Hampshire, and toponymics are more reliable as indicators of continuity between the two societies than the vagaries of settlement location in a steadily evolving landscape from the late fourth century onward. The only evidence for a British survival in the Micheldever area is the retention of Celtic river names and the possible identification of Walton as "Welsh-ton." Without greater sophistication in the archaeology of the post-Roman period, however, there is little chance that further light can be shed on the problem of British survival.

THE LATE SAXON SETTLEMENT

The period from the introduction of land documents in the eighth century to the beginning of the twelfth century may be treated as a single unit. Lying outside the Danelaw, Hampshire received no Scandinavian settlement, and "there is little evidence that the Conquest made a significant impact upon either village form or pattern."[28] Unlike much of England, many villages of the Micheldever region appear first in Saxon documents, often centuries before the Domesday Survey. Nearly all medieval settlements here were already recorded by the end of the eleventh century.[29] Caution about the unreliability of the Domesday Book as a guide to early medieval settlement is less important in the Micheldever region than elsewhere because here its role in the study of the early

---

[27] Yet pottery from the Mediterranean and southern Gaul continued as evidence of foreign trade in the sub-Roman west. For example, see Leslie Alcock, *"By South Cadbury . . . is that Camelot . . .": The Excavation of Cadbury Castle 1966–1970* (London, 1972), pp. 174–83, figs. 27, 28, pl. XIII.

[28] Peter Bigmore, "Villages and Towns," pp. 154–92 in Leonard Cantor, ed., *The English Medieval Landscape* (Philadelphia, 1982), quote on p. 157.

[29] The exceptions are New Alresford on the "Alre" and Overton on the upper Test, both later medieval planned towns, and Godsfield east of the Candover stream, an establishment of the Knights Templar.

medieval settlements is supplementary.[30] Domesday Book is a listing of manors, not villages, and the subsequent confusion and irregularities of its coverage are due to local topography and tenurial associations.

Late Saxon villages show both a strongly linear distribution and a propensity to be located on alternating sides of streams. It is therefore difficult to suggest a meaningful figure for inter-settlement distances. Many sites were three-quarters or one and a half miles apart, and the former figure may represent settlements formed at the interstices of earlier village territories. The early medieval settlement pattern of the Micheldever area is significantly coherent, and falls within Peter Haggett's geographic category of "distortion by resource localization" of a regular lattice arrangement of settlement centers. In this case the settlement pattern is that which Haggett defined as having been caused by the localization of a *linear* resource, identified as a stream or roadway.[31]

Figure 3.3 reveals that the early Saxon pattern of valley settlement was not dramatically altered in the late Saxon period. The increased number of villages and hamlets recorded directly or indirectly before 1100 suggests a certain amount of infilling due to population growth. The nucleated village is associated with the central chalkland of Hampshire, while other parts of the county had "a combination of villages, satellite hamlets and dispersed farmsteads."[32] Subsidiary daughter settlements were created in valleys, but little settlement took place between the valleys, except perhaps at places bearing woodland names. Thus Woodmancott did not appear until Domesday (though it could be the Saxon *Ticcesham*), and Crawley and Sparsholt turned from wood names into the names of settlements. Aside from the forest hamlets, the late Saxon period shows the land above the 250-foot contour to be devoid of activity, including burials, for by this time churchyard cemeteries were the rule.

The rarity of upland hamlets in the Micheldever area at this time is only partly attributable to topography. While some of the slopes can be steep, most of the terrain is relatively gentle, and is on a much smaller scale than the upland valleys of Wales and Northumbria. Soil types also do not fully explain the settlement pattern. Although Clay-with-Flints deposits are more prevalent on higher elevations and on northward facing slopes, late Saxon settlements appear at equal frequencies on both sides of the valleys.

---

[30] See P. H. Sawyer, "Introduction: Early Medieval Settlement," pp. 1–10, and S. P. J. Harvey, "Evidence for Settlement Study: Domesday Book," pp. 194–99, in *Medieval Settlement*.

[31] Haggett cautions that "the actual development of regional settlement patterns is a multi-variate product in which social conventions play as big a part as environment." Peter Haggett, *Locational Analysis in Human Geography* (London, 1965), pp. 92–95.

[32] M. F. Hughes, "Settlement and Landscape Change in Medieval Hampshire," pp. 66–77 in Shennan and Schadla-Hall, *Archaeology of Hampshire*, p. 68.

The settlement pattern can be explained by the remaining natural factor determining land use, the availability of water, which was in turn affected by the poor soil conditions proposed for the late and sub-Roman periods. The water table dropped because of overworked soil; the light chalk soils lost their tilth, and shallow ploughing of the Clay-with-Flints formed a hardpan of mineral salts that impeded water percolation and led to the drying out of the chalk substrata. With adequate rainfall, the tilth of the upper soil would have been replenished after several generations, even though the iron pan under the clays might remain. However, the early medieval change from an Atlantic climate to a Continental climate sharply reduced the amount of rainfall in western Europe, leaving the exposed chalk downs as dry as before, with little chance to raise the water table again. Continuous agricultural exploitation since that time, and increased demands upon the hydrofer, have continued to reduce slowly the water table of the Wessex chalkland.[33]

The early Saxon patterns of settlement that were related to the Roman roads and the former Roman city and royal center at Winchester had disappeared by the end of the early Middle Ages. Roman roads and towns were products of earlier modes of transportation and administration and were not necessarily factors in the physical expression of medieval economy and government. At the same time, new agricultural techniques opened up lower elevations to permanent cultivation and encouraged the growth of valley habitation sites. The late Saxon settlements were therefore an extension and elaboration of an embryonic early Saxon "valley pattern." This evolutionary development took place in an area spared the traumatic changes made by Danish and Norse invasions and landtaking north of the Thames.

THE CONTRIBUTION OF PLACE-NAME STUDIES

Dating of the villages of middle Hampshire should help reveal the stages by which the early Saxon settlement distribution took on the pattern of the eleventh century, a pattern that typically continued through the Middle Ages until the recent past. A problem is that documentary references to individual villages in the early Middle Ages are rare, and few settlements offer enough archaeological detail to permit a secure dating. Even so, the chronology revised by scholars of the English Place-Name Society for the appearance and currency of toponymic elements can assign relative dates for the origin of certain village names, and, in the absence of information to the contrary, to the settlements themselves.[34] The new chronology of place-name usage em-

---

[33] The geographic conditions of early medieval Hampshire have been described in Chapter II, where the works of Stamp, Limbrey, Lamb, and others were cited.

[34] A survey of the prominent place names of the Micheldever region appears in "Micheldever," Appendix A, pp. 453–84.

phasizes landscape features and the economic particulars of estates.[35] The earliest were the (1) fifth- and sixth-century topographic, Latin, Celtic, and *hām* elements. Then followed the habitation names, in order: (2) *hamtun*, (3) *-ingtun*, and (4) *tun*. By the seventh century, (5) *stoc*, "worth," "cot," "bury," and Christian elements came into use. With the latest element as the deciding factor, the village names in the immediate vicinity of Micheldever can be placed in the following sequential groups:

Stream names: Micheldever, Candover, Somborne, Itchen, Tichbourne, Headbourne, Cranbourne.

Other topographic elements: Bullington, Totford, Chilland, Alresford, Leckford, Axford.

Hām names: Popham, Waltham (plus *Ticcesham* and *Herpesham*).

Hamtun names: Northington (*Northameton*).

-ingtun names: Avington, Lovington, Ovington, Yavington.

Tun names: Drayton, Barton, Sutton Scotney, Norton, Wonston, Weston, Stratton, Swaraton, Abbotston, Preston, Chilton, Bighton, Grundleton, Bishop's Sutton, Hinton, Cheriton, Easton, Littleton, Chilbolton.

Later elements: Worthy, Beauworth, Burcot, Woodmancott.

The chronology of place-name usage is not immediately transferable to that of settlements. One must not assume that the naming of a *place* can be applied to a *village*. Most difficult in this respect are the wood names (e.g., Sparsholt, Crawley), which were given to forest tracts long before settlement took place within them. Similarly, a stream or topographic name does not necessarily imply a settlement at that location. Yet valleys, streams, and downs (*dun*) were certainly the sites of early Saxon settlement; archaeology proves that central Hampshire was occupied throughout the period, even if few habitation sites have been located. The difference, it seems, is in specificity. The earliest names may have pertained to wider areas rather than to particular sites. Both the smaller side valleys (e.g., Bramdean, *denu*) and the larger catchment areas took their names from the streams watering them, of which Micheldever is a prime example.

What then do these toponymic developments tell of the early medieval settlement pattern of the Micheldever region? First, early place names record not only the location of settlement but also the type of settlement. The eleventh-century distribution of settlements reveals a compact, evenly spaced pattern of mainly nucleated villages. But was this pattern present in the eighth century or earlier? Medieval settlement types are classified as either nucleated or dispersed, and there is increasing archaeological evidence for an originally dispersed Anglo-Saxon settlement in Hampshire.[36] Indeed, the instance of pottery found at locations

---

[35] The following comments are based largely upon Margaret Gelling's synthesis of recent toponymic research, *Signposts to the Past: Place-Names and the History of England* (London, 1978).

[36] See David A. Hinton, "Hampshire's Anglo-Saxon Origins," pp. 59, 60.

near Micheldever for which there is no dispersed settlement are likely indicators of early Saxon dispersed settlement in the form of farmsteads and hamlets.

On the other hand, climatic and soil conditions seem to have caused the movement of most settlement to the valleys. The earliest Hampshire sites include those on exposed hilltops, so it is possible that regardless of the particular soil conditions on sub-Roman sites the water table declined, slowly or irregularly at first and then rapidly, following the drop in precipitation accompanying the climatic change of the eighth and ninth centuries. The drier climate must have coincided with a change in agricultural practices, favoring the arable use of heavier, lower soils. Both factors were stimuli for the abandonment of the downland sites and the conversion of former streamside hamlets into more populated, nucleated villages.

The villages bearing stream names have been identified as the earliest in other parts of Wessex and are treated as such here. Local studies in Hampshire have suggested that the river valleys were the means by which early Saxon settlement was made.[37] Many Hampshire stream names have Celtic origins or contain Celtic elements, testifying to their antiquity. The dispersed settlements discussed above have left little trace for archaeology individually, but as groups they may be fossilized in the earliest toponyms. Stream names were used not only for villages, but more importantly, for settlement territories that were much larger than the extent of the fields and woods of the later medieval village manors. As late as 904, in a charter drawn up in Winchester, less than ten miles away, the lands that later became the manor of Wonston (S374) were identified simply as "at Micheldever." Wonston lies in the Dever valley three miles downstream from Micheldever. Valleys thus went by the names later documented for at least some of their component parts. An originally uniformly dispersed settlement would not in fact have had separate parts. As a conglomerate collection of landholdings and farmsteads, it could readily be identified by a group name like the *Meonware* (dwellers by the river Meon) of southeastern Hampshire.[38] The stream/valley name "Meon" was no doubt originally applied to the entire area of dispersed settlement, while later, upon the nucleation of settlement, it referred to the major habitation center as well as the group as a whole. By the end of the Saxon period further changes in administration and landholding removed the original meaning of the name, and for the compilers of Domesday Book there was no suggestion that the villages with stream names were constituted any differently from their neighbors.

Place names with other topographic elements (e.g., Totford, Bulling-

---

[37] See F. A. Aldsworth, "Pre-Domesday Geography of Hampshire."
[38] Hinton, "Hampshire's Anglo-Saxon Origins," p. 63; *A.S.E.*, p. 294.

ton) were usually given at an early date. Some of these locales were no doubt the sites of early farmsteads, but it must be noted that place names for natural, topographic features need not have been given to the sites of settlement until much later, or not at all. All topographic features would have been assigned descriptions/names by local inhabitants, as is apparent from the details of the charter bounds. In the absence of documentary and archaeological evidence, it is problematic just when it was that a topographic place name was first applied to a habitation site rather than the natural feature.

Along with settlements having topographic place name elements, there are those that received from the start a name with a habitation element. The element *hām* (as opposed to *hamm*) is considered to have been used earliest, in the fifth century.[39] Here Popham is the prime example. Significantly, Waltham lies a few miles to the northwest, and two minor *hām* establishments were recorded on the bounds of Popham. Peter Sawyer has found instances where place names in -*hām* were originally applied to an area, not a particular site.[40] It seems that, as in the case of stream names and perhaps other toponyms, the use was applied first to areas, then to both areas and specific points within them, and finally to the settlements alone. It is possible that the habitations associated with the *hām* locales originated in sub-Roman military settlements sited on or near a Roman road. Popham does not lie in a valley, but at the point where the Silchester-Winchester road crosses the high ridge north of the Micheldever watershed. Popham's location certainly suits Sawyer's hypothesis, having a certain portion of upland between the valleys as a dependent territory.

Following the appearance of place names in *hām*, a series of secondary and tertiary settlements were given toponyms with habitation elements. The secondary settlements are represented by "hamton" (Northington, *Northameton*, on the Candover) and "-ington" (the four examples of which lie together on the south bank of the Itchen). They probably represent two steps in the recognition of outlying or dependent settlements (*tuns*). First was the *tun* pertaining to the *ham*, then came the *tun* of a leader or his dependents. The creation of these originally small settlements was probably a stage in the eighth- and ninth-century abandonment of the upland sites and the movement of rural population into discrete settlements.

Place names ending in "ton" alone were the next stage of nomenclature. The most common English place-name element, the *tun* had by the late Saxon period lost the sense of being necessarily a dependency or outlier; it was no longer combined with the personal "-ing" as

---

[39] See J. M. Dodgson, "Place-Names from *hām*, Distinguished from *hamm* names, in relation to the Settlement of Kent, Surrey, and Sussex," *Anglo-Saxon England* II, pp. 1–50; and Rhona M. Huggins, "The Significance of the Place-Name *Wealdam*," *Medieval Archaeology* 19 (1975), pp. 198–201.

[40] P. H. Sawyer, *From Roman Britain to Norman England* (London, 1978), pp. 157–59.

"-ington." The frequency of personal names, however, shows the new importance of the landowner. These names are known to have sometimes been altered, in that the personal-name element was exchanged for that of the most recent owner. One wonders to what extent these name changes appear in the documents solely for administrative purposes. Nevertheless, the village usually bore the new manorial name, just as other villages came later to accept, in some form, French names imposed by Norman administrators.

The other habitation elements (worth, cot, wick, bury, etc.) were used contemporaneously to describe places that were different from the typical *tun*. In this sense they were specialized terms, but they referred to the original condition of the site when it served as a farmstead with a particular function or attribute and not to its later state as a hamlet or village. Consequently, these habitation elements, as with all place-name elements, can be used as clues to the nature of settlements only for the moment at which they received the name. Beyond that, the identification of settlement type must be extrapolated from supporting documentary and archaeological evidence.

CONCLUSIONS

What can be inferred about early medieval settlement from the pattern of its distribution, and what is its significance for rural development? Analysis of settlement in the Micheldever region yields several points of interest (see Fig. 3.4).

The oldest English place names are those with topographic elements, and those bearing Celtic stream names must have especial antiquity. In the Micheldever region, villages with these early names appear at approximately two-mile intervals, with specific locations determined by the course of the streams from which the names were taken. It is perhaps significant that every stream name here was also a settlement name, a rare situation in England.

The two large pagan cemeteries of the survey area lie close to the only two villages in the area considered the sites of Saxon royal halls (Micheldever and Kings Worthy). Northwest of the Micheldever region another large Saxon cemetery is associated with a royal center at Andover, where King Ethelred II baptized Anlaf the Dane.[41] This is not to suggest that royal control dictated pagan burial practices but rather that early Saxon cemeteries lay at social and political centers.

There is some evidence for selection in the siting of early medieval villages. Only villages with the latest pre-Conquest place names lie out of the river valleys and above the 250-foot elevation. The elevated site

---

[41] *A.S.C.: s.a.* 664.

of Popham is an exception, chosen perhaps because of its strategic position on the Roman road north to Winchester.

The position of Popham is also an exception to another observation—that Anglo-Saxon farmers clearly preferred some soils over others. Popham is the only village of the survey to lie directly upon the Clay-with-Flints (though at a locality near several Iron Age and Romano-British farm sites). The value of its strategic position must have outweighed the unsuitability of the land upon which it was placed. Elsewhere, villages are more likely to have been settled on gravel terraces than upon the chalk or valley loams, but while many of the gravel beds along streams such as the Dever were occupied by early medieval settlements, others were not. Nevertheless, some villages, such as Barton Stacey and Newton Stacey, were sited clearly upon very small areas of gravel in large zones of chalk subsoil. The proposed sites of deserted early medieval hamlets or farmsteads also avoided the Clay-with-Flints; of the seven sites, none was on or close to this type of soil.

To conclude, the pattern of settlement distribution at the end of the early medieval period represents a maturation of the trend observed at the beginning of the period, and both patterns contrast strongly with the Romano-British settlement distribution. Put simply, the Romans lived upon the chalk downs, while the Anglo-Saxons came to inhabit the valley bottoms. Pagan Saxon settlements may mark not an overlap between the Roman and medieval patterns (with both elements present), but a "patternless" period of political and economic instability. In the fifth century Roman agricultural and settlement patterns disintegrated. Thenceforth, the presence, authority, and ethnicity of landowning magnates would determine the placement of local populations. In the eighth century, the lengthy formative process of coalescing habitations began to transform manorial foci into villages.

Post-Roman settlements are notoriously hard to find; there are only a handful of sites in the Micheldever area. The several early Anglo-Saxon rural settlements excavated in Hampshire were located on high chalk promontories, and all appear to have been nucleated villages, not dispersed settlements.[42] Yet the conditions of the fifth to eighth centuries are appropriate for dispersed settlement. A very low population was spread thinly over a landscape that contained light soils exhausted by overuse and heavy soils too difficult for simple agricultural technology to exploit successfully. The result was a settlement pattern based upon individual farmsteads, occasionally clustered into hamlets.

The confusing, even contradictory, evidence that prohibits a clear

---

[42] See Hinton, "Hampshire's Anglo-Saxon Origins," pp. 59, 60. The argument is that many later village sites would have been inappropriate for early Saxon settlement, and they have no evidence of pagan occupation.

view of post-Roman settlement and land use may be due to the fact that the scarcity of habitation sites has led archaeologists to place a greater reliance on burials. While many pagan Saxons were interred in large, communal cemeteries, others were buried individually or in pairs at sites away from the cemeteries. Large cemeteries may indicate the religious or social focus of communities, but there is at present no correlation between cemetery type and settlement distribution. The rarity of early Saxon settlements discovered so far may well be an indication that they were in fact dispersed. Such homesteads may have been impermanent; after the resources around habitation sites were depleted, poverty of soil and lack of manpower could have forced farmers to move every few generations. Complicating the picture is the obscurity of Celtic ethnic identity. Because the only domestically produced pottery in the post-Roman period, a crude, grass-tempered ware, has been attributed solely to the Anglo-Saxons, no settlements have been identified as Celtic. One may conclude that historians must give greater weight than they have supposed to the specific tribal background of the Germanic inhabitants of an area, the amount of residual Celtic population, and the geographic specifics of a locality.

Two additional factors appear in the following centuries. A drier climate from the eighth century onward lowered the central Hampshire water table, drying up springs in the upper chalk valleys and forcing the population into the watered lower valleys. Freed from the effects of sixth- and seventh-century epidemics and bolstered by improvements in agricultural techniques (the heavy plough with moldboard and the use of naked wheat varieties), population grew substantially in the early medieval period. This increase led to a centralization or nucleation of settlement, made possible and indeed necessary as agricultural practices simultaneously changed from independent to cooperative farming.[43]

By the tenth and eleventh centuries the process had created the fully developed classic manor and village. The large estates of middle Hampshire left little room for the establishment of unitary manors (one manor for one vill), which elsewhere was a further factor encouraging the nucleation of villages. Because of the incomplete development in the Micheldever region of what was a standard pattern in the Midlands and elsewhere, Micheldever has several instances of a "retarded" village pattern, i.e., settlements too close together to develop individually into fully formed villages with self-sustaining populations and attendant churches, independent manorial courts and customs, etc. They are therefore similar to the "polyfocal" villages that Christopher Taylor be-

---

[43] This view is corroborated by David Hall's proposed late eighth-century date for site abandonment and the formation of strip fields. See D. Hall, "The Origins of Open-Field Agriculture—The Archaeological Evidence," pp. 22–38 in T. Rowley, ed., *The Origins of Open-Field Agriculture* (London, Totowa, N.J., 1981).

lieves coalesced in the mid- to late Saxon period.[44] Micheldever village itself may have had three foci— Northbrook, Southbrook, and one on the Dever itself. East Stratton appears to have moved away from an original settlement on the Roman street, and West Stratton likely resulted from a counter movement. Outside the Micheldever valley, the tithing hamlet of Chilland on the north bank of the Itchen, and the sites of Lovington and Yavington on the south bank, are three examples among many of early medieval settlements that never had the opportunity to expand and whose lands were absorbed by larger neighboring communities.

Comparative Settlement Studies

The historical geographers A. Ellison and J. Harriss inaugurated the use of locational models for early Anglo-Saxon settlement in southern England, but unfortunately their work was largely based upon outmoded notions of toponymic chronology. By considering place names ending in "ing" as evidence for primary settlement, and by grouping "ton," "ham," and "ford" names together as representing secondary sites, Ellison and Harriss organized their material according to criteria no longer considered valid. Their conclusions are thus unlikely to be of much current value, but their premise that settlements should be conceptualized as nodes of movement did offer a new way of examining medieval rural settlement. By this concept, they held that:

a village implies not merely a community but an area of land, exploited by it and necessary to it for its subsistence. With a given technology and economic regime there would have been an optimal size for the units of exploitation and one might expect to find some regularity in the size of areas of land accessible from each village.[45]

Ellison and Harriss used idealized circular catchment areas as the basis for their models, taking a 2-km radius as a likely limit to daily activities. Comparison of the inter-village distances based upon the model reveals that where villages are farther apart their territories are more evenly distributed around the centers, but where villages conform to a linear pattern (following a road or stream) their territories are elongated perpendicular to the line of settlements. These findings are perhaps pre-

---

[44] See C. C. Taylor, "Polyfocal Settlement and the English Village," *Medieval Archaeology* 21 (1977), pp. 189–93; and "The Anglo-Saxon Countryside," pp. 5–15 in Trevor Rowley, ed., *Anglo-Saxon Settlement and Landscape* (Oxford, 1974).

[45] A. Ellison and J. Harriss, "Settlement and Land Use," p. 941. But the limitations of this approach were set out by Christopher Taylor in "The Study of Settlement Patterns in pre-Saxon England," pp. 109–13 in Ucko, et al., *Man, Settlement and Urbanism*.

dictable, determined by the premise that villages needed approximately equal land areas for survival.

The concept of movement as the basis for settlement can be examined more closely. Two factors determine movement: natural resources and human activity. The former controls the direction and distance, the latter the frequency and variation of that movement. A change in one factor, if not offset by a correcting change of the other, will cause a shift in movement, with obvious effects upon its node, the settlement site.

This equation can be applied to some of the conditions in the Micheldever area. A dropping water table might have little effect upon a habitation site if it were offset by an increase in the depth of wells serving the site, but its effect upon the level of soil moisture in the summer could alter the productivity of field crops and change the pattern of movement in the effort to maintain the level of production. Similarly, a change in farming practice from mixed to more arable or to more pastoral would alter the customary daily movement of the agricultural population. The less fixed a village site was by tradition, manifest in the physical presence of other institutions (center of worship, place of tribute collection), the less likely it was that equalizing measures (acceptance of lower crop yields, changed labor demands upon a sector of the work force) would be preferable to a shift to a new habitation site. The considerable late medieval alteration of village plans and sites was the result of drastic changes in rural conditions, a combination of deteriorating climate and crop yields, population collapse from endemic plagues, and the conversion of communal arable production to sheep rearing and farm rental. But this well-known desertion of villages was no doubt a smaller shift in settlement than that which took place in the early Middle Ages, before a parochial church and seigneurial court existed to impede local population migration.

Ellison and Harriss proposed several models of settlement expansion in the fifth and sixth centuries. Although based upon the inadequate place-name chronology, these models took into account variations in land-use potential, as laid out in the Ordnance Survey *Map of Land Use Potential*. This material has relevancy for the areas studied by Ellison and Harriss but not for north-central Hampshire, where nearly all the land is chalk-based and has the same rating of land-use potential. Moreover, land-use definitions are generally likely to be misleading for the study of farming practices a thousand years ago, because the definitions concern twentieth-century soil conditions and agricultural interests. The recorded drift geology, for all its shortcomings in specificity, still remains a better guide to land type. But it alone is not enough to gauge adequately the background to settlement and land use; topography and hydrology have been shown here to be important factors for any survey of rural development.

Another employment of the "new geography" was C.J. Arnold's

polygon model building for Saxon settlement in southern England.[46] He constructed polygons, the sides of which were equidistant from village sites, and proposed that these geometric forms represented ideal village territories. The model does not take into account land value, terrain, and population density, and, because the polygons do not accurately portray the land units associated with the villages, it fails to explain the positioning of settlements. Corrective alterations, however, would change the function of this model, which is to analyze and explain spatial relationships between settlements, not between them and their territorial units. But even with the territorial adjustments it is difficult to see how geographic locational modeling alone can explain the location of early medieval village sites. Either villages were placed centrally in different sized territories, or the divisions between villages were established to create a certain equality of land. For the present, geographic modeling cannot distinguish between these alternatives because of its basic weakness, its assumption that all early medieval villages were of the same date.

Settlement studies that are directed more toward archaeology than to theoretical geography include those made by William Ford on the Avon valley in Warwickshire and by Peter Wade-Martins on Launditch Hundred in western Norfolk. Both surveys analyzed similar data from archaeological work, place-name studies, and later manorial and ecclesiastic records. Because the surveys are of such dissimilar geographic conditions, it is of little value to compare the details of the settlement patterns they present.[47] Similarly, Alan Everitt's mammoth study of the early medieval settlement of Kent undertook many avenues of investigation, but the breadth of its subject—an entire county—does not permit ready comparison.[48]

Blending both archaeological concerns and geographic modeling is Barry Cunliffe's important study of medieval settlement on the chalk downland around Chalton, in southeastern Hampshire.[49] The Chalton region is farther from the main river valleys and routes of communication than is Micheldever, and it lacks the latter's agricultural resources, but the two locales are only twenty-five miles apart and share the same general soil types and geographic formations. Here Cunliffe drew from

---

[46] See C. J. Arnold, "Early Anglo-Saxon Settlement Patterns in Southern England," *Journal of Historical Geography* 3:4 (1977), pp. 309–15.

[47] W. J. Ford, "Some Settlement Patterns in the Central Region of the Warwickshire Avon," pp. 274–94 in *Medieval Settlement*. Peter Wade-Martin, "The Development of the Landscape and Human Settlement in West Norfolk from 350–1650 A.D. with particular reference to Launditch Hundred," Ph.D. Dissertation, University of Leicester, 1971.

[48] Nonetheless, Everitt's case study of the lands of Milton Regis is on a comparative scale, with a minsterland of 17,000 acres and twelve parishes. Alan Everitt, *Continuity and Colonization: The Evolution of Kentish Settlement* (Leicester, 1986), pp. 302–32.

[49] Barry Cunliffe, "Saxon and Medieval Settlement Pattern in the Region of Chalton, Hampshire," *Medieval Archaeology* 16 (1972), pp. 1–12.

an intensive archaeological field survey to reconstruct an early medieval settlement pattern. The earliest phase of his model has central-place settlements as the foci for large hexagonal territories, elongated in shape to be centrally sited over the hilltop promontories on the south sides of the chalk downs. The central sites lay two to three miles apart, with two-mile by four-mile territories.

The early medieval movement of settlement around Chalton can be compared to the settlement chronology of the Micheldever area. Cunliffe proposed that the middle Saxon nucleated site at the center of the Chalton territory was abandoned along with its outlying farmsteads and hamlets in the ninth century. At the same time late Saxon settlements were formed ca. 900 at lower elevations, and their respective parish units fairly evenly divide the original territory. Later settlements were colonies of these sites, most of which remain as villages to this day.

The Chalton model is based upon the field survey of that parish, which found one nucleated early Saxon village and evidence for early Saxon period occupation at three Romano-British sites in the vicinity, and at a previously unoccupied site. The identification is based upon grass-tempered wares, pottery types which, as noted above, are thought to be associated with Saxon occupation from the fifth to the eighth centuries. Cunliffe matched these hilltop settlements to other excavated Saxon-period villages, and argued for a revision of the old view that Saxon settlement took place in the valleys. He did admit, however, that the grass-tempered pottery and the sites in which it was found might "represent the continuing sub-Roman population and owe little or nothing to intrusive traditions."[50] While it is likely that some small post-Roman settlements were Celtic rather than Saxon, there is no real doubt that the hilltop village was occupied by Germanic people, who had building techniques and house styles, as well as personal artifacts, that are typical of the early Saxon culture.

Cunliffe's conclusions present a full chronology: in the fourth and fifth centuries nucleated sites appeared in the Roman countryside; in the fifth through ninth centuries, nucleated villages were established on hilltops; in the tenth century population shifted to new locations often in the valley bottoms; in the eleventh to fourteenth centuries there was a gradual expansion of village lands and new farmsteads. The first two phases of settlement pattern may actually represent the insertion among late Roman colonate holdings, of a Saxon village at a strategic site dominating the vicinity. Perhaps a warrior leader with his dependents and

---

[50] Ibid., p. 5. This reveals a reluctance to adopt wholeheartedly the view that the British population reverted to a non-ceramic society after the collapse of the Romano-British pottery industries. He also notes the "friable nature of grass-tempered pottery, which tends to disintegrate on exposure to weather": pp. 2, 3. See also J. G. Hurst's recognition of grass-tempered wares in pre-Saxon contexts in western England: "The Pottery," pp. 283–348 in *A.A.S.E.*, esp. p. 294.

followers lived there ruling the local British population. By the ninth century all these sites were abandoned, and the new villages on lower ground probably reflected changing conditions—climatic, economic, and social. The desiccation of the chalk on the South Downs may not have been as intensive as in central Hampshire, because it is closer to the Channel and its wetter weather. Nevertheless, the improved plough and grain varieties, and perhaps the standard manuring practice that Cunliffe suggested, permitted successful arable cultivation on a wider variety of soils. Any separate Celtic identity appears to have disappeared by the early medieval period; ethnic groups must have become fairly hybridized. If villages were indeed segregated in the sixth century, it was probably no longer the case by the time the population shifted to the valleys—and, in fact, the movement itself may have been a factor in obliterating ethnic distinction.

The archaeological evidence from the Chalton region can be corroborated by place-name studies. Settlements abandoned in the early Middle Ages did not leave behind a record of their names, but the hilltop village two miles west of Chalton is called Catherington. It ends in an "ington" name element, thought to have been used in the sixth century or later, but its first element was probably the Old Welsh *cateir*, "seat" (from *cathedra*), which was commonly transferred to "hill" or "promontory."[51] Secondary settlement sites at Chalton have names with "ton" and "worth," while the last-founded sites have names ending in "dean" and "field."

Survey work at Micheldever suggests a continuing occupation of the downs in the first post-Roman centuries, just as Cunliffe found at Chalton. Both localities witnessed Anglo-Saxon site abandonment and movement, and the establishment of permanent village communities well before the eleventh century (Fig. 3.4). Peter Sawyer claimed that the late Saxon period was one of "shifting, not expanding settlement."[52] That view seems to be confirmed by the patterns of early medieval settlement at both Chalton and Micheldever, and at early medieval sites throughout England—a mobility of early Saxon settlement, coupled with a clear tendency toward a mid- and late Saxon concentration of population in nuclear villages.[53]

---

[51] *O.D.E.P.N.*, pp 90, 93.

[52] *Medieval Settlement*, p. 6.

[53] The two leading examples of this pattern are the excavations at Maxey in Northamptonshire and at Wharram Percy in Yorkshire: P. V. Addeyman, "A Dark-age Settlement at Maxey, Northants," *Medieval Archaeology* 8 (1964), pp. 20–73; M. W. Beresford and J. G. Hurst, "Wharram Percy: A Case Study in Microtopography," pp. 114–44 in *Medieval Settlement*.

IV. THE MANORIAL ECONOMY

The downland of central Hampshire has been for the past several centuries a typical "sheep and barley" land, where thin but well-drained soils are particularly suited for an alternating livestock and crop production. Early medieval Micheldever, however, was subject to a different climate and agricultural regime. Observations of local and regional land use in that period should help reconstruct the manorial economy of Micheldever. It should be noted that this study is concerned with the rural development of a locality and region, and is not an institutional economic history like the works of T. Ambrose Raftis and J.Z. Titow.[1]

AGRICULTURAL ORGANIZATION

The background to studying the earlier rural economy in the Micheldever region begins with the Romans, who made some effort to exploit local resources fully. Their villas emphasized cereal production, with some large-scale stock rearing in suitable areas, while the native Celtic villages retained a mixed farming economy. Created and then exacerbated by political authoritarianism and a deteriorating climate, an over-exploitation of the land is likely to have brought about the end of both Roman and British agricultural regimes during the fifth century.

Anglo-Saxon agriculture was based upon mixed farming, though by the late eighth century there was already some export of wool to the Continent.[2] Barley decreased as a dominant staple, and naked wheats largely replaced the hulled wheat varieties. The naked wheats prefer heavier soils, so that the transition in wheat types may reflect agricultural expansion into the clay lands, and certainly represents an increased productivity of those clay lands already under cultivation. Livestock served a variety of functions: oxen for ploughing, sheep and goats for milk products and wool, and swine for meat. The land use of most farming units comprised several elements: extensive open fields for cer-

---

[1] T. Ambrose Raftis, *The Estates of Ramsey Abbey: A Study in Economic Growth and Organization*, Pontifical Institute of Medieval Studies (Toronto, 1957), and J. Z. Titow, *Winchester Yields. A Study in Medieval Agricultural Productivity* (Cambridge, 1972).

[2] Recorded in the correspondence between Charlemagne and Offa, king of Mercia. The information on Anglo-Saxon farming practice is drawn from contributions in *A.H.E.W.*: H.P.R. Finberg for Anglo-Saxon agriculture before 1042, Vol. I, Pt. 2, pp. 385–583, and M. L. Ryder on livestock, Vol. I, Pt. 1, pp. 301–40.

eal production and stubble grazing; small fields and gardens for grass and vegetables, with fruit trees in the garden plot; and meadow and rough pasture for livestock, primarily sheep and cattle. Poultry consisted of geese and fowl, and were often housed. The woods beyond the fields contained herds of pigs as well as the game that was a likely addition to the peasant diet.

A family holding, the farmstead or hide, was the typical agricultural unit of the early Saxon period, though it need not have been the only type. The personnel of a hide is likely to have included slaves and dependents in addition to family members; a holding so composed was already on the way to manorial status.

The settlement pattern of post-Roman sites in Hampshire suggests an interpretative model whereby a large, nucleated Germanic village on the high downland overlooked small dependent British settlements. By this hypothesis, agricultural units were the individual hamlets or the clan divisions within them, but all would have been controlled to some extent by the central political authority in the dominating village. The earliest law code for Wessex, that of Ine (ca. 695), reflects an ethnic diversity of Saxon and Welsh (Briton) subjects, but only the beginnings of village life.[3] In later Saxon villages this early arrangement was replaced by a unity of agricultural organization and authority at the individual village level.

By 1100, all middle Hampshire was divided into identifiable manors that had both demesne and tenant land. Some were held at knight's service by royal demand; others may have been farmed out for profit. Details of the estates and land use in Micheldever Hundred at the end of the early Middle Ages reveal which manorial practices were being followed in the eleventh century, and suggest which forms of rural organization had been present as far back as the eighth century.

The Anglo-Saxon Manor

The Anglo-Saxon period saw the conversion of what had been an independent entity, the hide or *hiwisc* (household) into one element of a larger, integrated agricultural unit, the manor.[4] The limited documentary evidence suggests that pre-Conquest manors were substantially similar to their medieval successors. A major difference was that slavery still existed in the eleventh century, though it was declining and soon to be extinguished. Another important difference was that the mixed

---

[3] Most relevant laws concern the household as hide, but farmsteads are also manorial, and one entry (no. 42) concerns having "a common meadow, or other land divided in shares," which presumes a community settlement. Translated in *E.H.D.* I, p. 368.

[4] For the change in the hide, see Sir Paul Vinogradoff, *The Growth of the Manor*, 2nd ed. (New York, 1951), p. 140.

farming practiced by the Anglo-Saxons largely turned to arable production in the central Middle Ages. The later Anglo-Saxon manor comprised tenant and demesne lands, with common pasture and woods. It
functioned through the combined authority of customary rights as represented by a village assembly or hall-moot, and managerial control by
the reeve (*gerefa*) similar to the later steward or bailiff.

Three pre-Conquest documents give details of Anglo-Saxon manorial
organization: a survey of Hurstbourne, Hampshire, and the instruc-
tional essays, the *Gerefa* and the *Rectitudines Singularum Personarum*. The
first source is similar to later medieval custumals. It describes the services
due from the inhabitants of Hurstbourne manor only seven miles northwest of Micheldever.[5] Although copied ca. 1050, the survey probably
dates to the acquisition of the manor by the Old Minster after Alfred's
death in 899. Its details, moreover, might represent conditions at the
beginning of its history of tenurial exchange in the last quarter of the
eighth century. The list was probably drawn up because the owners,
the monks of the Old Minster, feared (or found) that the rapid succession
of landholders had enabled the ceorls of Hurstbourne to avoid their
traditional dues. These obligations consisted of money payments, services of labor, and supplies for the manor. The labor services were
ploughing, sowing, and carting cereal crops, and mowing and stacking
hay. The required supplies were quantities of ale, wheat, barley, firewood, and fencing. A further tribute of four sheep at Easter suggests
that before the tenth century sheep were already an important resource
in this part of the Hampshire chalk downs. A final demand that the
ceorls do the required work on all but three weeks of the year seems to
refute Stenton's contention that these ceorls were essentially free.[6] Ad-
mittedly, it could be largely a difference in semantics; the ceorls were
neither free nor slave. Clearly, however, they owed more than a limited
service. The Hurstbourne survey shows that the ceorls were an integral
part of the manorial economy in 900, and perhaps had been so as far
back as the late eighth century.

The Hurstbourne custumal is important because it reveals three significant details of Anglo-Saxon manorial organization. First, the unit of
tenure was the *hiwisc* which seems to have retained the dual sense of
hide and household, and represented a recognized portion or share of
the village lands.[7] Secondly, the estate of Hurstbourne had an arable

---

[5] J. Robertson, *Anglo-Saxon Charters* (Cambridge, 1939) pp. 207, 454. It is translated in
E.H.D. II, p. 879, where comparison can be made to the Tidenham, Glos., estate survey.
Note that David Douglas and George Greenaway consider the Hurstbourne survey to be
mid-eleventh century in date, while Finberg argued that it should be placed in the early
ninth century. Even though the survey was copied ca. 1050, the changes in ownership
that would have caused its initial compilation had ended by ca. 900. The use of the term
hiwisc, moreover, suggests an early date.

[6] *A.S.E.*, p. 476.

[7] See Vinogradoff, *Growth of the Manor*, p. 151.

demesne—where the service took place—which Reginald Lennard considered the requisite for a true medieval manor.[8] Thirdly, aside from the labor services and the farm produce, the 60-hide estate brought in an annual cash revenue, which, at 40 pence a hide, yielded an even ten pounds annually. Hurstbourne was a substantial rural estate, and the cash return in addition to its demesne production was a valuable asset at the time when a good horse or slave was valued at one-half pound.[9] H.P.R. Finberg proposed that the 40 pence from each hide could be the same as the "ten pence from each yardland" that were due from the half-free *gebur* in the eleventh century, because *ceorl* had only a general sense of "husbandman" and was used indiscriminately for cottager, freedman, or rent-paying tenant.[10] It may therefore have been more an economic term than a social classification. If Finberg's identification is correct, the particulars of the Hurstbourne custumal would therefore apply to a great many manors in late Saxon Wessex. It also suggests that certainly by the tenth century (and perhaps by the late eighth), the major change in rural economy and society was already taking place, with the creation of the manor and its dependent, permanent workers. The change in the late Saxon period may not have been that new manorial conditions developed, but an already well-defined norm of the manor spread far more widely.

The eleventh-century tract entitled *Gerefa* details the functions of a reeve, and includes a long list of tools and materials required for the normal functioning of a manor.[11] It portrays early medieval agricultural routine in a detailed account of manorial activities throughout the year. Above all, it demonstrates the multiplicity of products yielded by the ideal manor. The reeve managed an estate that could produce grain, beans, flax, dyes, vegetables, wool, butter and cheese, fish, pork, poultry and eggs, honey, and even wine. The absence of metalworking is noteworthy—there was no smith on the manor. Even in the eleventh century, a smith would not be expected on every manor, but perhaps certain workers, such as a ploughman, could repair their own equipment when necessary. The reeve must have acquired metal items, primarily iron tools, from itinerant smiths or local markets.[12]

---

[8] Reginald Lennard, *Rural England 1086–1135* (Oxford, 1959), pp. 213–14.

[9] These and other items appear in a mid-tenth-century list of compensations in "The Ordinance of the Bishops and Reeves of the Land District (VI Athelstan)," translated in *E.H.D.* I, pp. 387–88.

[10] Finberg in *A.H.E.W.*, Vol. I, pt. 2, pp. 441–51, 466.

[11] *Be Gesceadwan Gerefa* (Cambridge, Corpus Christi MS 383, f. 102) published in *Gesetze*, Vol. I, pp. 453–55. It has been translated in W. Cunningham, *The Growth of English Industry and Commerce*, 5th ed. (Cambridge, 1915), pp. 573–76.

[12] Ine's Law no. 63, however, states that when a *gesith* moves, he may have with him his reeve, his smith, and his children's nurse: translated in *E.H.D.* I, p. 371. An Anglo-Saxon rural smithy excavated at Warram Percy, Yorkshire, is considered by its excavators to have been "a focus of some longevity": *Medieval Archaeology* 27 (1983), pp. 208–209.

The *Rectitudines Singularum Personarum*, of eleventh-century West Midland origin (probably the Worcester diocese of Oswald or Wulfstan), is an account of the reciprocal responsibilities characteristic of the Anglo-Saxon manor.[13] The text details dues expected from each class of manorial worker and customary rights each claimed in return. Above the slave was the *cotsetla*, who paid no rent, but owed heavy services. Next, the *gebur* was provided a house with stock and tools. He held a yardland, paying ten pence rent (the same as a Hurstbourne *ceorl*),[14] but also doing some demesne work. The highest ranking individual was the *geneat*, a rent payer who still owed some field labor and produce from his holding, but does not seem to have been supplied with a home or tools.

The *Rectitudines* listing of worker types from oxherd to cheesemaker to woodward serves as a reminder of how varied were the functions of the complex manorial economy. Villagers and manorial authorities were interdependent; the manor could not continue to produce in diversity and quantity without the contribution of both elements. Failure on the part of "management" in overseeing the results of required work and in ensuring the customary rewards for this effort, would lessen that productivity and soon reduce the manor's value. Perhaps because of this mutual responsibility, early medieval agriculture was stable. Yet the depredations of raiding and warfare could easily disrupt the surplus production that permitted the political and cultural achievements of the Old English secular and religious leadership.

The Norman Manor

The Norman Conquest brought with it no new agricultural regime.[15] English manors remained generally as before, and by Domesday can be seen to have changed very little, beyond the nearly wholesale replacement of the Anglo-Danish aristocracy by a predominately Norman ruling class. The great ecclesiastical estates continued largely intact, and new ones were created from confiscated lands by the Norman dynasty and its confederates. The proportion of royal estates to the total number of holdings, however, was at a height not seen for centuries. But because of the many church holdings in Hampshire, there was less royal land (excluding forest territories) in the Norman period than there had been during the early tenth century.[16]

---

[13] See *Gesetze*, Vol. I, pp. 444–53, for the standard edition. The *Rectitudines* is translated with a bibliography in *E.H.D.* II, pp. 813–16.

[14] As noted by Finberg, *A.H.E.W.*, Vol. I, pt. 2, p. 514.

[15] Agricultural developments by the thirteenth century appear in Walter of Henley's *Hosebondrie* and other guides in Elizabeth Lamond, ed., *Walter of Henley's Husbandry Together With an Anonymous Husbandry, Seneschaucie and Robert Grosseteste's Rules* (London, 1890).

[16] The reconquest by Alfred of course preceded the bequests made in his will. The gifts made by Edward and his descendants in the tenth and eleventh centuries came to en-

By 1100, however, significant but subtle changes were occurring. The great Norman lords had taken over the scattered holdings of their Anglo-Danish counterparts. The spread of land tenure by knight's service was creating a complicated pyramidal structure of obligations and relations. Yet on the local level, it soon became usual for a knight to hold a single manor, to occupy it for much of the year, and to plan for his son to inherit it. There developed a new local land-holding class, the possessions of which became effectively inheritable early in the twelfth century.

In the early Norman period, there was another common method of landholding, distinct from that of feudal tenure. Reginald Lennard has claimed that "farming-out of manors on stock-and-land leases was so common that this mode of estate management, which was inherited from Anglo-Saxon England, must at least rate in importance with the system of tenure of knight-service introduced by the Normans."[17] Those instances where a landlord leased the demesne of a manor to a *firmarius* for a fixed rent, Lennard contended, were only rarely identified in Domesday Book because the survey had no interest in the manner in which the estate was administered, only in its economic potential, but such arrangements do appear in the contemporary records of ecclesiastical institutions. The multiple term leases that are found in the late tenth century continue through the eleventh century. One of the rare Domesday references to this type of holding occurs in the entry for Headbourne Worthy, south of Micheldever, where a Norman, Radulf de Mortemer, had taken over the last life term of the three-life lease of the estate of the Old Minster.[18]

Lennard found it particularly revealing that most of the *firmarii* of the first Norman century had English names.[19] Most of them paid very high rents, likely the result of their weakened political status. He contrasted the reports of William's having offered manors to the highest bidder regardless of existing arrangements, to the example of a lease of 902. This Anglo-Saxon lease specified that the lessee could not be turned out in favor of someone offering a higher rent, a condition not present in later leases.[20] The Normans thus appear to have granted leases with no security of tenure, while the Anglo-Saxons granted full-term leases. The Normans apparently considered market values to be more profitable

---

compass as large a part of central Hampshire (including Micheldever) as had been earlier assigned to the bishop and cathedral. By the end of the eleventh century, a large majority of manors in central Hampshire belonged to the church, and only a handful were held directly by the Crown.

[17] Lennard, *Rural England*, pp. v, 105–41.

[18] *Domesday Book*, 46d.

[19] Lennard, *Rural England*, pp. 154–55.

[20] Ine's Law, no. 67, concerns a landlord's attempt to add service to a fixed rent, which Dr. Whitelock assumed, perhaps unjustifiably, took place at the expiration of the original base: translated in *E.H.D.* I, p. 371.

than long-term secured leases, an appropriate attitude in that conditions of 1100 imply a greater money economy than those of 900.

Lennard reasoned that much of the farming-out was caused by the absence from England of the Norman kings and large numbers of lay and ecclesiastical nobles, resulting on the one hand in a reduced need for food supplies from their demesne lands, and on the other hand, a greater need for ready money.[21] And the Conquest likely had other consequences for farming-out. The ineligibility of most English to receive land in knight-service tenure must have an impact on leasing practices. The English had no alternative but to accept lands in leasehold under whatever terms the Normans offered. The increased farming-out of estates was therefore a result of the Conquest and the conditions it created—the near-total dispossession of the English aristocracy (creating demand), and the logistics of the Anglo-Norman duchy-kingdom that encouraged cash revenues and short-term leases (fostering supply). These developments in early Norman landholding are indicative of the increased rate of post-Conquest economic change, a change in tempo that marked the end of the early Middle Ages.

MICHELDEVER HUNDRED IN DOMESDAY BOOK

Details of medieval field systems, their physical arrangements, work force, and products can be found in administrative surveys and in the records of individual manors. Later medieval and even post-medieval manorial documents are potentially informative, as they often contain references to field names and landscape features that were already part of the manors' physical structure in the eleventh century, if not earlier. For the early medieval period, only one general survey is pertinent, the Domesday Book, an invaluable source of information on the English manor of the late eleventh century. However, the goals of its creators and compilers, and irregularities in the record-making process, make the survey a source to be used with some discretion. R. Wheldon Finn has enumerated some of the difficulties encountered when applying Domesday entries to historical geography. He noted that unified vills with equal hidage could have widely varying populations, values, and agricultural resources.[22] Some of these manors appear to have been valued at two shillings per hide, while others were valued at six shillings per hide. Finn proposed several explanations for these and other discrepancies.[23] First, he agreed with Maitland that the demesne land was often exempt from hidage assessment. He also thought that perhaps

---

[21] Ibid., p. 139. The theme of the dual realm was taken up by John Le Patourel to explain administrative evolution, in *The Norman Empire* (Oxford, 1976).

[22] R. Wheldon Finn, *Domesday Book: A Guide* (London and Chichester, 1973), p. 26.

[23] Ibid., pp. 31–36.

only a portion of the land available for ploughing was actually cultivated each year. Further, a widespread practice of hiring plough teams would account for the commonly recorded discrepancy between the number of plough teams for which there was land available, and the number of teams actually on the manor, either in demesne or belonging to the vill. And because the number of *servi* on the manor was often double that of its plough teams, Finn argued that these slaves were demesne ploughmen, two for a team, one for the plough and one for the oxen. Whatever the intricacies of the Domesday Book, the entries for the Micheldever area do contain information that can be applied directly to its economic structures, in particular, to its field systems and the land use upon which they were based. The Domesday figures for the entries of Micheldever area manors have been compiled in chart form (see Appendix B), and provide the computations and comparisons that follow.[24]

Social Factors

The creators of Domesday Book were interested in the vill only as it related to the make-up of the manorial work force and to the customary dues and rights of those workers. The Inquest noted how many workers there were and of what kind. In the Micheldever area, it distinguished between *villani, bordarii,* and *servi.* The distinctions were of social and legal status, as determined by the degree of dependence. The everyday effect of this distinction was in the individual's working week, but the terminology suggests a differentiation based on domicile: *villani* as villagers, and *bordarii* (or *cotarii*) as cottagers. *Servi* described the remaining workers, the slaves of the lord's farm or household.[25] Perhaps agricultural workers were formerly typed according to their work and residence: those living in their own village and coming onto the demesne for customary labor, those supplied with cottages, (perhaps scattered among newly cleared lands), and the slaves presumably assigned quarters on the home farm.

Can the settlement pattern of each vill be interpreted from the Domesday Book figures for types of agricultural workers? Unfortunately, the data cannot be used effectively for Micheldever itself, because the numbers given for *villani, bordarii,* and *servi* are the combined figures for several villages and hamlets within the manor, and other smaller holdings have obviously been included in the totals as well. The attempt to compare villages, rather than manors, proves unsuccessful. Some locales

[24] These figures are based upon the relevant entries in *Domesday Book: Hampshire,* Julian Munby, ed. (Chichester, 1982), which is a correction of Abraham Farley's 1783 edition.

[25] See the definitions offered in R. E. Latham, *Revised Medieval Word-List from British and Irish Sources* (London, 1965), pp. 53, 119, 436, 513.

have only a couple of *villani* listed (e.g., Hunton), but many more *bordarii* and *servi*.

The basis for comparing worker types is by manors, not villages. Simple computations give figures on the relative numbers of worker types. Of seventeen manors with both *villani* and *bordarii*, in eight there were more *villani* than *bordarii*, in five they were equal, and in four there were fewer *villani* than *bordarii*. Therefore, twice as many manors had more *villani* than *bordarii*, than the reverse. Even so, there were nearly as many manors with equal numbers or fewer *villani*, as those with more *villani*. The quantifications may be better expressed by percentages: *villani* dominant manors = 47 percent, equal class manors = 29 percent, and *bordarii* dominant manors = 24 percent. If the categories of domicile implied in the terminology are extended to settlement types of the eleventh century, the first group of manors would have had nucleated village settlements, the second hamlets and farmsteads, and the third perhaps only scattered farmstead groupings. Unfortunately, the scarcity of information about eleventh-century settlement types prohibits a detailed comparison of each manor, but this deduced pattern does correspond (at nearly 50 percent) to the overall prevalence of villages in this part of Hampshire.

Manors with *servi* are also available for analysis. *Servi* were nearly always the smallest group of manorial workers. More *servi* than usual appear in a group of manors in the west Dever valley (Wonston, Sutton, Hunton, Stoke Charity), at two manors on the lower Candover (Northington, Swarraton), and at a single manor upstream (Chilton Candover). These localities are indistinguishable from neighboring estates in land value, village density, or history of land holdings.

The reported figures for all types of agricultural worker indicate that the proportional amounts of peasant type varied greatly among manors and even among holdings of a single manor. There is no overall geographic pattern to the distribution of relative number of *villani* and *bordarii*. Manors with high numbers of *servi* form no geographic or tenurial pattern. An anomalous entry for manorial workers is the appearance at the royal estate of Barton Stacey/Kings Worthy, of six *coliberti*, a worker type defined as recently freed teams of *servi*.[26] These six *coliberti*, however, do little to alter the ratio of the other 90 workers listed in the entry for that double estate. Finn noted that *coliberti* are found in Hampshire Domesday entries for royal and ecclesiastical manors, and he placed them socially between serfs and villeins.[27] They should represent, then,

---

[26] Finn, *Guide*, p. 35.
[27] R. Welldon Finn, "Hampshire," pp. 287–363 in H. C. Darby and Eila M. J. Campbell, ed., *The Domesday Geography of South-East England* (Cambridge, 1962), esp. p. 314. But see also P. Vinogradoff, *English Society in the Eleventh Century* (Oxford, 1908), pp. 468–69; and *A.S.E.*, pp. 468–70.

the late eleventh-century extinction of slavery on the estates of the king and the church, which might be expected to take the lead in this social change.

Finally, Domesday figures for peasant workers and landholders serve as a basis for estimating the rural population, a measure by which villages and manors can be compared. These estimates are presented in Appendix B and Figure 4.1, and are based upon Lennard's contention that the notations of *villani* and *bordarii* represented heads of peasant households, which he estimated to have contained an average of five members.[28] Listed in the Domesday entries for economic resources, between the entry for plough teams and that for meadow acreage, the numbers of *servi* (and presumably *coliberti* as well) are likely to have been counts of individuals. In addition to the estate workers, the manager of each manor (the reeve, bailiff, or *firmarius*) would usually have a family, which if large enough, shared some of the day-to-day labor. These persons would have been considered "management," however, and were thus not recorded by the Domesday assessors. For the sake of standard computation, the formula: *villanus* = 5, *bordarius* = 5, *servi* = 1, will yield an approximation of the inhabitants of a vill, though it does not include the family of the reeve or other agents of the manor.[29]

R. Welldon Finn, in the *Domesday Geography of South-East England*, argued that a multiplier of 4 or 5 of the Domesday figures yielded an approximate population total, but he used the workforce figures alone to examine the relative population level in Hampshire.[30] He compared worker totals for Domesday hundreds, grouping them in relative pro-

---

[28] Lennard, *Rural England*, p. 7. Josiah Cox Russell proposed a 3.45 ratio of population per household for the later Middle Ages, but this included urban properties with smaller households: *British Medieval Populations* (Albuquerque, 1948), pp. 22–23. Russell has recently repeated that figure (at 3.5), defining his unit as the nuclear family only: *The Control of Late Ancient and Medieval Population*, American Philosophical Society Memoirs, Vol. 160 (Philadelphia, 1985), pp. 147–51.

What remains to be determined, though, is the frequency of solely nuclear families in early medieval society. At Montaillou, in early fourteenth-century southern France, Emmanuel Le Roy Ladurie observed that the "evidence for 'more than nuclear' families concerns chiefly old widowed mothers living with their sons," but he also reported several instances of other family members and servants. The second most wealthy peasant household had at least seven members. See *Montaillou: The Promised Land of Error* (New York, 1978), pp. 42–43.

With typical acuity, Maitland recognized the difficulties in setting a ratio: "One must multiply . . . by four, five or six according to knowledge or taste": *D.B.B.*, p. 408.

[29] Manors were normally run by a reeve or bailiff, or if *ad firmam*, by the farmer himself or an estate manager. While some of these persons may have been single, most represented a family group unmentioned in the Domesday Survey, but which could be added to the population total of the vill. It is possible that the number of *servi* at a manor was dictated to some degree by the size of the familial workforce of the reeve. Individuals without families would need domestic and farm servants to ensure the proper functioning of the home farm, even if some or all of the cultivation was undertaken by the villagers.

[30] Finn, in *Domesday Geography*, p. 310.

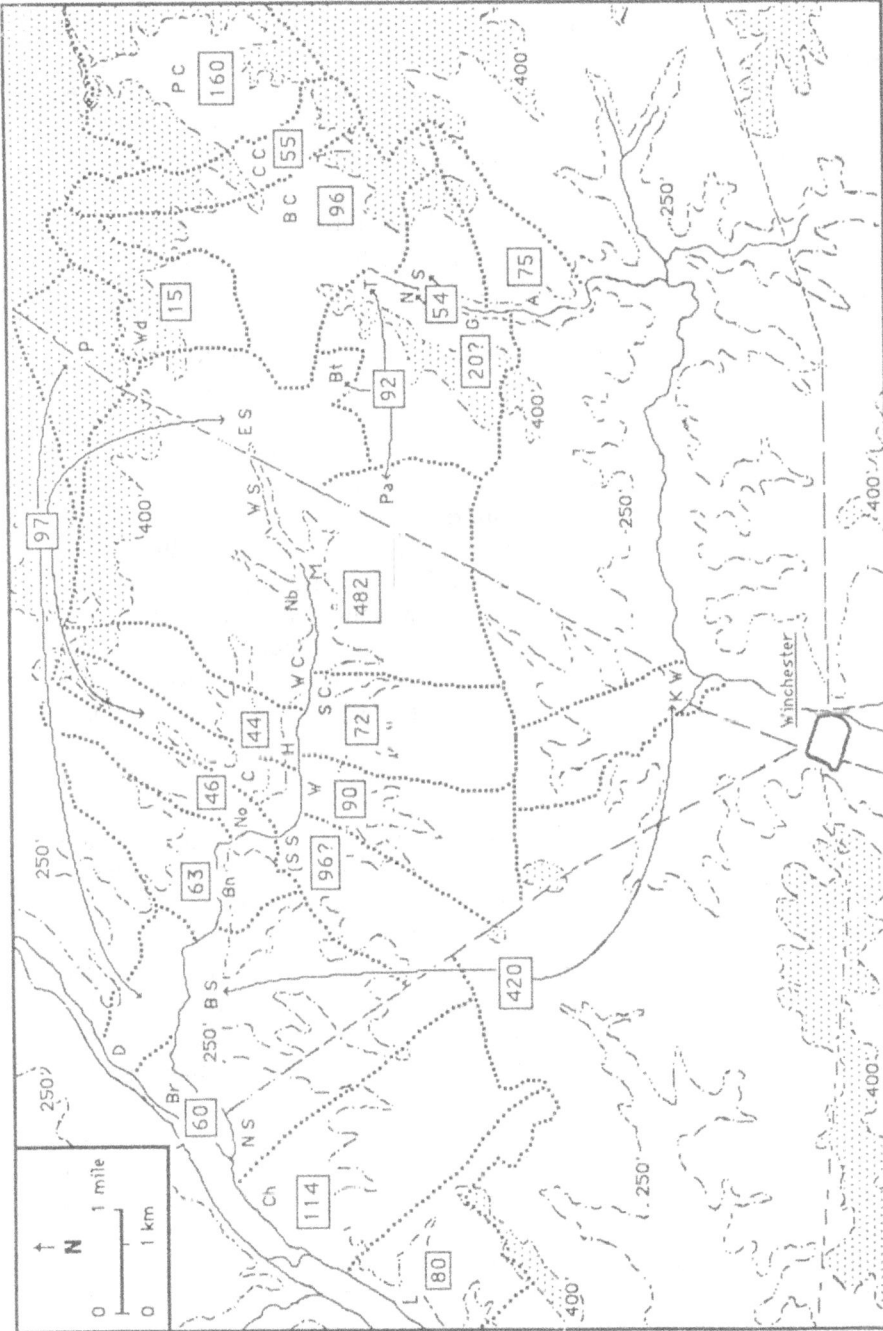

FIG. 4.1 Domesday Population Estimates

portion. The upper Dever valley and the Candover valley had average population levels, while the lower Dever and the Test valley villages nearby were part of the most highly populated area of Hampshire.[31] Finn assigned manorial populations to villages or localities; the manorial complexities of northern Hampshire were noted, but they do not appear in his analyses. The Domesday population of Micheldever, for instance, should not be placed simply in the modern village, but ought to be distributed among the thirteen identifiable components of the large estate.

In the case where a manor contained more than one vill, population size can be crudely approximated by dividing conglomerate totals by the number of vills in the manor. The results are in fact comparable to normally reconstructed village populations. Thus the 420 persons of Barton Stacey were also at Newton Stacey and Kings Worthy, giving an average 140 at each place. Similarly, Northington and Swaraton shared 54 estimated residents, averaging 27 apiece, and Totford, Burcot, and Papenholt held an estimated 92 persons, or an average of 31 per vill.

The population of Micheldever and its four associated manors of Stratton, Drayton, Popham, and Cranborne is more difficult to apportion, because medieval Micheldever included both the village of that name and the three hamlets of Weston, Northbrook, and West Stratton. The former royal manor of Micheldever is unlikely to have the same population as a hamlet. The average population estimate for each of the four vills adjoining Micheldever is 60. If we assume this figure for the average population of each of the four separate manors of East Stratton, Drayton, Popham, and Cranbourne, then the combined 240 leaves 242 to be divided among Micheldever and its three dependent hamlets. If the hamlets are rated at 31 apiece (the figure assigned to the adjacent Totford, Burcot, and Papenholt), their subtraction from the 242 estimate of the former royal vill leaves 149. This number is strikingly similar to the population of 140 ascribed to the royal vills of Barton Stacey and Kings Worthy.

The map illustrating the population estimates for the Micheldever area (Fig. 4.1) shows a wide spectrum of population levels per manor. It must be remembered that some manors had several settlements, and that manorial dues need not have been restricted to only the inhabitants of the closest vill. According to the formula used here, the manors with single vills generally had populations of 100 persons or less. A smaller village would have been closer to 50 to 60 inhabitants, representing perhaps a dozen families. The smallest settlement type above a single farmstead was the tiny hamlet with fifteen persons, just a few families living together. The estimations and averaging used for the Domesday figures reflect the spectrum of manor and settlement size in eleventh-

---

[31] Ibid., p. 312, fig. 94; p. 313, fig. 95.

century Hampshire. This organic diversity must surely be the consequence of a lengthy process of rural development and estate formation.

Economic Factors

The Domesday Book is an economic accounting of manorial fiefs, the component parts of the Anglo-Norman kingdom. The Book's economic interests pertinent to this study are three in number: the Danegeld tax that was due from each manor, the arable production measured in plough teams and land available for plough teams, and the monetary worth of the manor as an annual render or lease value. Entries sometimes listed non-arable resources: pasture, meadow, wood, and mills and churches. Each of these factors, through an examination of its geographic distribution, is a means of assessing the rural economy of the Micheldever area.

The Danegeld is a tenth-century military contribution that became an eleventh-century land tax. Alternating application of the Domesday terms *se defendit* and *geldavit* do not represent differences in the make-up of the manors or in their obligations to the state. Rather, they show a different wording of the questions put to each hundred moot by different teams of assessors. Here, all manors "defended themselves" with their money, except Bullington and Preston Candover, the only manors adjacent to the Micheldever estate that belong in Wellford and Bermondspitt Hundreds. One must therefore question Finn's observation that for Hampshire "a particular formula is not regularly associated with certain hundreds . . ."[32]

The survival of earlier royal grants with recorded hidage figures indicates that many estates in middle Hampshire had undergone an often substantial reduction of hidage assessment by the time of the Domesday Survey. This beneficial hidation was a form of tax relief, or with forged documents, tax fraud. It was common among the holdings of ecclesiastical institutions, and was a feature of the properties held by royal officers under William (see Appendix B) and his predecessors. The extensive hidage reduction that occurred during the course of the eleventh century makes the Domesday hidage figures unreliable guides to the size or economic potential of contemporary manors. In the area studied, Chilbolton, Leckford, Norton, Sutton, and Wonston seem to have received such beneficial hidation from the Crown after 1066. The hidages of Micheldever, Preston Candover, and Brown Candover, however, were reduced because of tenurial changes.

Figure 4.2 illustrates the hidage in 1066 and 1086 for the manors around Micheldever. It can be seen here perhaps better than in Ap-

---

[32] Ibid., p. 299.

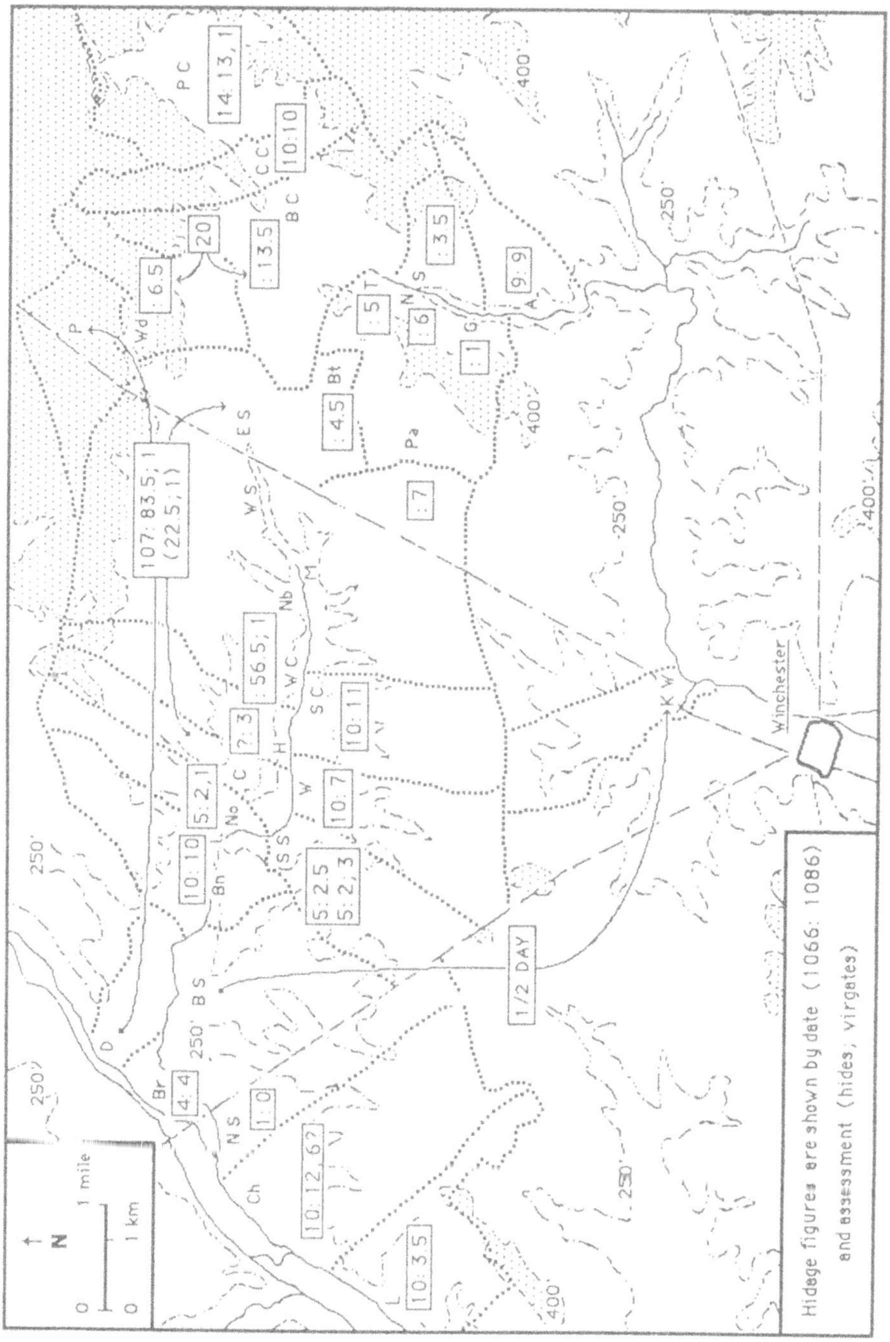
Hidage figures are shown by date (1066: 1086)
and assessment (hides, virgates)
Winchester
N
1 mile
1 km
1/2 DAY
107: 83.5; 1
(22.5; 1)
56.5; 1

FIG. 4.2 Domesday Hidage Figures

pendix B that at Micheldever itself hidage was not reduced after the Norman Conquest. The Book's confusing accounting system yielded results that are hard to verify, and scholars from J.H. Round on have used the assessment given in Domesday Book to explain eleventh-century circumstances, instead of inquiring exactly how each figure was derived.[33] The Domesday Book states that Micheldever had 107 hides in 1066, and 83½ hides 1 virgate in 1086. What it does not say is how the manor had changed territorially during the interval. Four manors traditionally attached to Micheldever (Drayton, Cranborne, Stratton, and Popham) were held from the New Minster by Hugh de Port in 1086. Their total hidage was 22½ hides 1 virgate, which can only be the difference between the Saxon 107 hides and the Domesday 83½ hides 1 virgate.[34]

Yet Micheldever did not lose or gain any real territory. The lands that Hugh de Port held of the Micheldever estate must have been used for the direct enfeoffment of an assigned number of knights, as such enfeoffments would make them immune to gelding and therefore not reported in that Domesday Book entry.[35] Other manors in middle Hampshire received reduced assessments, and for a few small ones, like Newton Stacey, all hidage was eliminated, but the exception of the 22 + hides of Hugh de Port is an immunity on the scale of the most generous of the West Saxon kings.

Domesday entries for plough teams (typically eight oxen) were intended to serve as a measure of arable production. The assessors listed the number present on each manorial unit and the number that such arable land would normally need. Contrary to the view that "usually the record of teams is complete and fairly straightforward,"[36] the information supplied by Domesday plough teams remains problematical for the Micheldever area. First, some of the land available for ploughing may have been at rest and unreported at the time the survey was taken. Secondly, it is common for a manor to have fewer plough teams than

---

[33] See J. H. Round, *V. C. H. Hampshire* I, pp. 449–526; and "Notes on Domesday Measures of Land," pp. 184–225 in P. Edward Dove, ed., *Domesday Studies* (London, 1888).

[34] The Micheldever Manor was not reduced in size. Hugh de Port held part of the Micheldever estate comprising the subsidiary manors northeast of Micheldever and those farther down the Dever to the west. East of Micheldever was a group of seven holdings (forming the later manors of Swarraton, Totford, Northington, Northington Grange, Burcot, and Papenholt). These lands were never held by Hugh de Port. Their 27 hides were included in the Micheldever estate in both 1066 and 1086, because the 107 (of 1066) less 27 gives a remarkably even figure for the Anglo-Saxon estate, and 83 ½ hides 1 virgate (of 1086) less 27 yields 56 ½ hides 1 virgate, a figure practically identical to the £56 value given the estate of Micheldever at Domesday. The lands over which Micheldever claimed superiority in 1086 were the same as the 107 hides TRE. F. W. Baring had suggested this in a note in *Domesday Tables* (London, 1909), pp. 192–93.

[35] The drop in geld assessment was due to Hugh's being a direct vassal of William. On *servicium debitum*, see H. M. Chew, *The English Ecclesiastical Tenant-in-Chief and Knights Service* (London, 1932), pp. 1–10.

[36] Finn, *Domesday Geography*, pp. 307, 318.

the number given as available, yet there are some instances (e.g., Abbotstone, Chilbolton) where the combined plough teams present on demesne and vill are greater than the potential plough teams. In these cases, the plough teams were owned by the lord or village, but must have been used at other locations. Because plough teams could be shared or hired, the number present on a manor may not necessarily reflect the actual production of the estate.[37] A better indicator of economic development is the land available for a given number of plough teams. Although it does not take into account other farming activities, it is a standardized measure of arable production, the most important element in the rural economy.[38]

Figure 4.3 illustrates the Domesday plough lands, measuring the number of plough teams for which there was adequate land in 1086. The widely differing figures are the result of the vastly different sizes of the estates examined. The actual amount of land under cultivation cannot be determined. Much of a manor was no doubt in woods, pasture, or perhaps unused wasteland. A very rough estimate, however, might be one hide, perhaps about 120 acres, per plough team.[39]

But there are some surprises. Stoke Charity had land for only four plough teams, though it was of a size one might expect to have had seven or eight, as did neighboring Wonston and Sutton Scotney. Perhaps at Stoke there was a greater emphasis on pasture. As part of an episcopal estate, might it suggest that the bishop's manors tended toward greater specialization: meat, dairy, or wool?

To determine the size of a demesne, Lennard tried to compare the number of plough teams held by the vill with the number on the demesne.[40] The appropriate figures for the Micheldever area yield interesting results.[41] Of the eighteen manors examined, eleven (61 percent) had more plough teams in the vill, two (11 percent) had equal numbers, and only five (28 percent) had more plough teams recorded for the demesne. The last five manors were Bullington, Woodmancot, Chilton

---

[37] Ine's seventh-century law code (no. 60) refers to a *ceorl* hiring another's yoke of oxen: translated in *E.H.D.* I, p. 371.

[38] Finn, *Guide,* pp. 107–15, describes the artificiality of ploughland figures and reviews the literature on the problem. More recently, Sally Harvey has reaffirmed the view that ploughland figures represent contemporary assessments: "Taxation and the Ploughland in Domesday Book," pp. 86–103 in P. Sawyer, ed., *Domesday Book: A Reassessment* (London, 1985).

[39] Maitland's detailed argument for an 120-acre hide is not convincing, yet the sheer weight of his evidence suggest that this size hide may have been used by many Norman administrators: *D.D.B.,* pp. 475–90.

[40] Lennard, *Rural England,* pp. 82, 91, 93, 97–98, 103, esp. 217–18, found the attempt unrewarding because the ratios vary considerably.

[41] The holdings at Preston Candover are counted as one manor, and the subsidiary manors of Micheldever are counted as one manor separate from Micheldever; the seven minor holdings east of Micheldever proper are not included in the figures.

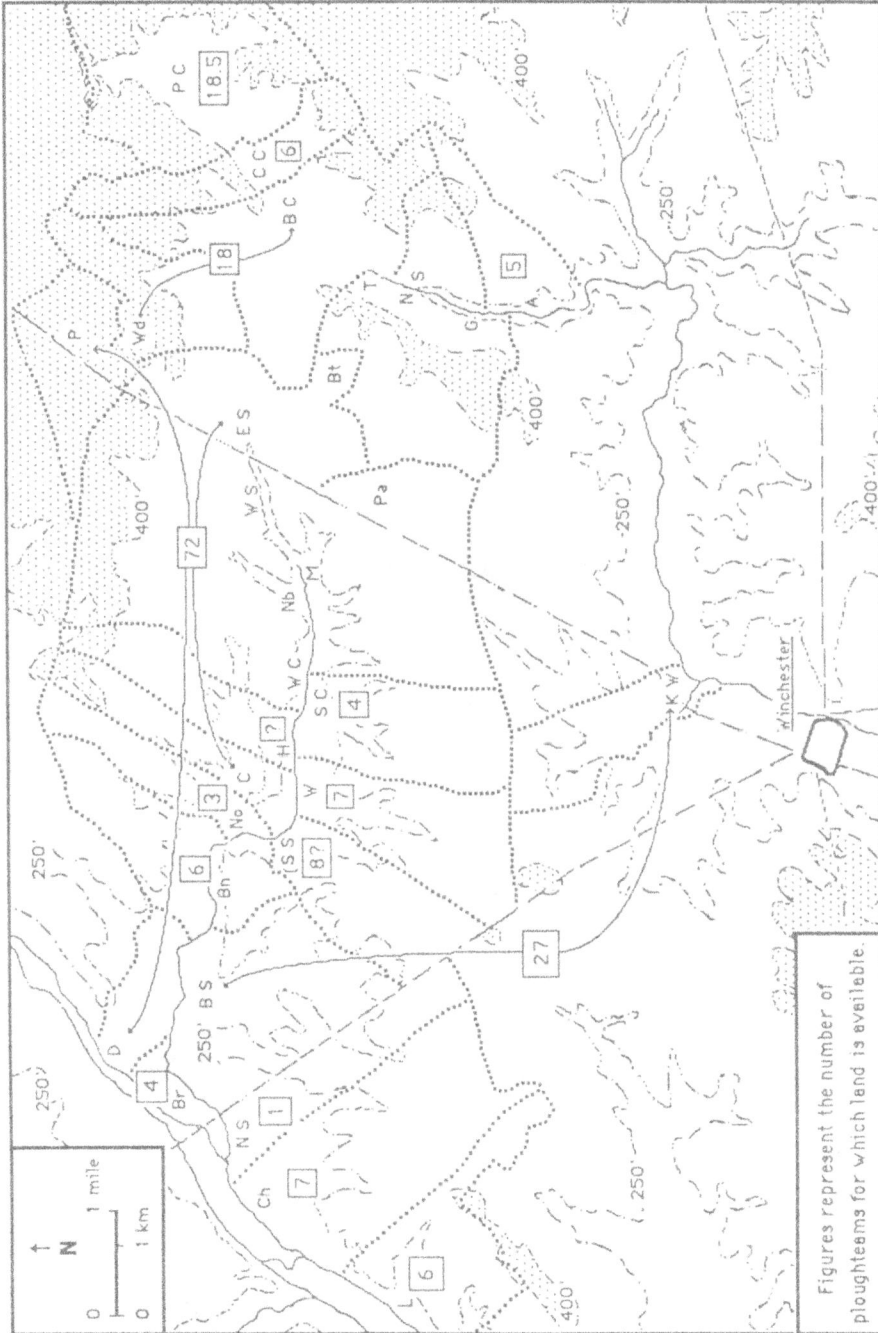

Fig. 4.3 Domesday Plough Lands

Candover, Stoke Charity, and Hugh de Port's manor comprising the four holdings in fief from Micheldever. The other properties belonged to Wherwell Abbey, the New Minster, and the Bishop of Winchester; ecclesiastical institutions in fact held the majority of the estates in Hampshire. The Chilton Candover manor, the detached Micheldever lands of Hugh de Port, and Stoke Charity had more *bordarii* than *villani*, as might be expected on a manor with extensive demesne. Yet, at Bullington and at Woodmancot, the work force appears to have been comprised solely of three *villani*. The two manors where the plough teams were equally distributed between vill and demesne, Leckford and Hunton, had combined numbers of *bordarii* and *servi* larger than, or equal to the number of *villani*, but so did many manors with more ploughs in the vill.

The comparative evidence reveals no pattern corresponding to plough team numbers. If the differences in plough team allocations (demesne plough teams were more numerous at only 28 percent of the manors) are indicative of large and small demesnes, then the Micheldever region lacked the extensive demesne that was necessary for a well-developed manorial economy. But there may have been other reasons for the lower number of demesne plough teams. Local custom may have required peasant contributions of both labor and plough team on the demesne land. Alternately, as suggested by Finn, there may have been considerable leasing of plough teams.[42] Inter-manorial transfer of plough teams might explain the discrepancies between plough land and actual plough teams. It is possible that the true ratio of demesne to village land is the proportion of demesne plough teams to available plough land, assuming that villagers were left to make their own arrangements for cultivation. But even this assumption is brought into serious question by the figures for Chilbolton and Leckford. There, demesne and vill had more plough teams than there was plough land available; they are likely sources of extra plough teams hired elsewhere. With all these variabilities, and the possibility that demesne land was often excluded from the hidage assessment, there is as yet no satisfactory answer to the question of what proportion of a Domesday manor was in demesne.

The royal agents compiling the Book in 1086 would have been especially interested in the figures of monetary valuation, because in the escheat or reversion of a manor to the Crown (either permanently in confiscation or temporarily in wardship), the Exchequer was responsible for getting the proper return from the sheriff who administered it. One may assume, therefore, that the valuations are reasonably consistent and accurate. The basis for a manor's valuation was its expected annual financial yield. The Domesday Book valuation generally consists of three figures: *tunc*, the last recorded Saxon yield, assumed to be in 1066; *post*, the manor's value when it changed hands after that (typically when it

---

[42] Finn, *Guide*, p. 31.

was given out in fief by William or his tenants-in-chief, or when it was bought back by its original landholders); and *moda*, the value of the manor in 1086. The figures often show a fluctuation, even a strong increase or decrease. Usually this was due to changes in the extent of the estate, but it may occasionally reflect other influences, e.g., weather or damage by warfare.

A fourth figure occasionally appears. It shows the actual financial yield in 1086, as compared to the estate value, and it represents the return from farming out the manor. All manors that have their *feorm* so recorded were actually worked by a *firmarius*, not necessarily their titular landholder, but lack of this notation is not proof that a manor was not held *ad firmam*.[43] Of the estates surveyed here, three reported a *feorm* in addition to their Domesday values: Brown Candover, Newton Stacey, and Barton Stacey with Kings Worthy. The first manor belonged to New Minster, while the last two were royal estates. The Barton Stacey amount of £52 6s 1d was the money equivalent of one-half a day's *feorm*, the ancient Saxon measure of the daily cost to support the royal court, and the origin of the term used for the later practice of annual leasing.[44] Newton Stacey was clearly a portion of the estate that had been split off at some point. Both manors were farmed out by William for their revenues, and were not kept for their agricultural product despite the ease with which it could have been sent to the Court at Winchester. These instances support Lennard's theory that the lengthy visits to Normandy created a preference on the part of the Anglo-Norman kings and their court for cash revenues over those in kind, which encouraged the farming out of estates.[45] Cash income from their middle Hampshire manors *ad feorm* certainly went to William, his Norman bishop of Winchester, and his Norman abbot of New Minster.[46]

The 1086 valuation of a manor seems to have been based upon its actual measure in hides at a return or assessment of £1 per hide. Excepting beneficial hidation, which was related only to fiscal dues, the valuation corresponded to an estate's true size by adding to the late Saxon hidation any increases in hidation from land acquisition since that time. Thus, Norton, Sutton, and Wonston are valued at ten hides TRE, and rendered £10 each in 1086. Stoke Charity increased from ten to eleven hides by 1086, and was therefore valued at £11. Newton Stacey was reduced from one hide to having no hidage assessment at all, but was still valued at £1. Micheldever follows the same formula. Its total

---

[43] Lennard, *Rural England*, pp. 116, 118.

[44] Ibid., p. 128; Finn, *Domesday Geography*, pp. 317–18; Round, *V.C.H. Hampshire* I, p. 401.

[45] See Lennard, *Rural England*, pp. 139–40.

[46] Walkelin was the bishop from 1070 to 1098; the abbot of New Minster was Rualdus from 1072 to 1091; E. Edwards, *Liber Monasterii de Hyda*, p. xli. Finn notes that the royal manors of Hampshire were valued at £350 in 1086, but rendered over £500.

hidage in 1066 was 107, but the separate assessment of its subsidiary holdings shows that Micheldever manor itself had 56½ hides 1 virgate, and it had a £57 value. Hugh de Port's four holdings came to 22½ hides 1 virgate, which less the 3 hides 3 virgates of Micheldever demesne land is nearly identical to the £19 assessment of Hugh's land. The other small holdings of Micheldever do not correspond, but the Survey may not have recorded all the details upon which their values were based.

The basis for Domesday monetary valuations is readily apparent, but no consistent relationships appear among the figures for monetary value, hidage assessments, and plough teams, present or potential.[47] While the land available for plough teams sometimes equals the number of hides assigned to the manor, the valuation varies from one-half to three times the plough team number or hidage. This disparity between hidage and valuation appears in the holdings of the Micheldever estate, for which plough team figures are unfortunately unavailable. At these holdings, a two hide parcel was worth 20s, one and one-half hides were worth 30s, four and one-half hides were worth 60s, five hides were worth 50s, and seven hides were worth 100s. This undeniable lack of uniformity can hardly be attributed to drastically different soil conditions in adjacent landholdings. The disparities between value and hidage could result from the post-Conquest competition that Lennard suggested took place among Anglo-Saxons bidding for lands made available to them *ad firmam*, and not *in feodum*, which was reserved for Normans and a few favored Englishmen.[48]

Figure 4.4 illustrates the valuations of the manors around Micheldever in 1066 and 1086. The few that lost value between these dates are Preston and Chilton Candover, and Sutton and Norton on the lower Dever. The combined loss of these four manors is £8 25s, while ten other manors gained £26 2s.[49] A further three manors had no change or no TRE valuation. Increases in manorial values in the Micheldever area were thus greater in absolute terms than decreases and were proportionally greater as well, with an average gain of £2 6s per manor.

Appendix B records the fluctuating values of the estates in north-central Hampshire between 1066 and 1086. Some may have been a direct consequence of the invasion, with Micheldever itself being on one of the routes connecting Winchester and London. It has been long sug-

---

[47] The small number of manors here studied does not permit the statistical analysis undertaken by John McDonald and G. D. Snooks in *Domesday Economy: A New Approach to Anglo-Norman History* (Oxford, 1986). Their argument that assessment was based on ability to pay does not alter the observable relationship between geld and hidage, which itself is a value of wealth or productive capability.

[48] See Lennard, *Rural England*, pp. 139–40.

[49] Kings Worthy was recorded as part of Barton Stacey. Excluded from these figures are the poorly reported entries for the four subsidiary manors and seven small holdings of Micheldever manor.

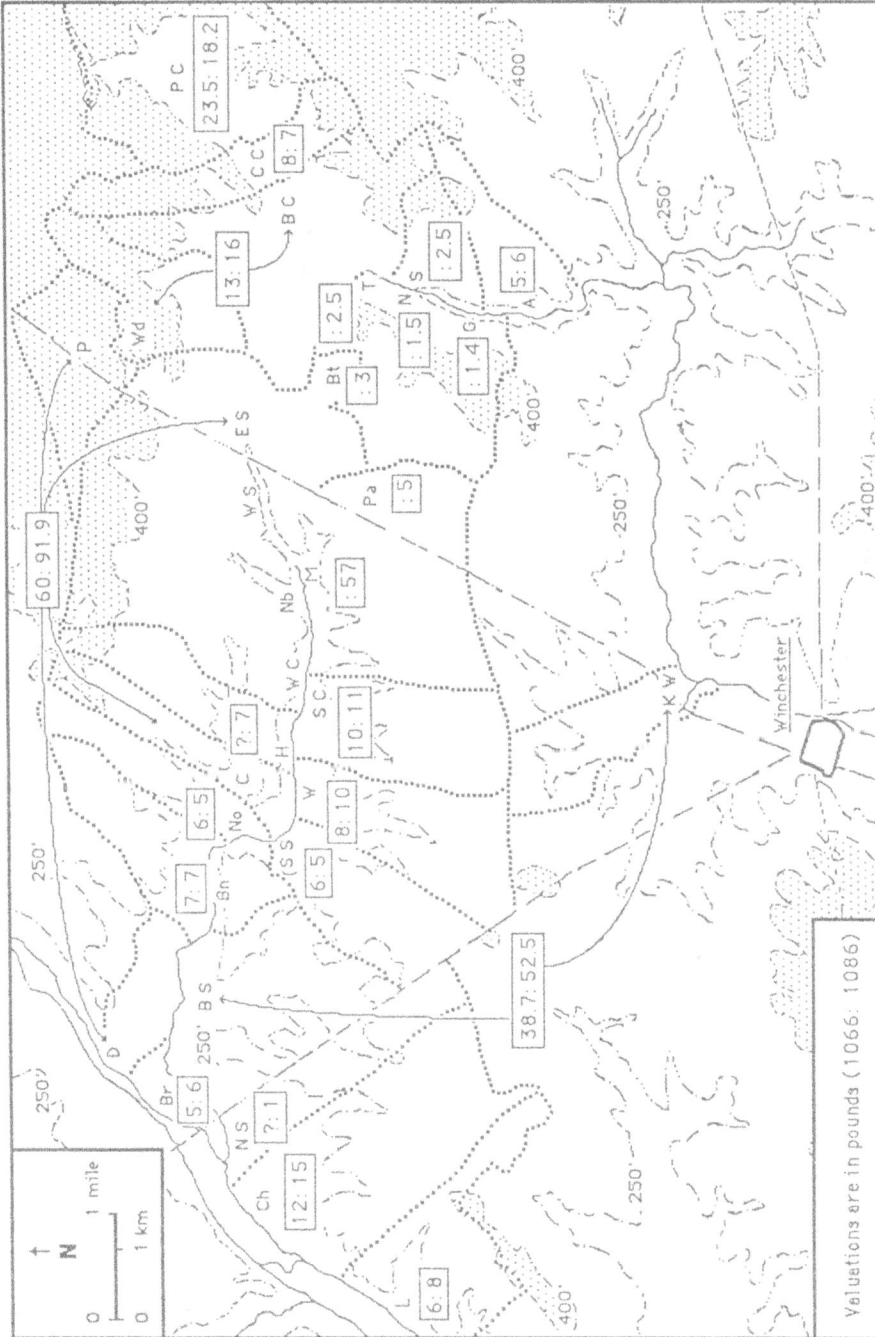

FIG. 4.4 Domesday Valuations

gested that the changes recorded in Domesday Book reflect the economic damage of the campaigns of conquest in the south, much as Yorkshire *wasta* entries record the later "harrying of the North."[50] It is unlikely, however, that the brief campaigns of the autumn of 1066 had effects that lasted a generation. The end of the Danish wars in 1016 witnessed the rapid recovery of English prosperity. Furthermore, in 1066 foraging and looting must have been particularly selective to have affected one manor more noticeably than another. If manors depreciated solely from damage suffered during the Conquest, their drop in value should be reasonably constant, as should be their rate of recovery. Similarly, even short-term climatic change would have resulted in a general trend of valuation changes.[51]

This is clearly not the case in the Micheldever region of Hampshire. Appendix B shows how variable were the fortunes (or at least the assessments) of the eighteen manors for which values were fully recorded.[52] There was in fact a general decrease in value following the termination of the Anglo-Danish regime of Edward and Harold. Only one manor (5.5 percent) gained value soon after 1066. Eight manors (44 percent) had the same value soon after 1066 as they had before it, and of these, two (11 percent) retained that value, while six (33 percent) gained in value. Nine manors (50 percent) lost value after 1066. Of the nine, two (11 percent) continued to lose value, four (22 percent) regained some of their pre-Conquest value, one (5.5 percent) recovered it all, and two (11 percent) became even more valuable.

The period, therefore, saw a general decline followed by a rise in the values of the manors of middle Hampshire. One-half the manors examined dropped in value soon after the Conquest; the ratio of total decreased to increased actual valuation is nine to one. But comparing the values of 1086 to those of 1066, 50 percent of the manors had increased values, 33 percent lost value, and 17 percent were unchanged. Therefore, despite a loss in value due to the Norman army's depredations, or more likely the Norman government's exactions, the manors

---

[50] F. H. Baring drew attention to a pattern of destruction, in *Domesday Tables*, pp. 207–16. Welldon Finn, in *Domesday Geography*, p. 316, considers campaign destruction "a reasonable hypothesis."

[51] In *The Norman Conquest and its Effects on the Economy: 1066–86* (New York, London, 1971), Welldon Finn sought to prove that Domesday entries reveal the physical damage wrought by the Conquest. His ingenuity in directing conjunctional routes of Norman armies and auxiliaries through manors that had lost value TRE (pp. 64–68) is not convincing. Strong evidence for a countering argument is the fact that the great Micheldever estate, which could hardly be avoided by Norman troops (lying as it was across the routes to Winchester from the north), incurred no loss in value following the Conquest.

[52] None of Micheldever manors had a valuation before 1086, as the hundredal manor was considered in its entirety. Sutton was apparently two manors, but their entries are nearly identical and Sutton 2 is entered next to Norton, suggesting a clerical error in copying. Because its reliability is dubious, Sutton 2 has been removed from the list. Bullington has no recorded value for the post-1066 period, and is assumed to have remained the same.

of the Micheldever region were generally more valuable at the end of William the Conqueror's reign than at the end of Edward the Confessor's.[53]

These changes in value are not easily explained. There is no discernible relationship between change and manorial lordship, population, or economic resources. The manors in the Candover valley generally fared worse than those in the Micheldever valley, but the manors along or near the Test valley did better. Chilbolton, Barton Stacey, Bransbury and the two Leckford manors all increased in value. This difference might result from the presence of Norman armies, if they marched between Winchester and London, and not along the Test. But it could also result from the geographic specifics of the estates. The broad lowland of the Test valley when drained and channelized would provide good pasture and even better meadow, the source of the winter fodder for the additional plough teams necessary for increased arable production. A drier upland valley, the Candover lacked this potential for expanding its productivity. The difference in values may therefore suggest that the Test valley manors were economically well developed. Finn noted that the Test valley had the highest density of population and plough teams at Domesday.[54] As most of the manors there were retained by their pre-Conquest ecclesiastical owners, this economic activity may have been part of a wider process. One may hypothesize that religious houses had earlier started long-term physical improvements on their properties, and this estate management paid off in greater productivity, and therefore values, in the late eleventh century.[55]

Non-Arable Resources

In addition to figures on hidage, plough teams, and monetary values, the Domesday record for each holding may contain information on its non-arable resources: meadow, pasture, and woodland, plus the manor's possession of a mill or church. In each instance the type of resource was identified, and its amount specified. Those estates with land along a stream were the ones with more meadow, though it is possible that detached properties existed for fodder, e.g., the single acre of meadow belonging to Woodmancot.

The completeness of the reporting is questionable, however, because

---

[53] Comparisons of Domesday monetary figures are based on the assumption that no appreciable change occurred in the value of the currency between 1066 and 1086.

[54] Finn, *Domesday Geography*, p. 319.

[55] To suggest a primary cause, the increase in value from 1066 to 1086 may have been part of a general rise in productivity of monastic and episcopal lands in Hampshire. The late tenth-century church reform saw the expulsion of the canons from the New Minster in 964 and the reorganization of their prebendary properties into communal ownership, under a central authority that had the resources to develop its estates more effectively.

some low-lying manors that even today have riverside meadows without the need for plough-team fodder, had no meadow reported in Domesday Book. The water meadows of the Dever stream pass directly through the manor of Bullington, for instance, but there was no entry for a meadow, only a mill. The same absence appears in the Bransbury, Wonston, and Hunton entries, while other manors along the Test, Dever, or Candover do report adequate amounts of meadow. It is probably a simple case of omission in the instances cited. Geography might have been a factor, but these manors were not contiguous. Management is also unlikely, because they were not tenurially related. One holding belonged to Wherwell Abbey, another to the bishop of Winchester, and the others were the New Minster's.

Pasture was recorded much less often than meadow. It occurs only once in the entries under examination, at the royal estate of Barton Stacey/Kings Worthy (*De herbagio: xlvi sol.*). Extensive pasture land until recently existed in both places, on what are today Moody's Down and Worthy Down. The other manors must have had considerable pasture land as a matter of course. Downland pasture in middle Hampshire may not have been converted to arable land until the thirteenth century.[56] One must conclude that pasture was normally not recorded, and the instance at Barton Stacey indicates a special situation.[57] As it is the only royal manor among those here surveyed, it is likely that the Domesday commissioners were more interested in the render of 46s than in the fact that it came from pasture land. The separate income from the pasture at Barton Stacey should indicate that it was leased out. It was an important asset, valued at more than many entire manors. The Barton entry thus reveals that the Crown not only had manors at farm, but probably also leased out specific areas in pasture. It is also possible that the extensive pasture here had some connection with the proximity of Winchester, perhaps supplying meat (and even parchment) to its civil and religious institutions, as well as wool to its nascent cloth industry.[58]

Woodland was also rarely recorded.[59] Again, the Barton manor lists it as a resource. Here it was measured or valued in the number of swine it supplied, as is typical for Hampshire entries in Domesday book. This

---

[56] M. M. Postan, *The Medieval Economy and Society. An Economic History of Britain 1100–1500* (Berkeley and Los Angeles, 1972), p. 23.

[57] Finn, *Introduction to Domesday Book* (New York, 1963), p. 177. For Hampshire, he concluded that "the greater part of pasture in the county was unrecorded": *Domesday Geography*, p. 340. This must be an understatement, as entries for pasture appear in only 7 percent of the Domesday manors of the Micheldever area.

[58] See Martin Biddle and D. J. Keene, "Winchester in the Eleventh and Twelfth Centuries," pp. 241–448 in Biddle, *Winchester in the Early Middle Ages*, Winchester Studies, Vol. I (Oxford, 1976), pp. 435, 438.

[59] Finn in *Domesday Geography*, pp. 329–22, found it to be proportional to the present geography, with little wood on the Chalk downland. He wondered what amount of wood was in royal forests and therefore not inventoried in Domesday Book, yet he did not openly consider the possibility that this resource was omitted in many hundreds.

number is most probably the render from the annual culling of the herd, not the total number of pigs in the wood.[60] Thus Barton Stacey/Kings Worthy had a large amount of woodland, enough for a render of 80 swine. Micheldever is recorded as having wood for the mast of four pigs. As one section of Micheldever Wood later had pennage for 60 swine, the low number for such extensive woodland must be an error. Another entry was at one of the Preston Candover manors, where *silva ad clausura* (for fencing) is noted but not quantified. Finally, at Hunton, there was a wood valued at 6d, indicating that it was leased out from the estate, like the pasture at Barton Stacey. In the remaining manors, it is unlikely that the survey failed to recognize woodland on the scale of the four manors so noted. It may have been thought an unnecessary and unwarranted detail where woods were still an integral part of the manor, supplying timber, fuel, and pannage to the lord and the vill according to customary arrangements. Perhaps only those instances where woodland had some commercial value were entered into the survey, and presented in terms of a render, in kind or in money.

The low level of commercial development suggested by the Domesday entries for pasture and woods is not applicable to mills and churches. Thirteen and one-half mills were recorded for the thirty-five manors surveyed here. Nearly every manor that had been valued at five or more hides TRE had a mill in the 1086 survey. By the early Norman period, any manor with sufficient resources and a stream large enough to power a mill could be expected to have one. Archaeological evidence argues increasingly for an early appearance and perhaps widespread use of water mills in England, as the remains of well-designed structures can be assigned by radiocarbon dating firmly to the eighth and ninth centuries.[61] The ubiquity of the water mill in eleventh-century Hampshire should not be attributed to a sudden investment in newly acquired properties by Norman landlords, lay and clerical, but is more likely to have resulted from long-term manorial improvements, which are only fully revealed in the Domesday Book.

The Hampshire mills were usually given a standard value of 15s. Alternate figures are often multiples or fractions of that value. The one and one-half mills at Leckford rendered 22s 6p, and the three mills of Barton Stacey/Kings Worthy at 42s 6p came slightly below an even 45s. Perhaps one of the mills was decayed or usable only during the wet months of the year. At Micheldever, the 30d value of the mill must be a clerical error for two mills rendering 30s. Otherwise this large estate had only a single facility, which was worth only $\frac{1}{27}$th (3.8 percent)

[60] Ibid., p. 320.
[61] See David M. Wilson, "Craft and Industry," pp. 253–82 in Wilson, *A.A.S.E.*, esp. pp. 276, 281.

of a normal mill.[62] No mill appears at any of the Candover manors, eight holdings of various sizes, divided among Brown, Preston, and Chilton Candover. The absence of a mill here might reflect the fact that the upper Candover valley was as dry as it is now, with a running stream only during the winter and spring. This was not necessarily the case in the eleventh century, and the absence may be the result of a decision or oversight on the part of the Domesday commissioners. The three manorial blocks of the Candover valley lay in Mainsborough and Bermondspitt hundreds, and their details were probably recorded by a different team of assessors than those at Micheldever.[63] There was a different phrasing to the hidage assessment in Welford and Bermondspitt hundreds. The absence of mills is further evidence for differences between survey teams, or between hundred appearances at shire sessions of the Domesday Inquest.

The ownership of churches in the Micheldever region is recorded much less often than that of mills. Only six churches are listed, and here again the reason may be a difference in recording hundred returns. Churches appear only in Barton and Buddlesgate hundreds; the compilers of Domesday must not have received information on the renders from churches at manors in the other hundreds of middle Hampshire. One church of the six is given a value; it was at Stoke Charity, was held by "Mauger," and was worth 15s, the same value as a mill. Elsewhere in Hampshire, churches were valued from 5s to 20s.[64]

A final example of middle Hampshire Domesday entries of non-arable resources is the presence of *hagae* (burgage property) in Winchester. One *haga* worth 17d belonged to a Preston Candover manor, and Norton manor had 5 *hagae* worth 10s. The practice of attaching Winchester tenements to rural manors is well attested and is thought to have been so widespread that Martin Biddle and Derek Keene, plotting the distribution of such holdings, suggested that it was a means by which "inhabitants of the country were guaranteed accommodation within the defences of Winchester in times of trouble."[65] They based their views on Domesday Book, early charters, and the two surveys of Winchester

---

[62] Finn suggested that the absence of mills could indicate the local use of handmills: *Introduction to Domesday*, p. 188. This is unlikely; compared to the Iron Age or Romano-British period, querns are not an integral component of the eleventh-century Hampshire village artifactual assemblage. A donkey or ox mill, however, is an obvious alternative, which could also be listed among those entries assumed to be water mills.

[63] Finn observed that Bermondspitt Hundred had no recorded mills, and assumed it was due to the altitude of the hundred: *Domesday Geography*, p. 348. He did not mention that Mainsborough Hundred farther downstream also lacked mills.

[64] Finn, *Domesday Geography*, p. 349, recognized the poor recording of churches, but did not treat it at the hundred level.

[65] Biddle and Keene, "Winchester in the Eleventh and Twelfth Centuries," *Winchester in the Early Middle Ages*, pp. 382–83, Table 12. Compare figure 20 (p. 385) of Biddle and Keene with the unpaginated map in *Domesday Book: Hampshire*. See also Welldon Finn, *Domesday Geography*, pp. 353–54.

of the early twelfth century. A closer inspection of the Domesday entries for middle Hampshire manors with Winchester tenements, however, reveals that these can be found in only five of the fifteen hundreds into which the region was divided: Ashley (1), Barton (3), Basingstoke (2), Bermondspitt (2), and Somborne (2). That the ten manors of middle Hampshire with Winchester *hagae* were concentrated in five hundreds, while ten other hundreds had no such manors, seems good evidence for another discrepancy in the Domesday Book. In those five hundreds (including Barton and Bermondspitt for which recording differences have been noted above), Winchester properties were among the items included on the survey, while in the other ten hundreds, this information does not appear and was probably not recorded.

The preceding review of the non-arable resources noted in Domesday Book partly reveals the particulars of the eleventh-century manors around Micheldever; it even more fully illustrates the dangers that beset interpretations of the Domesday Book entries. Figure 4.5 depicts the recorded presence of non-arable resources in the manors around Micheldever: meadow, pasture, wood, and mills and churches. Of these five resources, only meadow land is noted with regularity, and even here there are curious gaps. The inclusion of the other four elements in the Domesday Book (and the *hagae* in Winchester) depended upon the hundred in which they lay—and upon the interest taken in those items by some combination of testamentary jury, survey team, and clerical compiler for that hundred.

Figure 4.6 illustrates the types of items found in the entries for the manors around Micheldever, divided into their respective hundreds. The geography of these manors is generally similar, though with more potential meadow land in the low-lying terrain along the lower Dever and Test. The royal hundred of Barton had the most extensive list, while Bountisborough and Buddlegate had somewhat fewer items, and the remaining hundreds recorded little in the way of non-arable resources.

Regional or national comparison of these economic, tenurial, and social data is unreliable. Because the particulars were unequally collected and recorded on a hundred-by-hundred basis,[66] broadly quantifiable figures, as appear in *The Domesday Geography of England*, are therefore highly suspect, but some approaches to quantifying the material may not be as misleading. The Domesday entries can be successfully compared if the manors lie in hundreds that were surveyed by the same criteria in 1086. The result might be applicable to only a portion of the total number of manors in a region, but it would be more reliable.

---

[66] The Domesday assessors used information supplied by the tenants-in-chief, but it was certainly checked and compiled at the hundred court sessions. See Frederick F. Kreisler, "Domesday Book and the Anglo-Norman Synthesis," pp. 3–16 in *Order and Innovation in the Middle Ages: Essays in Honor of Joseph R. Strayer*, W. C. Jordan, et al., ed. (Princeton, 1976).

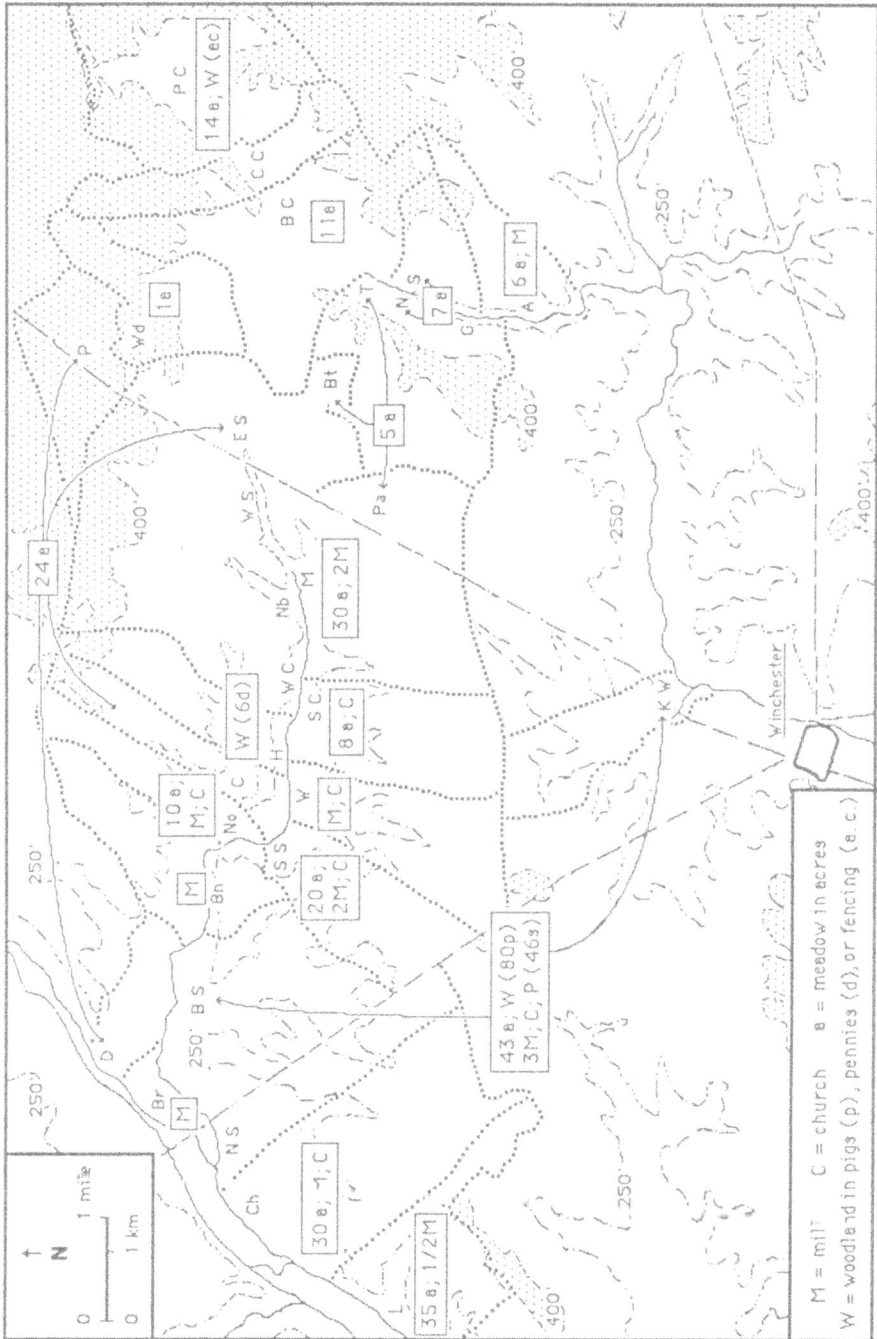

Fig. 4.5 Domesday Non-Arable Resources

M = mill   C = church   a = meadow in acres
W = woodland in pigs (p), pennies (d), or fencing (a.c.)

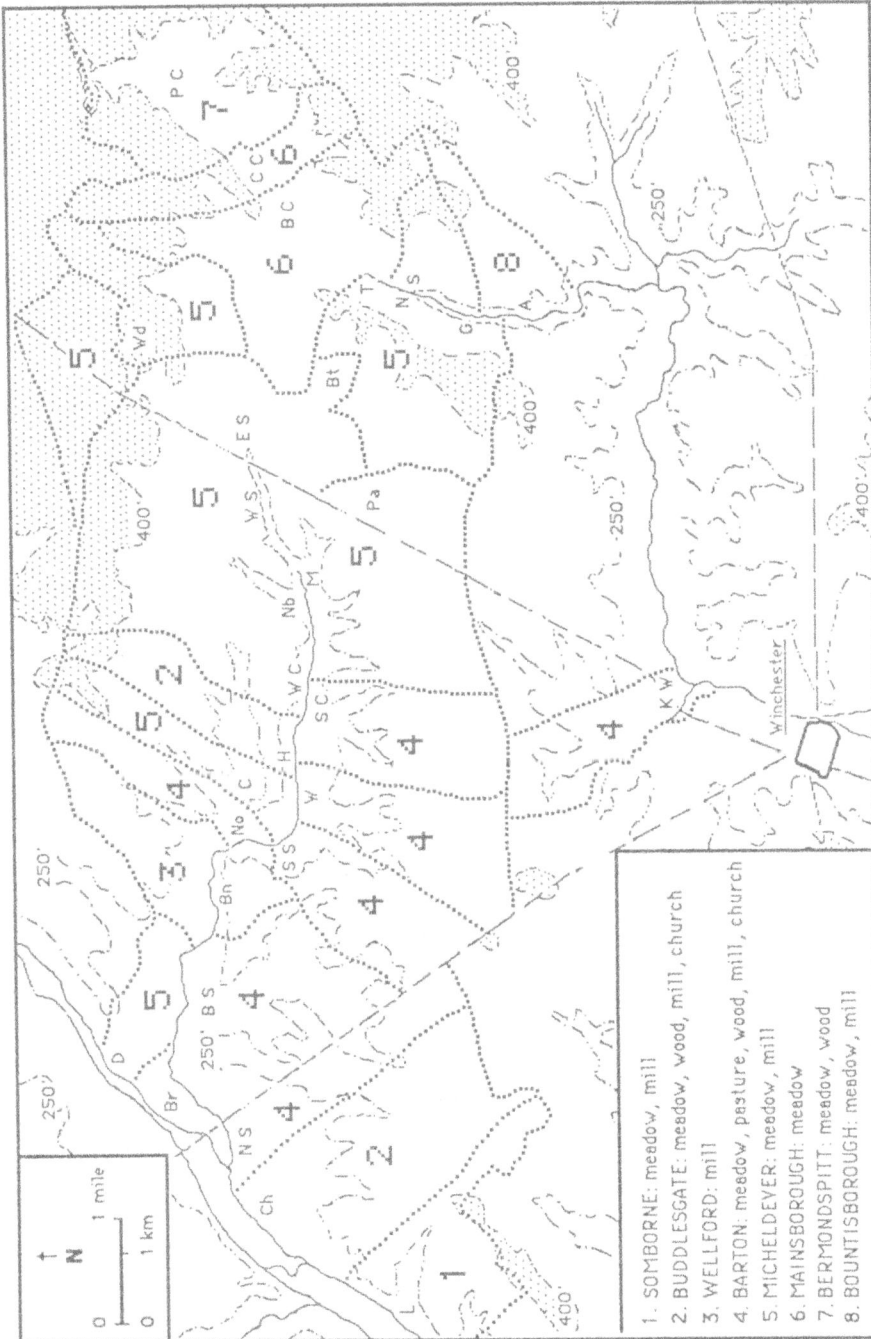

FIG. 4.6 Domesday Criteria, Reported by Hundred

1. SOMBORNE: meadow, mill
2. BUDDLESGATE: meadow, wood, mill, church
3. WELLFORD: mill
4. BARTON: meadow, pasture, wood, mill, church
5. MICHELDEVER: meadow, mill
6. MAINSBOROUGH: meadow
7. BERMONDSPITT: meadow, wood
8. BOUNTISBOROUGH: meadow, mill

Conclusions

The information in the Domesday Book respecting the manors of the Micheldever area serves as a guide to their size and value, but only conditionally. The Domesday hidage figures are not fully comparable, since the hidage of many if not most middle Hampshire manors was beneficially reduced. Moreover, the figures for manorial renders or values show disparities between similar-sized manors, suggesting that other, unrecorded factors contributed to a manor's assessment or render. Also, the criteria for recording workers and their categories were poorly defined and may have been used differently by each team of assessors. These difficulties must seriously qualify conclusions made by comparing manorial valuations and population figures. The recorded entries for plough teams may be a firmer indicator of economic value, but only for arable production. Even so, a manor's production cannot be readily gauged because of the poorly understood differences between the number of plough teams for which there was land available, the number on the demesne, and the number in the vill.

Another area for cautious use of Domesday material is the non-arable resources of the manor: meadow, pasture, wood, mill, church, and urban property. The recording of these items was haphazard, with such resources surveyed for some hundreds and not for others.[67] As a consequence, these types of resources can be used properly only when comparing manors in hundreds that were similarly surveyed in 1086.

Keeping these limitations in mind, some observations can be made. A pattern appears when the number of ploughs or plough lands is compared to the valuation or render of a manor, TRE, later, or in 1086 (see Appendix B). It is more likely than not that one of the first figures (arable) will be similar or identical to one of the latter (monetary) figures. In seven of fifteen cases examined, one of the plough team sums equaled one of the values in pounds silver. In other cases, the figures were close, though not identical. It seems that at some stage, there existed a rough—or direct—equivalency of £1 value/render for each plough team.[68] Other factors or assets no doubt came to contribute to a manor's worth, and altered the equivalency. As with other problems in the Domesday Book, this is an area where detailed quantitative analysis on a large scale could isolate conditions common to manors with the original equivalency and other conditions common to those manors whose values have changed.

---

[67] These findings therefore support and expand Finn's general observation on the Domesday Survey, that "in some Hundreds, the authorities do not seem to have troubled to make a return of certain items": *Introduction to Domesday*, p. 168. Baring had noted that the proportion of teamlands to hides varied widely in different hundreds, and in different villages within the same hundred: *Domesday Tables*, p. 7.

[68] Maitland found a similar tendency. He concluded that conflicting assessments were based on different formulae: 1 hide = 1 team land *vs* 1 hide = £1. *D.B.B.*, pp. 470–73.

In the Micheldever area, the unitary manors most often retained the equivalency, while the large multiple estates did not. Further, the small manors within the large estates (such as Micheldever) showed no equivalency, but perhaps here the Domesday Survey was not equipped to inquire into complicated intra-manorial arrangements. Perhaps typical of administrative record keeping, it seems that only those answers in response to specific questions were required or desired, despite how incomplete or inappropriate they may have been.

Analysis reveals a second pattern in the Domesday records. Population estimates made by this study often appear in a similar mathematical ratio to the figures for the 1086 valuations. Abbotstone with 75 inhabitants rendered £6. At Bransbury 60 rendered £6. At Bullington 63 rendered £7, and the three manors of Brown Candover, with populations of 94, 3, and 15, rendered £10, £1, £7 respectively. Chilton's 55 rendered £7. The Preston Candover holdings were 53: £5; 14: £1.5; 18: £4; 59: £5; 16: £2.5. Owing to variations and exceptions (e.g., Chilton and Brown Candover), the equation is imperfect, but it appears that in many cases, each £1 of a manor's valuation corresponded to 10 members of its estimated population.[69] This confirms the expectation that the size of the village community generally corresponds to manorial value.

These observations can be applied to the broad question of early medieval economic levels. The following argument proposes a conjectural figure for economic growth: If each £1 of a manor's value corresponded roughly to ten inhabitants, and if a household on average had five members, then each family was responsible for the render on £½ (or 120 pence). According to the early eleventh-century formula noted above, ten pence was the return (as rent) for each yard land (¼ hide).[70] A hypothetical Micheldever peasant family would therefore account for three hides. This does not include other types of manorial workers and their contribution in cultivated yard lands, but if the figures are not too far off, they point to an increase in agricultural productivity beyond the original 1:1 equivalency of household to hide that is connoted by the word *hiwisc* of the earliest records. The implication is that farmland and/or productivity increased three-fold in the four centuries 700 to 1100.

---

[69] As a check on the population estimate, the recorded free workforce comprising *villani* and *bordarii* for these villages was examined. It was found to be twice the valuation (plus or minus 10 percent) in six (50 percent) of the above twelve manors. Even as great variables as the recorded work force therefore had a significantly standard arithmetical relationship to the monetary renders.

[70] In the *Rectitudines Singularum Personarum*, the *gebur* was provided with a house and farming capital for a ten pence rent: *Gesetze*, Vol. I, pp. 444–53; translated in *E.H.D.* II, pp. 813–16.

V. THE EARLY MEDIEVAL LANDSCAPE

EVIDENCE OF LAND USE

Anglo-Saxon charters and Domesday Book entries describe estates and their components, but information on field systems *per se* is generally restricted to later medieval manorial records. Those of the hundredal manor of Micheldever are a good source for early medieval land use. References to field systems, woodland development, village extents, and the road network appear in the material incorporated in the late medieval copies of the Hyde Abbey Cartulary.[1] Most of the records are of thirteenth- and fourteenth-century date, and consist of abbreviated notes of land transactions, donations, and leases directly involving the abbey. (This material is presented in condensed form in Appendix A.) The named agricultural units, the fields and woods, were usually accompanied by a location or description by which one can recreate their physical lay-out. The sections of field systems associated with such field names can be compared to the land units and fossilized field boundaries recorded on estate and tithe award maps of the eighteenth and nineteenth centuries. Little in the way of pre-Conquest patterns of land use could survive directly the millennium from 800 to 1800, but the later evidence can explain and clarify earlier references. Because later medieval field names occasionally contain names or references from the pre-Conquest period, details particularly suited to long-range study are landscape features and manorial and parochial boundaries.

Estate and Tithe Award Maps

The Hampshire County Record Office contains several maps that bear upon the study of the field systems of Micheldever Hundred. Foremost is the series of maps accompanying Tithe Awards, undertaken in the early nineteenth century when the government restructured the financial basis of parishes. Maps exist for most of the parishes in the Micheldever region, and each presents a large scale plan of a parish (at 25 inches to the mile), with a list of the names of all fields and woods. On

---

[1] Anglo-Saxon charters were collected in B. L. Lansdowne MS 717; the major cartulary is B. L. Harleian MS 1761, and its copy is in B. L. Cotton MS Dom. A xiv. Edward Edwards reviewed the cartularies in *Liber de Hida*.

the maps appear field and wood boundaries, roads, tracks, and buildings, as well as certain natural features, such as streams and ponds. For
this study, scaled copies of the Tithe Award maps were made for parishes that cover the medieval manors of the Micheldever valley: Sutton
Scotney, Wonston, Stoke Charity, Bullington, Hunton, Norton, Cranbourne, Popham, Stratton, Woodmancott, Micheldever and its dependencies.[2] These maps were supplemented by a series of eighteenth-century estate maps for Micheldever lands and others detailing the late
eighteenth-century enclosure of village common pastures.[3] The Micheldever estate maps show that the manor included all the present Micheldever parish, i.e., Micheldever, with the tithings of Weston Colley,
Northbrook, West Stratton, East Stratton, and the smaller units of Godwinsdown and Burcot. The early medieval property of Papenholt had
by then become Micheldever Wood, part of Southbrook Tithing of Micheldever. Details of both groups of maps were compared to the larger
scale Ordnance Survey first edition 6″ map (1869) and to Isaac Taylor's
map of Hampshire (1759).[4]

Manorial Records

The Hyde Abbey Cartulary (B.L. Harl. MS 1761) contains entries of
rents and quitclaims to Micheldever lands from the late twelfth and early
thirteenth centuries to the end of the Middle Ages. These records concern only Micheldever Manor, and indicate that in the late medieval
period Micheldever was kept as a demesne manor, while subsidiary
manors at Woodmancott, East and West Stratton, Bransbury, Popham,
etc., were farmed out, or held by knight's fee only. The Micheldever
lands were divided into several tithings corresponding to "vills": Weston, Northbrook, and Southbrook, as well as the smaller holding of
Godwinsdown and Papenholt. The cartulary also records leases and
quitclaims of pasture and woodland in the Micheldever tithings and in
the Strattons, Popham, and Woodmancott. The field, pasture, and wood
names have been collected and assigned to their respective land units
(see Appendix B). Many of the names appear in altered form on the

---

[2] H.R.O.: Map Index, Tithe Award List. Entries there are not numbered, but entered
according to the nineteenth-century parish name.
[3] **Micheldever:** H.R.O. 11M52/488 Burcott Coppice (17C.), 516 Beckhurst land (1698),
519 church crofts (n.d.); 2M51/3 Southbrook tithing, 11 East Stratton, 12 West Stratton, 14
Micheldever, 15 Stratton Park and Home Farm (19C.).
   Wonston: H.R.O. 38M48/62 Tithe Award tracing. (1859 parish), 33M62 Enclosure Agreement (n.d.).
   Bullington: H.R.O. 5M64/24 Tithe Award copy (n.d.), 76 tracing of West Bullington
estate map (n.d.).
   Barton Stacey: H.R.O. 8M61/26–28 three tracings of map. Tithe? (n.d.), 62/75 Bransbury
Manor Farm (1857).
[4] H.R.O: 1M4e/10,11; 34M62.

eighteenth-century estate maps and the nineteenth-century Tithe Award maps. The names and locational descriptions in the cartulary entries permit some of the place names to be firmly located, and they are so indicated on Figure 5.1.

The late medieval manorial records make two important contributions to the understanding of medieval land use at Micheldever. First is the nature of the field systems themselves. Each medieval settlement or manorial division had its own field extending up from the valley bottom to include pasture and woodland on the flanking ridge lines. The post-medieval estate maps for Micheldever recorded the field subdivisions and their names in the tithings of Weston, Northbrook, and Southbrook. There is a major difference in the fields of the thirteenth-century cartulary records and those of the eighteenth-century estate. In the post-medieval period, all the vills have three fields (West, Middle, and East Common Field), but the thirteenth-century land transactions refer to only two fields at each vill. The placement of identifiable field section names on Figure 5.1 shows that a previous middle field could not have passed unrecognized.

The introduction of the three-field system to Micheldever can have occurred no earlier than the second quarter of the fourteenth century, the latest firm recording of the two fields alone, and no later than the beginning of the fifteenth century, when a document of 1415 refers to triennial rotation (see Appendix A, Wriothesley Documents, No. 177), as does another of 1651. The change followed a local expansion of arable. The lands of the vicar of Micheldever (Appendix A, No. 118, ca. 1310) have field names that can be found later in the Southbrook Cow Down (East) Common Field, including Midfurlong (Middlefurlong), La Schulve (The Shelves), and the land of St. Johns of Winchester (St. Johns Croft east of the highway). These identifications may mark the earliest appearance of arable land in what before had presumably been a large pasture, the Cow Down. The expansion of arable land at Micheldever is likely to have taken place in the early fourteeth century, and was followed by a redistribution of lands aong three fields. This redistribution was unrecorded, but it is certain. Equally certain is its absence from East and West Stratton. The estate maps show that East Stratton retained a simple two-field system, and West Stratton an infield-outfield system. The conditions on these five land units substantiate Joan Thirsk's contention that the medieval field system fully evolved only in the thirteenth century, and in many places the classic form never appeared.[5]

The second set of information supplied by medieval manorial documents concerns the extent of woodland. While the records are far too

---

[5] Joan Thirsk, "The Common Fields," *Past and Present* 23 (Dec. 1964), pp. 3–25. Postan, *Medieval Economy and Society*, p. 55, proposed that most localities employed both the two-field system and the three-field system.

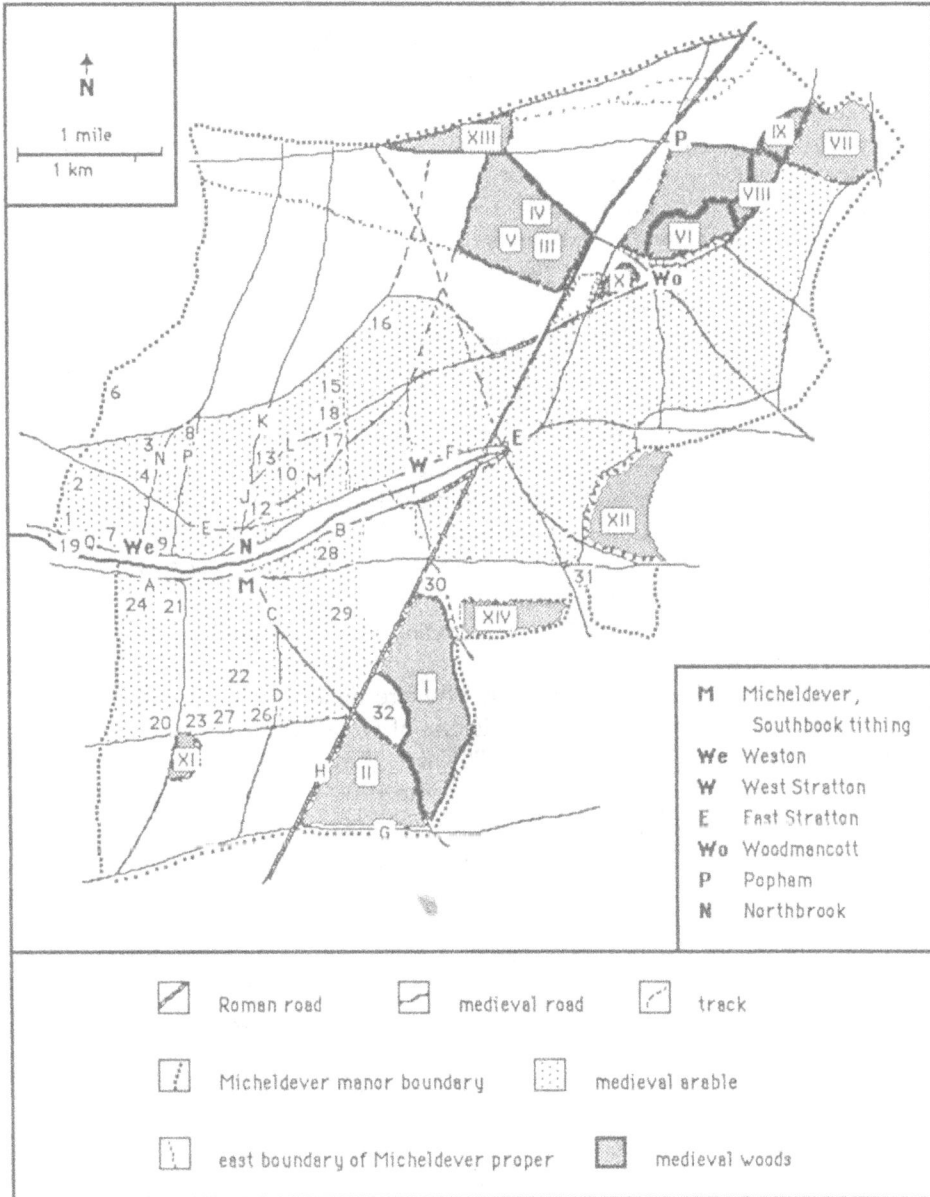

FIG. 5.1 Landscape Features of Medieval Micheldever

sketchy to describe accurately all the woodland in Micheldever manor, there is a series of references to assarting from the late twelfth through the fourteenth centuries (see Appendix A). There were *vasti* of woods called: the Hurst, Elvenholt of Woodmancott; Lessewood, the Sturt, and Bradley of West Stratton; Rowehurst of East Stratton; Baldredsely (Bazely Copse) and Papenholt of Micheldever. *Frussico* (friscus, newly cleared land), *sefrem, solum, kekum,* and *hacio* (enclosures) are terms used to describe the results of the assarting. Papenholt contained an enclosure called *Wlfladecrofte* (Wulfleda's croft), and ca. 1320, two hundred oaks were illicitly removed from the forest, so it was still a large wood.

The later Middle Ages saw the extensive clearance of woodland in Woodmancott, East and West Stratton, and in Papenholt. All these places lay in the upper reaches of the Dever valley, and it is likely that the high, often poor ground of the watershed between the Micheldever and Candover valleys had been heavily wooded in the early Middle Ages. The cleared land that belonged to early settlements like Burcot and *Ticcesham* (Woodmancott) had probably been restricted to narrow fields and pastures along the valley bottoms where chalk soils were flanked by higher ground of Clay-with-Flints. The boundary points of the Micheldever charter (S360) that pertain to the east side of the estate are sixteen in number, of which seven are wood names. The lands along the watershed here would have been the last to be cleared. There were wide areas of intractable Clay-with-Flints, and no streamside meadows that could provide enough winter food for the oxen required to support a village-size population. The few settlements in the woods were to remain small and unimportant.

The medieval field systems and woodland of Micheldever are recon-structed on Figure 5.3. Field names indicative of land use are the basis for the suggested reconstruction of the pre-Enclosure medieval land-scape, illustrating the land-use divisions of wood, pasture, arable, and meadow (see Appendix A). The 1730 estate map supplies the common fields for each village, and they are identified as W (west), M (middle), and E (east), where appropriate. Figure 5.3 also depicts the known lo-cation of medieval mills, at which all local grain would have been pro-cessed. Where evidence is lacking, the land use of some areas has been extrapolated from that recorded for adjacent properties. After the Middle Ages, further woodland was cleared, and by the eighteenth and nine-teenth centuries, most of the land here came to be cultivated as arable.

Increased population permitted and necessitated the expansion of ar-able land in the post-Conquest period, but before then population had not reached the level needed for arable dominance. Much smaller fields, and corresponding larger pasture and woodland, had comprised the early medieval landscape. Meadow land probably changed little. It could be argued that the field name evidence for former woods and pasture (downland) refers only to conditions at the end of the Middle Ages, when a lower population and a higher demand for wool caused else-where a sharp reduction in the amount of land under cereal cultivation.[6]

---

[6] Late medieval population and economic changes are best described in Maurice Beres-ford, *The Lost Villages of England* (London, 1954). His arguments are refined in his contri-bution to Maurice Beresford and John G. Hurst, ed., *Deserted Medieval Villages* (London, 1971). See also John Hatcher, *Plague, Population, and the English Economy 1348–1530* (Lon-don, 1977); and M. M. Postan, *The Medieval Economy and Society: An Economic History of Britain 1100–1500* (Berkeley, Cal., 1972).

Yet, the Micheldever estate map shows the common fields surviving until 1730, with only small areas having been enclosed. Moreover, land documents of the twelfth and thirteenth centuries indicate that woodland was being converted to arable land and pasture land at that time. The evidence therefore suggests no late medieval pastoral movement at Micheldever, and the general outline of post-medieval land use reflects that of the medieval manor.

Hedgerow Dating

Elements of medieval landscapes can sometimes be recreated without the use of documents. Archaeological examination of the relationship between field boundaries can often establish a relative chronological framework for portions of the field system. Another method of dating field systems is that proposed by Dr. M.D. Hooper, Senior Scientific Officer of the Nature Conservancy, by which hedgerows can be dated by the number of plant species within them, thus supplying a *terminus ante quem* for the fields they enclose.[7] Using hedgerows that appeared in medieval documents as the basis for computation, Dr. Hooper arrived

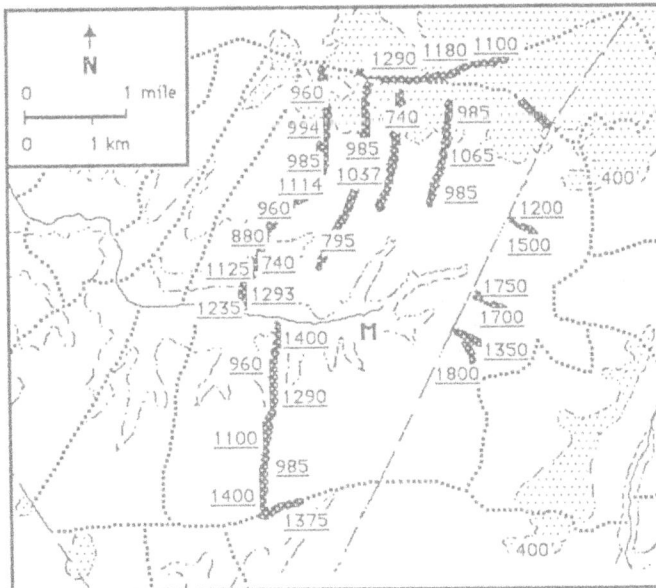

FIG. 5.2 Hedgerow Dating at Micheldever

---

[7] See M. D. Hooper, "Hedges and Local History," pp. 6–15 in *Hedges in Local History*, The Standing Conference on Local History, National Council of Social Service (London, 1971).

at a formula of general application: Age of hedge + 50 years = (110 years x number of plant species in a thirty yard section) + 30 years.[8]

A number of hedges in the Micheldever manor have been studied and sampled following the Hooper formula.[9] The results of the hedgerow sampling are presented on Figure 5.2. They consist of five north-south continuous hedges, a type which W.G. Hoskins considered a good indicator of an early date,[10] and eight short east-west hedges, most of which lie in East Stratton, east of the Roman road. Portions of the two hedge lines that mark the western boundary of Micheldever manor may date back to the Anglo-Saxon period. Late medieval dates appear for the hedges on the northern and southern extremities of the manor, areas where common pasture land was partially enclosed at the end of the Middle Ages. Yet the northern portions of Weston Colley tithing, a holding called Godwinsdown, and Northbrook tithing were downland pasture throughout the Middle Ages, and were only converted to arable land in the modern period. The tenth- and early eleventh-century dates for the hedges there suggest that the common pasture downland was divided in late Saxon times among the lands of the individual villages and hamlets. The western and eastern sides of the Godwinsdown holding suggest an even earlier origin for these field systems.[11] In contrast, portions of a hedge bordering former woodland north of East Stratton may date ca. 1200, while the east-west hedges south of the village have species counts indicating an origin in the 1700s, which corresponds well to enclosure changes marked on the 1730 estate map.

The dates of Micheldever hedgerows derived from the Hooper hypothesis formula are supported by the historical data. Godwinsdown, for instance, can be traced back to at least 1222–49. The application of

---

[8] Early medieval hedges were usually made of a single shrub (e.g., hawthorne), but were colonized naturally by other species at the approximate rate of one every century. Dr. Hooper cautions that the formula is not applicable to certain areas where farmers traditionally planted mixed hedges (e.g., Shropshire). He also notes that his formula is not accurate within the past two centuries, nor above ten or twelve species.

[9] In 1973–74, Dr. Hooper himself, assisted by me, examined a series of hedges running perpendicular to the Roman road (modern A33) in Popham and East Stratton. In 1976, hedgerows on the north and the west sides of the Micheldever estate were sampled as part of a survey of that parish. P. J. Fasham, Director of Excavations for the M3 Archaeological Rescue Committee, sponsored both surveys and has kindly permitted the use of this material from the M.A.R.C.3 files in the offices of the Wessex Archaeological Unit, Salisbury.

[10] W. G. Hoskins, "Historical Sources for Hedge Dating," pp. 14–19 in *Hedges and Local History*, esp. p. 17. Professor Hoskins was supportive of the Hooper approach, and considered hedges "valuable evidence" that was being destroyed at a great pace through urban expansion and agricultural change.

[11] The greater number of species at these points must be accepted with caution. They may have been the locations of earlier field boundaries, not necessarily on the same alignment as the later Saxon divisions. Similarly, the very early date of 660 for the boundary between Popham and West Stratton is at the limit of the dating formula's range. Forest edges are always possible sources of contamination, and the Blackwood (*Blakewud*) across a track south of the hedge appears to be of ancient origin.

Hooper's formula to the Micheldever manorial boundaries suggests that the territorial entities of Weston Colley, Godwinsdown, and Northbrook have been in existence for one thousand years. These poorly documented tithings are equivalent to most parishes of the Micheldever area. Both are strips perpendicular to the stream, complete economic units with proportional amounts of available land types and land uses. The boundaries of both types of manorial unit continued north from the arable through what was common pasture and woodland on the high downs. The presence of hedgerows here dating back at least to the tenth century would mean that the pasture of each unit of the Micheldever estate was not open, common land, but was available only to the inhabitants of the particular tithing hamlet. It is tempting to associate the creation of these divisions with the late tenth-century appearance of land tenure for money rents or military service.[12] Eighth-century dates suggested by several sections of hedgerow might reveal the presence of earlier field systems which overlapped or coincided with the lines of the later arrangement of perhaps more thoroughly hedged divisions. That period saw great changes in the countryside, especially in the movement and establishment of new settlements.

PATTERNS OF LAND USE

The general distribution of medieval land-use types closely followed the geography of the Micheldever valley. Meadow land was confined to the valley bottom, i.e., along the banks of the Dever, and in the Cranbourne side valley. Arable lands extended throughout the base of the valley and along the lower slopes. Pasture was at the higher elevations where it competed with woodland, which was usually confined to the more exposed positions. An exception to the pattern is the upland village of Popham, where there was no meadow, and the arable land seems to have been the result of woodland clearance from the village center. Burcot and Woodmancott lie in branch valleys of the upper Dever drainage system. Their shared toponymic element and their small size reveal that they were satellite settlements. If the relation of their field systems to the habitation center is indicative of the direction in which their original manorial association lay, Woodmancott was originally associated with Stratton, and Burcot with Totford or Northington.

When used in the context of local estate development, the details of charter boundaries can reconstruct the basic elements of an Anglo-Saxon landscape. Some boundaries were ancient, important territorial divi-

---

[12] Military tenure and rents are best documented by the bishop of Worcester's Liberty of Oswaldslow, the literature on which is reviewed in Eric John, *Land Tenure in Early England* (Leicester, 1960), pp. 80–161. It is John's contention that the cathedral's liberties included military service, and that this combination was the beginning of English feudalism.

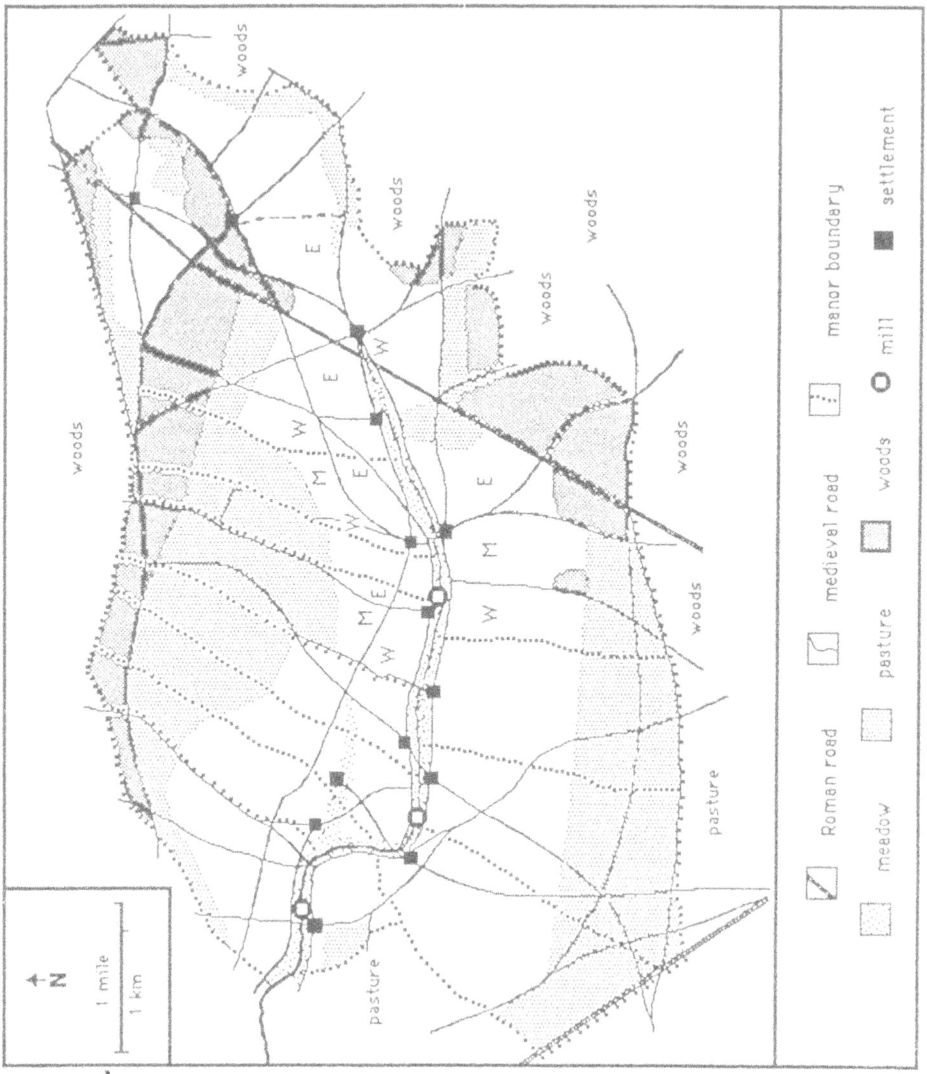

Fig. 5.3 The Reconstructed Early Medieval Landscape

sions, while others reveal themselves to be arbitrary sections of previously integral properties. Place names on the latter bounds, therefore, should indicate the sort of conditions that would be found *inside* an estate. Wood place-name elements on the Anglo-Saxon charters of the Micheldever valley show that its northern and eastern sides were heavily wooded in the early Middle Ages. In the thirteenth century, certainly, widespread assarting took place in Woodmancott; there was still room for agricultural expansion. Because Papenholt was never cleared for arable land, it became the post-medieval Micheldever Wood.

There is no such evidence for woodland on the southern and western sides of the Dever valley. South of the Dever, where now only one small wood remains west of Micheldever village, there is no indication that woodland had been much greater in historic times. The pattern of medieval agricultural expansion, where arable replaced pasture, and pasture replaced woodland, has no documentation in the southwestern Micheldever valley. Indeed, in the Anglo-Saxon charters, the common woodland terms *wudu*, *grafan*, and *leah* were not used for any of the place names on the boundaries there. One must conclude that this area had only minimal wood cover, probably restricted to small, scattered groves on patches of Clay-with-Flints. The smaller cultivatable area and the distance from the population centers suggest that the early medieval land use here was pasture, on a very large scale. The time frame for the extension of arable land and the clearance of woodland is less definite for the entire Micheldever valley. Yet the available evidence for the "woodland to pasture to arable" sequence here does not necessarily support Peter Sawyer's hypothesis that the Anglo-Saxon countryside was fully exploited.[13] Perhaps much depends upon the term "exploitation"— here it could be used in the sense that the pre-Conquest rural population was taking advantage of its resources. The amount of meadow land and the presence of watermills in the eleventh century suggest that capital was being invested in agricultural improvements, perhaps first on estates of the Church. Nevertheless, it was a process, not a state, a beginning to the growth that would lead to the full exploitation—and then over-exploitation—of the land in the later Middle Ages.

THE ROAD SYSTEM

The relationship of settlement and land use to other elements of the landscape was anything but static. Rural development can be seen to react continually to the influences of climate, technology, and socioeconomic demands. Yet the settlements and accompanying fields, pastures, and woods are necessarily reconstructed in isolation. The sources

---

[13] Sawyer's views are outlined in *Medieval Settlement*, pp. 1–7.

reveal the landscape features but not their part in a manorial or village unity, and each manor/village is treated in isolation from the regional whole. To integrate the other landscape elements and bind them together into a single unit of rural development, one further element of the landscape remains to be discussed: the early medieval road network.

The road system is in two ways valuable to the study of settlement and land use. As its primary function is of course communication, the relative importance of population centers is revealed by the status of the links between them. And as roads also typically served as major property and agricultural boundaries, they help identify those land divisions.

Certain roads in Micheldever Hundred can be identified by name from the late medieval and post-medieval sources (see Appendix B and Figure 5.1). The 1730 estate map of Micheldever names the route leading west from Micheldever village as "Sloe Lane" (A), the one leading northeast as "Coach Lane" (B), and that leading south as "Hawthorne Lane" (C). Because these names do not appear on earlier records, they may not have medieval origins. Along a track branching to the south from Hawthorne Lane were lands named "Millway" and "Drove Way" (D). This road may be identified as the "millweye" (*iter molendini*) of the manorial documents. The "Token Way" (E) of the 1730 estate map is the road leading northwest from Northbrook, and it is traceable farther west in the Tithe Award maps for Hunton, Wonston, and Bullington parishes.

Medieval manorial records mention several roads within Micheldever manor. The road between East Stratton and West Stratton (F) needed repair at the place called "le fforde." Traffic from Micheldever to Stratton went on the *regiam stratam*, presumably the same route as that of the *itineris regalis* appearing in several documents. South of Papenholt was the "Lundeneweye" (G) coming from Totford, and west of the wood lay the highway from Winchester to Reading, on the old Roman route (H). In Northbrook, lands in the west field bordered upon a "brodeweye" (L), that separated it from the west field, and "Stuvinghemeweye" (M) to Steventon. In Southbrook tithing were the above-mentioned "mill weye" (D) and "la Portweye de Westone," which should be the post-medieval "Sloe Lane" (A). In Weston tithing, lands in the east field bordered upon "la naperes weye" (N), the "tokingeweye" earlier referred to (E), and the *stratam regiam quae ducit versus Overtone* (P), Overton being a village on the upper Test.[14] Repair orders went out repeatedly for the *via alta regis* in the village of Weston called "traypath" or "tray pathway," for which ditches were to be dug on the northern and southern sides of the road. The description of the ditches proves that it definitely ran east-to-west, and of the two east-west roads at Weston, the

---

[14] "La naperes weye" could refer to a monastic official, the "naperer," the keeper of the napery, where the table linen was stored. The office of naperer of Hyde Abbey may have entailed business with towns on the upper Test, or had a particular field allotment, perhaps even reserved for flax growing for table linen.

upper one went by "Toking way," so the one by the bank of the Dever (Q) should be the "traypath" that was often flooded.[15] The medieval royal road thus passed along the south bank east of Micheldever, crossing there and heading via Weston on the north bank to ford again at Stoke Charity or continue to Hunton and Wonston. This apparent peculiarity is actually a sensible route for vehicular traffic, because the north bank of the Dever is fairly level, while the south side is a series of ridges and valleys considerably more difficult to traverse.

The reconstruction of the medieval road system of the Micheldever area on Figure 5.3 shows a dominant village-to-village pattern, a second group of tracks and lanes serving the fields, and a third series of herding "droveways" along the ridge lines.[16] Except around Winchester itself, Roman roads were no longer part of the local communication network. Even where a *straet* remained an important landscape feature, it is not known how much it was used, or indeed how suitable its surface was for medieval traffic.[17] Micheldever was the focus of a local road network, as would be expected for the *caput* of an hundredal manor. Above the flood level of the streamside meadow land, twin roads followed the banks of the Dever stream. These parallel roads were intersected at the Micheldever ford by two cross-country routes: one from the northeast, from Woodmancott, Popham, and eventually London; the other from the northwest, the "Toking Way" of the nineteenth-century tithe maps, leading to a crossing of the Test River, perhaps originally at Drayton, then later at Tufton (earlier "Tochington"). From Micheldever, the way to Winchester followed alternate routes south. Side roads went east and southeast through the woodland separating the Micheldever valley from that of the Candover. The Dever valley roads were also intersected at Bullington and Sutton Scotney, where routes from Whitchurch on the upper Test crossed toward Winchester. In the northeast of the Micheldever area, tracks connected Popham and Woodmancott with the Candovers. Other middle-distance routes passed through Hunton and East Stratton, where tracks obliquely cross the landscape southwest to the Somborne valley and southeast to the Candover valley.

---

[15] The boundaries of the Micheldever 901 charter (S360) came westward from Papenholt via a series of locations to follow a military road (*herpath*) to a tree (*Ecgulfes treo*) and from there along another road (*herpath*) to a Micheldever stream. It is possible that the later medieval "tray path" was the path by the tree of the charter, but it is difficult to explain how the boundary passed from Papenholt to Weston without mentioning the Dever or any of the settlements along it.

[16] The basis of the reconstruction is similar to that employed by Christopher Taylor in *Roads and Tracks of Britain* (London, 1979), i.e., documentary references plus structure and route. He recognized that a rural road system cannot be studied separately from the local field systems and the wider transportation needs. See pp. 103–110 for Saxon village communities, esp. p. 108 for the absolute necessity of walking the routes under consideration.

[17] Excavation of the Roman road by Stratton suggested that it was the site of a middle Saxon settlement and that the road had been repaired in late Saxon times. See P. J. Fashion, "Fieldwork and Excavations at East Stratton along the Roman Road from Winchester to Silchester," *Proc. Hants. Archaeol. Soc.* 37 (1981), pp. 165–88.

The medieval road network, as recreated from medieval and post-medieval sources, thus reinforces the observed settlement pattern of small villages occurring at regular intervals along the Dever stream. Alternate routes, perhaps of prehistoric origin, passed along the high ground forming the Micheldever valley watershed. The medieval road system reflects both the importance of Micheldever as a local center and the irrelevance of Roman roads to the local transportation network.

THE EVOLVING LANDSCAPE

Even with the integrating effects of the road system, surviving sources unevenly reveal the evolution of landscape features. Charters of the eighth and ninth centuries give only a few, general place-names. The lengthy lists of Anglo-Saxon boundary points are characteristic of the tenth century only, a change in charter detail contemporary with the smaller size of grant. Such detailed lists were apparently obsolete by the eleventh century, when charter boundaries were again restricted to a few major landmarks. This development may be related to the increasing acceptability of witness testimony, seen in the use of juries of presentment and in the Domesday panels of local witnesses.[18]

Boundary clauses often refer to natural features such as streams, valleys, and ridges, or smaller landmarks such as paths and poles, boulders and barrows. Less used are agricultural terms like "lynches" which indicate arable cultivation, and "ditches" which could also enclose pasture. More common in the charters of the Micheldever area are wood terms (*leah*, *wudu*, and *hurst*) which might determine the limits of uncleared land. Similarly, *dun* ("down," hill) refers to permanent pasture beyond the fields, and can be used to distinguish early pasture from that taken from woods or arable land in the late medieval and modern periods.

The earliest documents are also uninformative about the location and size of settlements from which the manors derived their labor force. The Micheldever charter of 900 (S360) mentions none of the villages in the eastern half of the Micheldever valley. It does refer to a *byrig* (the probably unoccupied prehistoric hillfort of Norsebury), two "hams" (small farmsteads or hamlets near Popham), and the *gemot hus* (the meeting hall, or possibly manor house, near Micheldever). The Cranbourne boundary clause (S360) does refer to Wonston village (*Wynsiges tun*), although the boundary passes by Sutton Scotney without a mention. The Hunton charter (S381) also has Wonston as a landmark (*Abbodes byrig*), but its bounds follow the Dever stream by Stoke Charity without mentioning that settlement. The charters thus contain no incidental in-

---

[18] For the separate topic of the decline of "bookland," see M. T. Clanchy, *From Memory to Written Record; England, 1066–1307* (Cambridge, Mass., 1979), p. 38.

formation; the only points named are those where a boundary makes a turn.

The broad pattern of early medieval land use in the Micheldever area suggests that its landscape was once bipartite: much of the eastern half of the valley was woodland, while large portions of the western valley seem to have been pasture land. This duality may reflect to some degree the geographic conditions of soil type, drainage, and elevation. But it also suggests that early Saxon zones of land use were broader than those of the late Saxon period. The Micheldever valley, it seems, could at one time have been a single economic unit. Woodland common to all inhabitants lay in a great arc centered on the eastern watershed, and common pasture land covered the southwest. Such a community-wide division of land use would have served a territory of dispersed farmsteads and small hamlets, with group responsibility for permanent pasture and woodland. It could have flourished only at a time before the demands of population growth brought about a discrete cooperative agricultural unit, the vill.

The division of the valley into separate vills and manors might have taken place as late as the charters of the ninth and tenth centuries, which first document the narrow blocks of land that became medieval parishes. If so, one could argue that it was the legal partition of the valley-unit into individual manors that caused the common resources to be converted into rights to pasture and woodland for each vill. The late Saxon charter boundaries, however, rarely appear as new, arbitrary land divisions. In most cases, the boundaries seem to be long-established divisions among land units based on vills. The latter view is supported by the information from hedgerow dating at Micheldever. The major field-system units in Micheldever manor had hedges which could date back to the late tenth century. In some instances, moreover, portions of these hedgerows appeared to be even earlier, from the eighth century. The combined sources of Anglo-Saxon charters, archaeology, toponymics, and hedgerow dating therefore indicate that the process of dividing the Micheldever valley into village strip-parishes probably started in the eighth century and was completed in the tenth.

The Micheldever area also seems to have had a mixed agricultural regime throughout the early medieval period. The four resources necessary for a balanced rural economy (meadow, arable, pasture, and woodland) were constantly available, though they varied in proportion over time and in different localities within the Dever valley. The Domesday Book gives a good account of the presence of meadow and arable land in the late eleventh century, but the amount of pasture and woodland is obscure. Some pasturage would always be found on the cropped fields, usually until Martinmas and the beginning of winter ploughing.[19]

---

[19] See W. O. Ault, *Open-Field Farming in Medieval England* (New York, 1972), pp. 40–46, for mainly later medieval pasturage. He notes that the use of legumes as a rotation crop came into use slowly, and was still limited in the thirteenth century: pp. 38, 39.

The presence of both cow downs and sheep downs in post-medieval Micheldever probably refers to an earlier division of pasture land between cattle for draught and ploughing, and sheep supplying wool and dairy products. Substantial acreage may have been given over to early medieval sheep raising, which is appropriate for a traditional wool producing region.[20]

Woodland was little mentioned in the Domesday Book, yet it must have been present at nearly every vill. The most likely answer for its absence is that only the woods that yielded revenue were noted. The rest must have been treated as manorial common, and probably had rules of usage established by tradition for each vill. A rough estimate of the swine herds of the Micheldever valley suggests the availability of woodland for at least a thousand pigs, yet the Domesday Book recorded only four. The Micheldever manors were never listed as possessing distant swine "denes," a common practice in Kent and Sussex, although it is possible that some of the small woodland settlements nearby had their origins in swineherd stations.

In conclusion, there is reason to believe that resources for sheep rearing and swine herding were allocated on the basis of the entire valley unit at early Saxon Micheldever. Between the eighth and tenth centuries, this primitive unity dissolved into separate village holdings, strip parishes that took in all necessary types of land. As economically independent entities in the late Saxon period, village lands were typically separated by banks, ditches, and hedges, landscape features that appear on charter boundaries and occasionally survive to the present.

This same period saw the rights and responsibilities of the wider community devolve upon new institutions, the manor and the hundred, topics beyond the range of this study, but which I have treated elsewhere.[21] The Domesday Book reveals an impressive regularity of farming communities along the banks of the Dever, as well as several small detached holdings scattered along the watershed between the Micheldever and Candover valleys. As lord of Micheldever, the New Minster directly controlled the extraneous parcels and lands that did not fit the pattern of equal-portioning among the strip-parish vills. Significantly, the regular strip pattern of land divisions was present throughout the entire Dever valley, as much in the eastern half, where most of the land remains to this day in the single, large manor of Micheldever, as in the western half, where separate manor/vills can be traced back to at least the late ninth century. As one-half the valley never adopted unitary

---

[20] M. M. Postan, *The Medieval Economy and Society. An Economic History of Britain in the Middle Ages* (London, 1972), p. 23, observes that in the bishop of Winchester's manors on the Chalk down land north of Winchester, the permanent pasture on the high ground was converted in the thirteenth century to arable land.

[21] Eric Klingelhöfer, *Manor, Vill, and Hundred: The Development of Rural Institutions in Early Medieval Hampshire* (Toronto, 1991). See also "Micheldever," pp. 268–418.

manors, the strip-pattern cannot be attributed to the spread of the "classic" manor. At Micheldever, therefore, the evolution of village lands was unrelated to manorial typology.

Irrespective of the type of manor or jurisdiction involved, the socioeconomic forces that caused rural population to converge onto village sites also concentrated its resources—its lands. Ancient royal estates may have been dismembered into small, "private" holdings or left largely intact, like Micheldever, but the economic basis for such landholdings was permanently altered by the appearance of the vill. Similar changes fundamentally affected settlement and land use throughout Anglo-Saxon England. Yet the focus of regional or county-wide studies of settlement has been too broad to detect the nuances of local geography and to treat the development of every vill or township territory. The study of Micheldever, significant for the variety of sources used and for the coherent patterns they yield, may stimulate other local studies of early medieval rural development. It remains to be seen if localities with different geographies and traditions will duplicate the findings presented here or will yield alternate patterns. Only a comparative grouping of local studies can provide a regional or even national perspective of English rural economies and communities in their formative period, the four centuries from the effective establishment of Christianity to the completion of the Norman Conquest.

Beyond the context of historical investigation, the clinically neutral terms "settlement" and "land use" actually signify the homes and lives of villagers who created and maintained perhaps the most powerful single institution in English history. Despite changes in custom and law, despite its physical transformations and economic obsolescence, the village born a millennium ago survived in spirit into this century. And we still may sometimes glimpse its fading image—in the church, on the common, and along the parish bounds.

APPENDIX A

REFERENCES FROM MANORIAL DOCUMENTS

The study of the medieval field systems and land use at Micheld-ever is based largely upon three types of documents: Anglo-Saxon charters with their lists of boundary landmarks; thirteenth- and fourteenth-century quitclaims of small holdings; and fifteenth- and sixteenth-century leases of large blocks of land by Hyde Abbey and its successors. The three types of document roughly mark the three traditional periods of the Middle Ages, or more concretely, the three phases of medieval rural economy. In archival terms, however, the first two types of document are found together in cartularies, while the latter appears among the muniments that accompanied the post-medieval lay manor in its dynastic descent. At Micheldever, one is fortunate to have landownership by only two families after the Dissolution: the Wriothesleys and their descendents from the 1500s to the early 1800s, and the Baring family since that time. An associated manor, Woodmancott, has been in the hands of a single entity, Winchester College, since Henry VIII forced its exchange for a more profitable property.

The foremost source for manorial references to Micheldever is the *Registrum Cartarum Abbatiae de Hyda*, B.L. MS Harleian 1761.[1] This bound, quarto volume of 191 folios is a fifteenth-century combination of annals and cartulary. The 88 entries of the cartulary comprise royal charters and confirmations; grants of liberties and privileges; lists of church tithes and taxes; copies of inquisition and *quo warranto* proceedings of royal courts; and grants, bequeathals, and quitclaims to the abbey from Hampshire landholders and others. Specifically manorial documents are grouped by manor, following a rough chronological order, and those of the Micheldever estate occupy ff. 38r–74r. A contemporary table of contents (ff. 3r–9v) lists the entries by manorial sections, by numeration, and by *tituli*. Harl. 1761 is a revised version of B.L. Cotton MS Domitian xiv (see below), continuing its list of entries to No. 154, and containing in subsequent folios late medieval notes on knights' fees, assessments, and royal inquisitions and directives.

The Hampshire Record Office possesses a transcript of Harl. 1761, which employs the numeration of the entries of ff. 38r–74v. The nu-

---

[1] See *A Catalogue of The Harleian Manuscripts in the British Museum*, Vol. II (London, 1808), pp. 205–207.

meration and dates assigned to some of the cartulary entries are retained here, though examination of the original in the British Library revealed numerous minor errors in the H.R.O. transcript which have been corrected here.

B.L. Cotton MS Domitian xiv a, is a small quarto of 121 folios, containing a section, *Cronicon Monasterii de Hyda*.[2] This chronicle is followed by *Registrum Cartarum Monasterii de Hida juxta Winton*, ff. 22–237. Micheldever charters occupy ff. 46–110, and are numbered 1 through 111, in chronological sequence until the fourteenth century, when a lack of order appears. Most of the writing is in a thirteenth-century hand, with later entries and corrections.

Another charter list is found in B.L. Stowe 58, *Liber* (or *Registrum*) *Abbatiae de Hyda*.[3] It is a sixteenth-century 70 folio paper copy of a lost original. It consists of copies and translations of Anglo-Saxon and Norman charters. It is similar, but not identical to the *Liber de Hyda* (a portion of which was copied by John Stow in 1572 and is Landsdowne MS 717). Stowe 58 contains a chronicle that ends in the eleventh century, and is divided into reigns of West Saxon monarchs. At the end of each is appended charters and confirmations of the reigns, an unusual arrangement.

In addition to these sources, Winchester College muniments include four original and pseudo-original Anglo-Saxon charters to the New Minster, of which two concern Micheldever properties, No. 12090 from Edward and No. 12093 from Canute. Winchester College also has some miscellaneous medieval and post-medieval land grants and leases for Micheldever (Nos. 12188–89, 12192) and Woodmancott (Nos. 12188–92, 19475–756, 21441–48).[4] The Winchester Cathedral cartulary contains much material about lands around Winchester, but its only references to Micheldever concern its church and chapels.[5] In addition, the Hampshire Record Office contains a large collection of manorial records in its Wriothesley Collection (H.R.O. 5M53). They include copies of some late medieval rentals, post-medieval letters patent, leases, and other land transactions relating to the Micheldever estate. The London Public Record Office contains the original documents of the Dissolution for Hyde Abbey lands and adjacent episcopal properties (Min. Accts 6 Henry VIII, Nos. 3341, 3343). The National Register of Court Rolls contains no additional references to those already noted.

---

[2] See *A Catalogue of the Manuscripts in the Cottonian Library deposited in the British Museum* (London, 1802), D 1047.

[3] Edited and partially translated in Edward Edwards, ed., *Liber Monasterii de Hyda* (London, 1866).

[4] Interesting unpublished medieval records in the College archives include: a 1293 court roll of (Preston) *Candevere* (Nos. 14490–94), a 1469 paper account roll of Hyde Abbey estate expenses (No. 12189), a 1282 inventory of livestock on Hyde Abbey estates (No. 12192), and a 1292 account roll of the bailiff of Candover (No. 12193).

[5] The cartulary has been published: A. W. Goodman, *Chartulary of Winchester Cathedral* (Winchester, 1927).

THE FIELDS OF MICHELDEVER

The following place names for the fields of Micheldever manor are taken from quitclaim entries in the Hyde Abbey cartulary (Harl. 1761). They have not been altered for spelling or copyist errors. By comparing the contents of the cartulary entries, it is possible to find the physical context for many of the field names mentioned. They are here arranged by tithing, field division, and cartulary entry number. Known dates are given; otherwise the documentary reference may be assumed to be of the thirteenth century. Identification of these names with the field names of the Tithe Award maps are given in parentheses at their first mention. Arabic numerals with an asterix, following an identification, refer to its location on Figure 5.1.

An immediate finding of the cartulary study is the absence of a thirteenth-century Middle Field in the Micheldever tithings of Northbrook, Southbrook, and Weston. Closer examination of the field names reveals that not only was a Middle Field not recorded, but one could not have existed in these manors, because some names refer to a specific locality that was bisected by East and West Fields, e.g., *Kenelonde* in Weston. Also notable is the number of medieval field names that appear on the post-Enclosure Tithe Award maps of early nineteenth-century parishes. It is probable that many more local names did survive to that time, but did not become the officially recorded names of the newly laid-out fields. To take one of the tithings as an example, Weston Colley had 24 individual field names given in medieval field descriptions. Of these, 9 were recorded nineteenth-century field names and one was a road name, giving at least a 42 percent field-name continuity at Micheldever manor between 1250 and 1800.[6]

FIELDS

WESTON TITHING

West Field

No. 28
markfurlong [Markfurlong]*1
sorhalne ad shevingdich
norgfurlong
nosebury [Norsebury piece]*2
holdene [Holdene shot]*3
clehull [Clay hill]*4
? in westland
gretediche [great bank]*5
teticom
nosethorne
hundeshull [Hound's Hill, in Hunton]*6

East Field

No. 4
kenelonde
tokingeweye [The Toking Way]
Abbots meadow

No. 39
garstone
kurielande

---

[6] For a listing of place names of fields and woods of the five villages of the eastern Dever valley, see "Micheldever," pp. 484–87.

No. 71
markam [?Markfurlong]
holdene
sup. la hulle [?Clay hill]
la naperes weye [Drove lane]
brofurlong [The Furlong]*7

No. 93
brocfurlango

No. 106
Nosebury with ditch around it
Kenelonde [Coneyland]*8
?la volte vicce

No. 40 1221
Kunlande
hokedene
lentesgarstone
godwynesdoune [Godwinsdown]*9

No. 93 1270
a la stapele
ab tuckingisweye
stratam regiam quae ducit versus
  Overtone

NORTHBROOK TITHING

West Field

No. 1
stikele next the pit [Sticles Hill Piece]*10
estone [Stones]*11
papenacre [Popesland]*12
chalg hulle [Chalk Hill]*13
ribworlande
west ditch end
crytethorne and ditchende
hu(f)thorne
grit thorneslade
hundesflode
magpilonde w/ veteram fischam
goldhourde

No. 2
stone
chakhulle
suttbrodelande
brodeweye
papenacre
stapele [Staples Croft]
huenethorne
ditchoke
?trepedelle
sortelond
horghelond
gretethorneslade
hundesflode
marledelonde
dounfurlonge
poukeputte (poss. in Dumner?)

No. 5
brodeweye
holdene
buttuke
godwynesdowne

No. 9
dounfurlong
combe
pappanacre

East Field

No. 1
medfurlong
est briggarstone
buttuke
fernhille
putteworth [Putworth in W.S.]*16
?estone
ditchende
burdene
brochenbruge

No. 2
wodeweye [to Woodmancott?]
medfurlong
gosemere [Goose Hill Shott]*15
fernhulle
langefurlango
stikele [Stikles Furlong]
stone
Hosente (Gosemere?)
putteworth
stratton field [Stratton Dean]
dengravethorne   *17
brockenbruge, northfurlong of
  morghenatesthorne
dou(n)efurlango

No. 9
gore
gosmere
south of wodeweye
fernhulle
putteworth
swindenelonde [Hog louse bush shot?]

No. 23
east side of highway from Micheldever to
  "hogas"
hundesflode
coppedesthorne
brodethorne
maghethielande

ditchende
stikele
riboughelonde
arghelonde
ditch hoke
gretthorneslade
ditchend
goldhourde
magnethielond

No. 10
west side of the bradeweye
holdene [Holdern, Hoddern]
buttuke
godwinsdoune [Sheep House Field]

No. 23
west side of highway from Micheldever to
   "hogas"
godwinesdoune
Jyrelonde
holdene
lentesgerstonesthorne
bruethorne
combe
brechiae (enclosures) of the Abbot
dene

No. 41   1223
stone
chalkhulle
schortebrodelonde next the land
   ?penistragers
bradeweye
papenacre
stapele
hunethorne
dichowk
schortelande
argelone
russedelle
grethorsesslade
marledelonde
hundesslade
downforlange
poukeputte

No. 42   1230
cumba
sub stikele
grethornneslade
hundesflud
dounfurlang
maghethielande
russedelle

No. 58
dounfurlong
?scipelonde
stapelforlang

No. 61   1254
west of brodewey

russdelle
schortefurlong
brodeweie
dichende
?dichbre
hargeland
dicheholze
solbrodelande
chalhulle
stone
burdoune
stratlingemarca
burdun
brokenbruge
dengravethorne
putworth
hosenet
?surnetebelond
fernhulle
hangindelande
above gosmere next osmundhams
langefurlange

No. 25
1/2 hide in Mich., on N. side
of village on east side of way
leading to godwynesdoune

No. 41   1223
west side of wodeweye
medfurlang
gosmere
fernhulle
lange furlango
sub shelve
?luisicot in hangendelonde
stikele
stone
?hosescote
puttewirhe
campo de stratton
?hosenote
denegravesthorn
dichende
brokenbrughe
morghemede
doun furlango

No. 42   1230
medefurlang
stikele
hangendelonde
dichelie
brondesdelle
dengravesthorne
dichende
burdene

No. 50
apud schicereshulle
buttukes

holdene
buttuk
godwynesdoune

No. 63
gosmere
putteworthe
burdene by denegroffesthorne & ext. ab
  the stuvinghemeweye [Steventon way]
la stone
la dichehocke
huarselonde
grithorsseesslade
in the brodewye & voc. gore
la coppedthorne
dichebye
russedelle
langegarston
le maizelonde

No. 65   1258
bosco voc. le blakewood
dounfurlong
middlefurlong
?for helva
acre voc. la brode
la rygge
schiplonde

No. 74
medfurlang in est langegarstone
buttuke
chakhulle
ad caput fosseti
largelonde

No. 75   1217?
sup. terram de stratton in wodeweye
in the helvam of Mich.
hosenet
?scarnelande
sonelbrodelond

No. 83
putteworth
?bukele
hundesflode
gosmere
la wydeweye
bordene
dengravesthorne
stywingemewye
la dichehoke
hyareslonde
suthorsses slade
la brodeweye, voc. gore
coppedesthorne in la dichelye
grethorseslade
estlangarstone
russesdelle
la my(z)elonde

No. 118   ca. 1310
in brokfurlong, acres voc. Knapaker
  [Naperes way]
le combe
sturyecrofte [Study croft]*19

SOUTHBROOK TITHING

West Field

No. 27
pidfurlong
schortefurlango
la butlyr [Butlers Close]*25
lewe'sburgh

No. 29
kattesbrahen [Cattsbane]*20
hungerdun
le wardesburch [Borough Farm]*21
kenelfsgartsone near parsonland [Gaston
 Hill]*23
mulwey [Millway shot]*26
la rigge
downfurlong
midelfurlong

No. 52
alwoldes lynch
kattesbraghon

No. 53
hungerdene

No. 54
wethergrove
wudeward
kenlesgartsone
cattesbraghone
mortefurlong
le porteweye de westone
west mas(t)dene
la mit'furlang
le wardesburghe

No. 62
markfurlong
la porteweye de westone
kenellesgartsone

No. 66   1250
kattesbraghene
la westdene contra westone *24
la merefurlong
hungerdene
la chetacre
swynenedene [Hogbourne?]
la wardesburghe

No. 83
iter molendini [Mill Way Shott]
?wesergose
?famiham
kenelfesgarstone
cattesbrahen
westmastedene
markfurlong
la hokkediche
war(d)esburghe
alwoldeslinche

East Field

No. 27
millweye
denedell [Den Dell shott]*27

No. 47
le myre
hokededyge [The Crooks]*28
iter molendini

No. 48   1259
le mire pasturam

No. 49   1250
schiceres hylle
buttokes

No. 54
houkededich
iter molendini

No. 66   1250
kenelvesgartsone
sullonde
wethersgrove
la mulweye
alwoldeslynche
la dounfurlong
fizdelle [Den Dell Shott?]
la rigge [Ridge Field]*28

No. 118   1310 (Vicar of Mich.)
smokaker
land of house of St. John [St. Johns Croft]
?foksinge
kenelonde
dounfurlong
?wychene sup. la schulve [The Shelves in
 Cow Down F.]
bagedene
midfurlong
hennethorne
mulleweye
?katteslonde
scyplond
hungerdene
fysheresthorne
la ferme
?apud tray

No. 147   1328
le hokededych
mulweye

ROADS

Further references to village tracks and field access lanes appear among the field references above. Numbered items are from the numerated entries of the Hyde Abbey Cartulary (B.L. Harl. 1761). Folio references are from unumerated entries.

No. 13: highway that runs from Micheldever to *hogas*.

No. 85: Northbrook, east side of *intineris regalis*.

Nos. 139, 140: Micheldever message N. of *regiam stratam*, from Mich. to Stratton.

F.121b (1408) *via alta regia . . . duc de vill westone vocatur traypath*, flooded carriages of the king. Ordered ditches to be dug, N. and S.; (1415) Orders repeated, high road of king in village of Weston called Tray pathway repaired with two ditches N. and S.

F. 37b *inqui. alta via dom. regis, jacens in villa de Mich. per quam iter de villa de Estratton usque villam de Westratton in quodam loco vocatur le fforde ruinosa*, etc., flooded, in disrepair.

WOODS

Roman numerals and paranthetical numbers are identifications illustrated on Figure 5.1. Numbered items are entries of the Hyde Abbey Cartulary (B.L. MS Harl. 1761); folios refer to unnumbered entries.

Micheldever Cartulary

No. 15 *Parva Papeholt* (I)—wood of Peter de Fraxino to head of Wolflede Crofte (32) on the south; by the way to wood of Galfridus Niger; to Lundenweye; by that way to highway from Winton to Reading; by that road to wood of Peter de Fraxino.

No. 16 *Parva Papeholt*—same description, wfladecrofte (sic).

No. 21 *Magna Papenholte* (II)—from Lundenweye that comes fr. Totford; by road between Abbot's wood and wood of Galfridus Niger; by road to head of W. Croft to wood of Peter de Fraxino, so to highway to redehone (30); thence by ditch east into the ditch that runs south into Pinkdene (31); thence by bank of Pinkdene to the lands of the monks of Waverley called Smalerigge.

No. 22 *Magna Papenholt*—same description.

No. 26 Pannage of *Parva Papenholt*, 60 pigs.

Nos. 31 and 31—same description as No. 15.

No. 33 *Magna Papenholt—sefrem* (hedge) of wolfledecrofte and the field of Little Papenholt . . . *magna viam* to redehone; thence by ditch of Stratton which runs east *usque vallem de Pinkdene.*

No. 35 Part of wood of West Stratton called La Sturte (III), the part lies on the east side of the wood, *sicut via dividit et extendit de Bradeleleghe* (IV) *usque ad Brodecrofte ex parte aquil. de la Brodecrofte et ex parte austr. de Bradeleghe et bosci Rich. Scutari.*

No. 65 (1258) Aldvenus de Niger q.c. to Roger Abbot . . . *cum toto bosco meo qui vocatur le Blakewood* (V).

No. 104i (1276) Woodmancote *hacio ext. ab angulo bosci Abb. voc. le Hurst* (VI), by *ter. voc. Popham Crofte.* New ditch dug to enclose.

No. 104ii (ca.1300) *Solum ext.* fr. wood of Abbot called Le Hurst *usque metas* of Dummer [a neighboring parish], in width fr. field of Ab. called Holt field on west to arable land of Ab.; 5' wide ditch; and a *kekum* at north end beside Alvenholt (VII)—to enclose wood of Woodmancote called le Hurst except 2 entrances.

No. 122 Fine for *bosco vastato*—old wasted forest called Alvyneholt west of Woodmancote.

No. 123 Idem for wood le Hurst.

f.121 (1276) *hacium prostrata per Ab. in Wodemancote, ext.* . . . Popham Croft, length 24 perch, . . . repair dirches; new dirch 3' wide and deep.

f.150i (ca.1190) Q.C. to Ab. *custodiam bosco de la Hurst* . . . pertaining to Micheldever, and is between Woodemancote and Popham.

f.150ii (ca.1190) Q.C. to Ab. bosco de Hurst and the Holte and bullokeswye and buteleya (VIII) and severleya (IX) and gateweye, up to *metas* of Dummer; Ab. gives 20 acres *in frussico* and 5 acres in Butleya *mensuratas.*

Inquisitions Post-Mortem: 1299 Pamber Forest—Wood of Hyde Abbey in Micheldever, beasts not able to enter (for hunting).

Forest Rolls, Box 5, Bag 1, Southampton 10: No. 171 (1298/9) Persons entered the wood of westrattone called lessewode, cut down saplings. Charges for old *vasti* of wood called hurst, 12d. *cellarium* of Hyde; Wood of Rowehurst (X), 12d.; woods called baldredsle and papenolte, *vasti* 2s.

Forest Rolls, Box 5, Bag 1, Southampton 10, No. 172 (ca.1320) Ab. of Hyde cut down in Papenholte 200 oaks, fine ½ mark. Persons came into Papenholt and stole 2 oaks, carried them to Hangtone with a wooden wheeled cart and 2 horses.

Post-Medieval Manorial References

Patent Rolls, 35 Henry VIII, p. 23: Thomas Lord Wriothesley, leases *Micheldevre, mansio rectoriae cum pert.* Cawsemede *pratum* 4 acres; *boscus voc.* Babisley Coppices (XI), Hanadlys C. (XII), Cohordis C. (XIII), Dottesley C. (XIV), Hogdown [Hogbourne?] C. (Magna Papenholt) and le Frethewood C. (Parva Papenholt).

Patent Rolls 35 Henry VIII, p. 36: Thomas Lord Wriothesley, receives Micheldever; all rabbit warren called Godwinsdoune; in Micheldever, Stonwey Coppice, 16a.; Grindells C. 13a.; Holme Hill C. 14a.; Harflete C. 30a.; Blakewood C. 13a.; the more Pingdon C. 12a.; the less Pingdon C. 11a.; Gusmedeheth [?] C. 2a.; Godwinsdown heath 28a.; Hogsdoune . . .; Bushelds C. 20a.; and Lowes C. 11a.

P.R.O. S.C. Henry VIII Ministers' Accounts, Nos. 3341, 3343: originals of the above.

H.R.O. 5 M 53 (Wriothesley Collection):

No. 143 (1537) Indenture by John (Salcot) Bishop of Banger and Commendatory of man. of St. Peter of Winchester [Hyde Abbey] to T. Wriothesley of Michedledever; site of parsonage, etc.

No. 176 (1308) Ordinance for fixed tithes of Micheldever. reference to tithes of *cardinum* (teasles)—The number of acres of teasles in unenclosed fields shall not exceed the number under grain (*grannarium numerarum*), Sturye Crofte meadow.

No. 177 (1425) . . . pasture of a certain field called le hycroft in which the Ab. and his tenants of West Stratton in 2 years of 3 have claimed after corn has been removed there until it has been sewn afresh, and during the whole of the third year.

No. 409 (1607) in Northbrook tithing: Colhay wardis, Pannys.

No. 419 (1651) Manor of East Stratton, 40 acres arable land, parcel of demesne lands lying together in the west field between the Farme Meade of West Stratton, a close adjacent to and belonging to West Stratton farmhouse, and lands of several copyholders . . . Covenant to not plough more than two years together, but will suffer them to remain untilled in the third year according to the custom of husbandry in those parts.

No. 416 (1595) 99 year lease by Henry Earl of Southampton, manor house of Mich., great farm, etc.; Goodwynnes D., Burnt Heathe, and Burnt Heathe Coppice.

No. 417 (1649) Goddens Downe Lodge and warren in Goddens D., Burnt Heath, and Burnt Heathe C.

No. 420 (1647) Agreement to build new barn, and have part of farm called Sheephouse.

No. 421 (1649) Barn newly erected, etc. . . . called Sheepe House, and land called Brook Furlong . . .

No. 422 (1649) Named husbandmen of Micheldever to hold parcels of enclosed land called Croftes lying near Hogdoune, the parcels called Pikes, the Playne, Lunways, lower party of New Downe, and part of Bushy and Heathy Ground fr. new sewn part to hedge running parallel to way from Winton to Stratton, the close called Whites at lower end of the Home Field, and haybarn. 3 year lease. Covenant that they may plough one third of number of acres of Croftes, Pikes, and part of the Playne east of the way to the northwest corner of Little Copice, providing that the last be one part of what is sewn as for want of tillage and long rest, as it is not so healthy for pasture as the other lands. Covenant not to plough the Playne west of the way.

No. 425 (1649) in Southbrook tithing: lands by East Field, and also 60 acres of land in Micheldever, commonly called two yardlands, with perts.

No. 427 (1653) Ref. to Butlers land, Meere Pond, Gidgefield Close, Guttermede Dell Close, the Rippinge Close, the Lane Meade, Primmers Corner Close.

No. 605 (1546) Manor of East Stratton, ref. to Emley Coppice (XV) 15 acres, Rownes C. 20a.; Blackwood C. 2a.; common and waste called Straitley Common [later Stratton Park?].

APPENDIX B

DOMESDAY FIGURES FOR THE MICHELDEVER AREA

DOMESDAY ENTRIES

The tabulation of the Hampshire Domesday entries for the manors in the immediate vicinity of Micheldever consists of the entries for the manors in the Dever valley, the lower Candover valley, and the east bank of the middle Test valley. Most of the sixteen manors have subdivided entries in the Domesday Book.

The information recorded by the Survey falls into six categories: 1) context, the Domesday Book folio, hundred, and lord/landholder T.R.E. and 1086; 2) hidage, T.R.E. and 1086, described as either "defended" or "gelded"; 3) arable production, recorded as land for N ploughs (or plough teams), and N ploughs (or plough teams) present on the demesne and/or the vill; 4) work force, categorized as *villani, bordarii, servi, coliberti*, to which has been added an estimated population total; 5) non-arable resources, comprising meadow, pasture, woodland, mill, church, and city property; 6) monetary value, recorded for T.R.E., later, and 1086, plus occasional returns from a *firmarius*.

Abbreviations used in the tabulation are BW = Bishop of Winchester; EG = Earl Godwin; EH = Earl (King) Harold; HP = Hugh de Port; KE = King Edward; KW = King William; MW = St. Mary's Convent, Winchester; NM = New Minster; OM = Old Minster (Winchester Cathedral); QE = Queen Edith; WA = Wherwell Abbey. Entries for lordship indicate the tenant-in-chief and the specific landholder, if different.

147

TABLE OF DOMESDAY FIGURES

Manor	Abbotstone	Barton Stacey Kings Worthy			Bransbury	Bulllington
DB folio	40d	38c	46d	48c	41d	44a
Hundred	Bountisb.	Barton			Barton	Welford
Lord 1066	BW	KE	KE	KE	BW/OM	WA
Tenant				Sh'ff	A.Romsey	
Lord 1086	BW	KW	Ralf	HP	BW/OM	WA
Tenant	HP |Reg.			Walt.	Rich.Cler.	
Other inf.						
Hides def.	9h		1h	.5h	4h	
Hides geld.						numquam
Now	9h	.5day 1v		.5h	4h	
Other inf.	1.5h					10h
Ploughlands	5p	25p	2p		4p	6p
Demesne pls.	2p	5p	9 oxen		1p	2p
Vill pls.	3p	18p			2p	
Other pls.	1p					
Villani	8	28	1		5	8
Bordarii	6	47	5		7	4
Servi	5	8	1			3
Coliberti		6				
(Est. pop.)	(75)	(420)			(60)	(63)
Meadow	5a, 1a (R)	37a	6a			
Pasture		46s.				
Wood		80 swine				
Mill	15s. (1)	42s. 6d. (3)			15s. (1)	15s. (1)
Church			1			
City prop.						
1066 val.	£5	£38 8s.4d. £3			£5	£7
later val.	£5	£38 8s.4d. £1.5			£4	
1086 val.	£5 + £1	£33	£1.515s.		£6	£7
Farm val.		£52 6s.1d.				

TABLE OF DOMESDAY FIGURES—Continued

Manor	Brown Candover (Woodm.)			Chilton Cand.	Chilbolton
DB folio	42a,b			40d	41a
Hundred	Mainsbor.			Mainsb.	Buddlesg.
Lord 1066	NM		NM	BW	OM
Tenant		Elaf		Godw.,Leofw.	
Lord 1086	NM		NM	BW	OM (5h 3v)
Tenant		HP	Alfsi	Richere	
Other inf.					Ri. Sturmey holds rest
Hides def.	20h			5h + 5h	10h
Hides geld.					
Now	13h 2.5v	|2.5h|6h 2.5v		10h	5h
Other inf.	11h dem.	|1h demesne			
Ploughlands	18p			6p	7p
Demesne pls.	1p	1p	3p	3p	2p
Vill pls.	8p		2p		7p
Other pls.					
Villani	13		3	1	11
Bordarii	4			10	11
Servi	9	3			4
(Est. pop.)	(94)	(3)	(15)	(55)	(114)
Meadow	10a	1a	1a		30a
Pasture					
Wood					
Mill					15s. (1)
Church					(1)
City prop.					
1066 val.	£13			£8	£12
Later val.	£13			£6	£12
1086 val.	£8	£1	£7	£7	£15
Farm val.	£10				

TABLE OF DOMESDAY FIGURES—Continued

Manor	Hunton	Leckford		Newton St.	Norton
DB folio	40b	42a,b	43d	48c	49d
Hundred	Buddl.?	Somborne		Barton	Barton
Lord 1066	BW	NM	MW	KE	KE
Tenant	Alwin St.			Aelfric	Fulk
Lord 1086	BW	NM	MW	William	KW
Tenant	Hugh				Odo thegn
Other inf.					
Hides def.		5h	5h	1h	5h
Hides geld.					
Now		2.5h	1h	0h	2h1v
Other inf.	3h				
Ploughlands		3p	3p	1p	3p
Demesne pls.	1p	1p	2p		2p
Vill pls.	1p	1p	2p		1p
Other pls.					
Villani	2	4	5		3
Bordarii	5	4	2		5
Servi	9	2	3		6
Coliberti					
(Est. pop.)	(44)	(42)	(38)		(46)
Meadow		20a			10a
Pasture					12d.
Wood	6d.				
Mill		22s.6d. (1.5)			15s. (1)
Church					(1)
City prop.					5 hagae 10s.
1066 val.		£3	£3		£6
Later val.		£3	£4		£3
1086 val.	£7	£4	£4	£1	£6 10s.
Farm val.				£1	

TABLE OF DOMESDAY FIGURES—Continued

Manor	Micheldever	(1–4)*	(5–7)*	(8)*	(9)*	(10)*	
DB folio	42c,d						
Hundred	Micheldever						
Lord 1066	NM	NM	NM	NM	NM	NM	
Tenant		4 men	3 men	father	wife	SH	
Lord 1086	NM	NM	NM	NM	NM	NM	NM
Tenant		HP	HC OS WH	Alfsi	Aldred	SH	Alfsi
Other inf.	4 villagers pay for lands						
Hides def.	107h						
Hides geld.							
Now	83h.5v**	22.5h1v	7h 5h 4.5h	6h	1.5h 2h	1h	
Other inf.						else-where	
Ploughlands	72p						
Demesne pls.	9p	6.5p	__6p__	__6.5p__			
Vill pls.	25p	1.5p	__4p__	__1.5p__			
Other pls.							
Villani	64	6	__9__	__5__		84	
Bordarii	28	12	__9__	__2__		51	
Servi	22	7	__2__	__19__		50	
Coliberti							
(Est. pop.)	(482)	(97)	(92)	(54)		(725) Totals	
Meadow	30a	24a	5a	7a			
Pasture							
Wood	8 pigs						
Mill	30d.(1)***						
Church							
City prop.							
1066 val.	£60						
Later val.	£40						
1086 val.	£54	£19	£5 £2.5 £3	£1.5 £1.5 £1 = £23.5			
Farm val.							
	(4 villagers pay 7s. = 28s.)			Total rev. = £24 18s.			

* 1–4 = Cranbourne, Drayton, Stratton, Popham; 5 = Papenholt; 6 = Totford; 7 = Burcot; 8 = Northington; 9 = Swaraton; 10 = Northington Grange ** Error for 83.5h 1v. *** Error for 30s.

TABLE OF DOMESDAY FIGURES—Continued

Manor	Preston Candover	Stoke Ch.	Sutton	Won- ston
DB folio	44c 45c,d 47a 47c 49d 49d	40c	46d	41d
Hundred	Bermondspitt	B'gate?	Barton	Barton
Lord 1066	EH KE KE KE QE KE	BW BW	EG	BW
Tenant	God. Ch. Osb.P	vill	Tovi	
Lord 1086	KW HP Ralf KW KW KW	BW BW	Rob.F.	BW
Tenant	Ansk. Odi. Chi. P	Geof		
Other inf.				
Hides def.		10h	5h	10h
Hides geld.	5.5h 1h1v 5h 5h 2.5h 1v			
Now	5.5h 1h1v 4.5h 2.5h 2h	7h 4h	2.5h	7h
Other inf.	1v elsewhere			
Ploughlands	5p 1p 6p 6p ? .5p	4p	4p	7p
Demesne pls.	2p 1p 1p 1.5p 1p 1p	2p 1p	1p	2p
Vill pls.	2.5 .5p 2p 3ox	1p	2p	5p
Other pls.	.5v elsewhere			
Villani	9 2 1 7 3	2	4	10
Bordarii	1 2 2	8 2	4	6
Servi	3 4 3 14 1	6 6	8	10
Coliberti				
(Est. pop.)	(53) (14) (18) (59) (16) Total = (160)	(72)	(48)	(90)
Meadow	5a 5a 4a	4a 4a	10a	
Pasture				
Wood	*		6s.3d. (1)	7s.6d. (1)
Mill				
Church		15s. (1)	(1)	(1)
City prop.	Haga 17d.			
1066 val.	£10 £1.5 £8 £5 £4	£10	£6	£8
Later val.	£3 £1.5 £5 £3 £3	£8	£4	£8
1086 val.	£5 £1.5 £4 £5 £2.5 5s	£7 £4	£5	£10
Farm val.				

* silva ad clausura

VALUATION CHANGES OF DOMESDAY MANORS

The following chart is based upon the *valet* entries of Appendix B.1. The manors are grouped according to the direction in which their values changed after the Conquest, and by Domesday. At Preston Candover, the Domesday record was detailed enough to present its five sub-manors, but this could not be done for Micheldever or Barton Stacey, the other large "multiple" estates.

The eighteen manors analyzed here present some interesting patterns.

Two manors (11 percent) lost value after 1066 and continued to lose value. By 1086 four manors (22 percent) regained some of what had been lost. Another manor (5.5 percent) regained all its lost value by Domesday, and two others (11 percent) were then more highly valued than they had been before the Conquest. Of the manors that lost value upon the Conquest, two (11 percent) underwent no change at all in value, while the largest group, five manors (27.5 percent), had higher valuations in 1086. One manor (5.5 percent) did not lose value after 1066. While it had a lower assessment at Domesday, its farm return was higher still, so it may also be considered a more valuable manor. Finally, one manor (5.5 percent) actually increased in value soon after the Conquest; it retained that value at Domesday.

In the Micheldever area, only 5.5 percent of the manors had higher values soon after the Conquest, while 50 percent lost value. The ratio is nearly 10:1. Secondly, by 1086 33 percent of the manors still had lower values than they had before the Conquest, but 50 percent increased their overall value between 1066 and 1086. As might be expected, the Norman Conquest was immediately detrimental to manorial values and presumably regional prosperity. Its effect, however, was by no means universal, and by the end of the Conqueror's reign, fully one-half the manors were more highly valued than at its beginning. One may surmise that despite Norman depredations (perhaps administrative rather than military), the regional economic improvement revealed by the Domesday values was typical of overall early medieval rural development.

POST-CONQUEST CHANGES IN DOMESDAY VALUATIONS
(Assessment in pounds: 1066, ca.1070, 1086)

		£0	£5	£10	£15	£20
Preston	£8	xxxxxxxxxxxxxxxx				
Candover 3	£5	xxxxxxxxxx				
	£4	xxxxxxxx				
Preston	£4	xxxxxxxx				
Candover 5	£3	xxxxxx				
	£2.5	xxxxx				
Chilton	£8	xxxxxxxxxxxxxxxx				
Candover	£6	xxxxxxxxxxxx				
	£7	xxxxxxxxxxxxxx				
Preston	£10	xxxxxxxxxxxxxxxxxxxxxx				
Candover 1	£3	xxxxxx				
	£5	xxxxxxxxxx				
Norton	£6	xxxxxxxxxxxxx				
	£4	xxxxxxxx				
	£5	xxxxxxxxxx				

POST-CONQUEST CHANGES IN DOMESDAY VALUATIONS—Continued					
	£0 ·	£5	£10	£15	£20
Sutton £6	xxxxxxxxxxxx				
£4	xxxxxxxx				
£5	xxxxxxxxxx				
Preston £5	xxxxxxxxxx				
Candover 4 £3	xxxxxx				
£5	xxxxxxxxxx				
Bransbury £5	xxxxxxxxxx				
£4	xxxxxxxx				
£6	xxxxxxxxxxxx				
Micheldever £60	xxxxxxxxxxxx		}1/10 recorded values		
£40	xxxxxxxx				
£75	xxxxxxxxxxxxxxxx				
Bullington £7	xxxxxxxxxxxxxx				
£7	xxxxxxxxxxxxxx				
Preston £1.5	xxx				
Candover 2 £1.5	xxx				
£1.5	xxx				
Brown £13	xxxxxxxxxxxxxxxxxxxxxxxxxxx				
Candover £13	xxxxxxxxxxxxxxxxxxxxxxxxxxx				
(+Woodm.) £16	xxxxxxxxxxxxxxxxxxxxxxxxxxxxxxxxxx				
farm £18	fffffffffffffffffffffffffffffffffffffffffffffff				
Chilbolton £12	xxxxxxxxxxxxxxxxxxxxxxxxx				
£12	xxxxxxxxxxxxxxxxxxxxxxxxx				
£15	xxxxxxxxxxxxxxxxxxxxxxxxxxxxxxxx				
£eckford 1 £3	xxxxxx				
£3	xxxxxx				
£4	xxxxxxxx				
Wonston £8	xxxxxxxxxxxxxxxx				
£8	xxxxxxxxxxxxxxxx				
£10	xxxxxxxxxxxxxxxxxxxx				
Abbotstone £5	xxxxxxxxxx				
£5	xxxxxxxxxx				
£6	xxxxxxxxxxxx				
Barton £41.5	xxxxxxxx		}1/10 recorded values		
Stacey £41.5	xxxxxxxx				
(+KWorthy) £35	xxxxxxxx				
farm £52.3	fffffffffffffff				
£eckford 2 £3	xxxxxx				
£4	xxxxxxxx				
£4	xxxxxxxx				

INDEX

www.ingramcontent.com/pod-product-compliance
Lightning Source LLC
Chambersburg PA
CBHW080927100426
42812CB00007B/2389

.